Rereading Childhood Books

Bloomsbury Perspectives on Children's Literature

Bloomsbury Perspectives on Children's Literature seeks to expand the range and quality of research in children's literature through publishing innovative monographs by leading and rising scholars in the field. With an emphasis on cross- and inter-disciplinary studies, this series takes literary approaches as a starting point, drawing on the particular capacity for children's literature to open out into other disciplines.

Titles in the Series

Adulthood in Children's Literature, Vanessa Joosen

The Courage to Imagine: The Child Hero in Children's Literature, Roni Natov

Ethics in British Children's Literature: Unexamined Life, Lisa Sainsbury

Fashioning Alice: The Career of Lewis Carroll's Icon, 1860–1901, Kiera Vaclavik

From Tongue to Text: A New Reading of Children's Poetry, Debbie Pullinger

Literature's Children: The Critical Child and the Art of Idealisation, Louise Joy

Rereading Childhood Books: A Poetics, Alison Waller

Forthcoming Titles

Metaphysics of Children's Literature: Climbing Fuzzy Mountains, Lisa Sainsbury

The Styles of Children's Literature: A Century of Change, Peter Hunt

Rereading Childhood Books

A Poetics

Alison Waller

BLOOMSBURY ACADEMIC
LONDON • NEW YORK • OXFORD • NEW DELHI • SYDNEY

BLOOMSBURY ACADEMIC
Bloomsbury Publishing Plc
50 Bedford Square, London, WC1B 3DP, UK
1385 Broadway, New York, NY 10018, USA

BLOOMSBURY, BLOOMSBURY ACADEMIC and the Diana logo are trademarks of Bloomsbury Publishing Plc

First published in Great Britain 2019

Cover design: Eleanor Rose
Cover image © Riccardo Guasco

A catalogue record for this book is available from the British Library.

A catalog record for this book is available from the Library of Congress.

ISBN: HB: 978-1-4742-9828-5
ePDF: 978-1-4742-9830-8
eBook: 978-1-4742-9829-2

Series: Bloomsbury Perspectives on Children's Literature

Typeset by Newgen KnowledgeWorks Pvt. Ltd., Chennai, India

To find out more about our authors and books visit www.bloomsbury.com and sign up for our newsletters.

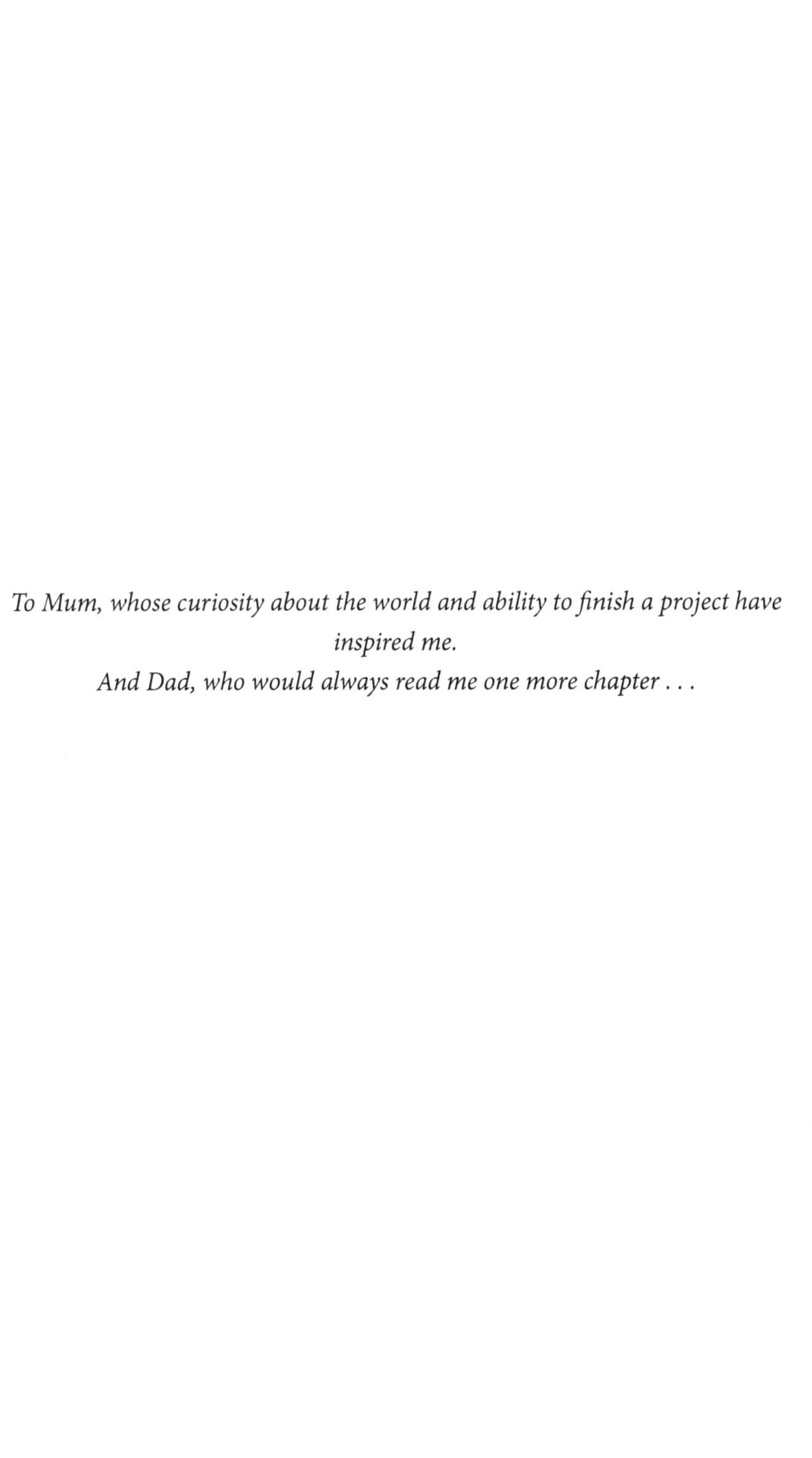

To Mum, whose curiosity about the world and ability to finish a project have inspired me.

And Dad, who would always read me one more chapter . . .

Contents

Acknowledgements

This book has been almost ten years in the creation, and in that time many generous people and institutions have helped and advised me. I am grateful to the University of Roehampton for allowing me leave to research and write. The Department of English and Creative Writing, the National Centre for Research in Children's Literature, and the Memory, Reading and Writing research group have afforded me much support and good cheer along the way, and I could not have asked for a better working environment in which to develop my interests. I was fortunate enough to receive a British Academy/Leverhulme Small Research Grant in 2014 to expand my collection of remembering and rereading interviews, and this financial help is much appreciated.

Major gratitude is due to the participants who took part in my surveys and subsequent 'rereading experiments'. I cannot name them individually, but each and every one generously gave me access to their memories and reading experiences, and many contributed concepts and insights that have shaped my own thinking. I loved working with them all. Particular thanks go to Bath Central Library and the University of the Third Age branches (Bath, Wandsworth, Hertford and Welwyn Garden City), for inviting me to give talks, helping me arrange contact and agreeing to advertise my research to their members.

A number of colleagues and friends have been kind enough to read my work along the way or offer their expertise and advice: sincere thanks to Joelle Adams, Jane Carroll, Susan Greenberg, Sarah Falcus, Nicki Humble, Jonathan Hope, Peter Hunt, Gilian Lathey, Fiona Maine, Laura Peters, David Rudd, Debby Thacker and Shelley Trower. Special credit is due to Lisa Sainsbury for her editorial wisdom, keen critical eye and general reassurance at all stages. Two of my wonderful PhD students worked as research assistants towards the end of the project, and have made the final stages much more bearable; so thanks also go to Erica Gillingham and Sarah Pyke. Susan Lumb helped me with transcription, and Riccardo Guasco created the incredible cover art. More personal encouragement has been forthcoming from friends and family, especially Sandra Byatt, Jenny Waller and David Waller. I have discovered five excellent co-reading subjects in Anna, Lucy, and Emily Byatt and Isobel and Ellie South. Dan South deserves a special mention for his emotional support, ace project planning and provision of treats when deadlines were completed. Borage and Marlow have known when purring is the most constructive criticism, and will get their rewards.

Finally, I would like to thank David Avital, Clara Herberg, Mark Richardson and all staff involved at Bloomsbury.

Introduction: Excavating

He who seeks to approach his own buried past must conduct himself like a man digging.

Benjamin, 1932/1999, p. 611

Polly sighed and laid her book face down on her bed. She rather thought she had read it after all, some time ago.

Jones, 1985/2000, p. 11

Nineteen-year-old Polly is lying on her stomach reading a collection of supernatural short stories. In the middle of a time-travel story called 'Two-timer' she is suddenly struck by an 'odd memory' of its ending and puts the volume down, realizing that she is not reading but rather *re*reading (Jones, 1985/2000, p. 14). The moment is unsettling for Polly, particularly since, when she returns to inspect the book more thoroughly, she discovers that 'half the stories she thought she remembered reading in this book were not there' (p. 11). The book becomes an uncanny marker of her recent childhood, which is, it turns out, not quite as she remembers it. When she first settles down to read 'Two-timer' Polly's past 'seemed a smooth string of normal, half-forgotten things' (p. 14). However, the experience of rereading this strange story, and re-encountering the partly familiar book in which it appears, releases new memories of her previous self and projects her 'across the jolt where she had done God alone knew what' (p. 14).

This opening scene from Diana Wynne Jones's *Fire and Hemlock* (1985) presents a dramatic account of what many adults might go through when they return to a significant book from childhood. For Polly, rereading 'Two-timer' is the catalyst for recovering earlier memories – of lived experience and textual encounters – that in turn launch her into a quest to rescue her enigmatic friend, Tom Lynn, from the queen of fairies. Few individuals in the real world outside of fantasy fiction will reread a childhood book as a precursor to battling supernatural forces as Polly does, but many return to books from the past with a sense of their potential as powerful talismans nonetheless. Adults recall snippets of poetry and prose read to them when they were little; they remember when and where they learnt to read words for themselves; they can sometimes recollect the way that the children's picture books and novels they consumed in their youth made them feel, and the meanings that characters, episodes and the general atmosphere of texts held for them as readers. Remembering and rereading are imaginative processes for reclaiming the private relationships that child selves once had with these texts. They can also be practical and professional acts for parents, grandparents, teachers, librarians, publishers and scholars of children's literature.

Little has been written about remembering and rereading childhood books as specific lived practices outside of individual memoirs.[1] In *Rereading Childhood Books*, I bring a new and systematic approach to the subject, establishing ways that cognitive, social and affective forces shape our personal attitudes to books from our early pasts, and look to understand some of the common purposes of returning to early reading experiences. I also seek to challenge the notion that nostalgia is the primary sense through which we might understand adult engagement with children's literature.

Paracanons and the lifelong reading act

Where previous scholars of memory and reading have glossed over early textual encounters, I bring them to the fore in this study. Italo Calvino has argued that we reread and remember certain texts because they 'exert a peculiar influence' (1991/1999, p. 4) over time and because we 'cannot remain indifferent' to them (p. 7). His interest in the way individuals relate to literature across the lifespan and how this literature can play a part in building self-identity is mostly confined to discussions of 'great works', particularly those encountered in adulthood. This is because youthful reading, in his account, lacks concentration and its practices and texts are thus often of 'little value' later in life (p. 4). Calvino recognizes the importance of childhood books, not in their own terms but as 'seeds' for future understanding. Matei Călinescu's 1993 study *Rereading* also views adult reading as 'normative' and adult rereading as inherently interesting, while childhood reading is important primarily as a stage building towards the proper faculties of 'maturity'. Călinescu's work is foundational for my poetics. However, while he acknowledges the importance of age in understanding reading phenomena and includes a short section on childhood, he does not actually explore many children's books. His discussion circulates instead around critical readings of a number of relevant literary texts for adults that invite multiple visits, such as short stories by Jorge Luis Borges, or Marcel Proust's *À la Recherche du Temps Perdu* (1913–27). In contrast, there is only fleeting reference to Lewis Carroll's *Alice's Adventures in Wonderland* (1865), described as one of the 'classics of children's literature' (Călinescu, 1993, p. 95), and a brief allusion to broad genres and subgenres such as 'fantasies à la Tolkien or C. S. Lewis' (p. 92). Instead of submitting these rich texts to scrutiny to broaden his sense of rereading, Călinescu relies on the idea that early readings 'may take on a disproportionate significance in our retrospective fantasies – disproportionate at least in regard to the intrinsic value of most of the books involved, if our mature self were to reassess it' (p. 96). The older reader is encouraged to 'reassess' books considered significant by his or her earlier reading self, rather than enjoy or otherwise re-experience them in a more integrated manner.[2]

Departing from these seminal critical commentaries on rereading, *Rereading Childhood Books* begins from the assumption that books encountered in youth have equal intrinsic value to those met in later life, and that early reading is not inherently less meaningful than that undertaken in subsequent years simply because the reader may display emergent cognitive skills or have relatively few life experiences. Since my study is primarily concerned with the intimate relationships between remembering reader and remembered childhood book, rather than ways that works become significant through forms of cultural memory, I am also not convinced that canonical texts represent the only material worth probing. Carroll's *Alice* books and other respected classics certainly act as markers of lifelong reading for some, simultaneously satisfying personal tastes *and* being accepted into the canon of children's literature as a representative body of texts widely valued and considered worth studying and revisiting; but other adults cite popular, marginalized and ephemeral fiction as a significant part of their early experiences with books. Indeed, in my own surveys, prolific author Enid Blyton was mentioned more often than any other author or single text, and her influence on a reader-based account of children's literature in the twentieth century should not be underestimated. I am therefore interested in the way childhood books function as *paracanonical* rather than canonical texts. The paracanon has been defined by Catharine R. Stimpson as a set of texts 'beloved' by individuals and communities of reading (1990, p. 957). Her definition can be usefully extended to allow for a more expansive conception of the 'peculiar influence' that childhood books might exert at the point of initial reception and beyond. This approach encourages a more complex consideration of the affective influence of literary encounters over time. The paracanonical books that feature in this study are not only 'love object[s]', as Stimpson puts it (p. 961), but also texts that have been and remain meaningful in all kinds of ways, not all of them positive. In *Fire and Hemlock*, Polly is initiated into reading for pleasure by Tom Lynn; however, the narrator sounds a warning note about the potential dangers of this activity: 'she read greedily, picking up another book as soon as she had finished the first one. She had read *The Box of Delights* and *The Lion, the Witch and the Wardrobe* too before she went home' (Jones, 1985/2000, p. 100). For any reader already familiar with the first in C. S. Lewis's *Narnia* series (1950–56), the mention of greedy consumption brings to mind Edmund's temptation at the hands of the White Witch and her box of Turkish delight. It is no wonder that Polly soon feels 'like a drug addict' (p. 100). For Polly, consumption of books leads her into dubious adventures and an overreliance on fiction; yet it is her rereading of such fictions that saves her and Tom at the novel's climax, when she finally learns what she needs to do about the faerie world by returning to *The Oxford Book of Ballads*. One message that might be taken away from this textual example is that childhood books can overwhelm, psychologically, emotionally and bodily, and that such reactions should be attended to as much as other forms of response based on intellectual, educational or moral grounds. I return to questions of how childhood reading can be remembered as oppressive and potentially risky in Chapter 3, where I consider affective responses such as grief and fear. In some cases, immersive encounters with childhood books can be so affecting that they result in those books being abandoned by the child and rejected by the adult rereader. Disappointment, frustration and boredom represent alternative dangers associated with rereading, and in Chapters 4 and 5

I tease out some of repercussions of these responses in relation to memory and nostalgia, suggesting that acts of returning to childhood books are necessarily constrained by the limits of what can be remembered, but also by ideological assumptions carried by adults about their younger selves (a point I will return to shortly).

I began with *Fire and Hemlock* partly because it is one of the novels I read in my youth. It sits within my paracanon alongside other books that disturbed or frightened me, such as Robert Cormier's *Fade* (1988) and Nicholas Fisk's *Grinny* (1973), and books that bored me, such as John Christopher's *The Guardians* (1970), as well as books that I loved and delighted in, including Blyton's *The Mystery of the Pantomime Cat* (1949), Frank Muir and Joseph Wright's *What-a-Mess and the Cat Next Door* (1981) and Lucy Bates and Diane de Groat's *Little Rabbit's Loose Tooth* (1975). These texts have '[come] along with me as I age' in Katharine Jones's formulation of what she describes as 'generational literature' (2006, p. 305), since I have remembered them, reimagined them and, in some cases, revisited them on multiple occasions into adulthood. Different points of engagement with childhood books span the life course, from the child's original encounter to the adult's return through memory or rereading, with potentially numerous instances of real and imaginative revisiting in-between. *Rereading Childhood Books* provides a poetics of what I call the *lifelong reading act*, a term I adapt from Louise Rosenblatt's definition of the 'reading act' as 'an event involving a particular individual and a particular text, happening at a particular time, under particular circumstances, in a particular social and cultural setting, and as part of the ongoing life of the individual and the group' (1985, p. 100). My concept of the lifelong reading act is a major contribution to the field of children's literature studies. Remembering and rereading, I argue, are not distinct from the reading act, but represent integrated elements that function on a micro level in each tangible, phenomenological encounter with a text, and on a macro level every time that text is conjured up through conscious reminiscence, involuntary memory, rereading projects or shared discourses about childhood books. This thesis underpins *Rereading Childhood Books*.

The categories of 'adult' and 'child' are threaded through the history of the academic study of children's literature and represent terms that define the field: children's literature is literature produced *by* adults *for* children.

The study of relationships between generations, what Clémentine Beauvais, drawing on the work of Maria Nikolajeva (2009), has called 'aetocriticism' (2015, p. 18), has also shaped research, leading scholars to enquire into the nature of power dynamics between adults and child readers and the hidden motivations produced within children's literature and its mechanisms of cultural production. These binary terms and power structures have always been of great interest to me, particularly because of the liminal spaces that exist between them (such as adolescence). However, in embracing the role of the remembering and rereading adult I have found it is necessary to soften boundaries and address ontological issues of readerly identity over time. *Rereading Childhood Books* offers an important alternative to binary notions of how adults respond to children's literature, moving beyond literary and educational divisions in the field to focus on what I have called *rereading attitudes*. These attitudes reflect the intricacies involved in recovering elements of the past when returning to childhood books in adulthood, and I hope I have provided some useful terms and ways of understanding such complexity (see Chapter 4 for discussion of *restorationist*, *preservationist* and *renovationist* attitudes).

Peter Hollindale's *Signs of Childness* (1997) represented a first step towards a process of opening up ideas about age and reading, critiquing the common assumption that childhood is a 'gradual, steady climb towards a plateau of achieved maturity' and positing that adults are also traversing a varied landscape that sometimes involves them 'climb[ing] back the way [they] came' (p. 38). Hollindale identifies a common ground where remembering adult and remembered child might come into contact instead, and where they may, indeed, find something to share through childhood experiences more generally. His notions of 'childness' and the accompanying adjective 'childly' are valuable concepts for the purposes of this book, since they provide ways of discussing experiences of childhood that are neither restricted to biological children nor weighted with nostalgia or implications of being something lesser or trivial, assumptions that would limit any serious exploration of autobiographical memory. Childness refers both to the qualities of being a child and qualities of remembering being a child, and encourages acknowledgement of continuities between older and younger experiences. More recently, Marah Gubar has articulated a related idea in terms of 'kinship', arguing that 'there is no one moment when we suddenly flip over from being a child to being an adult' (2013, p. 454). Recognizing ageing as a spectrum of experience and selfhood in this way, rather than as a sequence of distinct stages that act as barriers to each other, has helped me conceptualize reading as a lifelong act, accounts of which draw upon different autobiographical modes of being. Hollindale notes that on the whole adults are 'guests at the table of children's literature' (1997, p. 29), even if they are not necessarily hostile or destructive ones; however, I would counter that where that literature is made up of remembered childhood books the scenario shifts and adults must be seen as involved in ways that are primal and embedded. In this way, *Rereading Childhood Books* significantly shifts the field of children's literature as it stands, from a worldview in which adult critics and children exist in inherently separate spheres to one in which they exist simultaneously within individual readers. Katharine Jones has made some efforts to broaden terminology in the field to encompass some of these different possibilities. She recasts 'children's literature' as 'child literature' in order to include readers who are no longer in childhood within its sphere (2006, p. 306). I prefer to discuss 'childhood books' in this study, locating these books firmly within the life history of individual adults as texts that have in some way or other been understood as part of their childness, both in its initial experiential quality and in its quality as remembered state of being.

In examining autobiographical accounts or talking with adult readers I have generally considered childhood reading to be encounters that took place under the age of sixteen, while also recognizing that memories of poems read to a four-year-old self are bound to be different in kind to recollections of reading a chapter book for oneself at the age of eight or nine, or of studying a text in one's early teens at school. For clarity, where an autobiographical narrative clearly refers to adolescent reading experiences, I employ the term 'youthful', and elsewhere I use 'childly'. My reason for uniting this breadth of readerly experience where I may have previously drawn attention to boundaries and difference is that in terms of adults remembering and rereading, a distinction between self *now* and self *then* (or indeed a sense of continuity between these selves) is of most interest, whereas for children and young people reading a strong sense of self *now* and self *to be* is crucial (what Beauvais would call their 'might': 'the potent, latent future, to be filled with yet-unknown action'; 2015, p. 19). Further exploration of how the act of *rereading as a child* contributes to their might would be an interesting project, one that speaks to Walter Benjamin's interest in the way he dwelt on childhood books as a boy, 'abided between their lines' and 'reopening them after an interval, surprised [himself] at the spot where [he] had halted' (1932/1999, p. 632). Reading practices of contemporary children themselves fall outside of the scope of this study, which focuses instead on adult recollection and response, but some consideration will be given to memories of regular rereading of single texts or series within childhood.[3]

Nostalgia, memoirs and re-memorying

The now and then of autobiographical memory can present a rich source of information about the influence of childhood books and the processes of childly reading. Making use of autobiographical accounts presents various practical and methodological challenges, however, highlighting the instability of memory, the selective nature of written and oral recollections, and the limits of knowledge that can be gleaned from individual views of the past. Of particular concern throughout this study is the affective script of nostalgia, which attends so many narratives of childhood reading but which, I argue, does not always need to be at the core of lifelong reading. Nostalgia is conventionally conceived of as suspect, for philosophical, psychological, cultural and moral reasons. Couched as a strong desire to revisit the past for emotional sustenance, it can be critiqued for relying on realist assumptions about the stability of memory over time that have been undermined by theories of fragmentation and reconstruction. Moreover, for adults engaged in nostalgic activity, that urge can be read as solipsistic, 'childish' and even unhealthy in the sense it reduces the past to a source of gratification and reverses commonly held beliefs about the proper development of adult pleasure and taste. At a wider level, nostalgic practices might be blamed for insular and backward-looking attitudes infused through whole cultures. Even without subscribing to the strong moral agenda underpinning these assumptions, it is possible to identify individual risks attached to returning nostalgically to childhood books due to the distinct potential for them to reveal a mismatch between the adult rereader and child rereader and thus engender disappointment, irritation, or even embarrassment and shame. While acknowledging the powerful relationship between children's literature and discourses of nostalgia, and providing tools for understanding the nuanced way in which nostalgia manifests itself through narratives of remembered reading and rereading, *Rereading Childhood Books* also provides ways and means of discussing early reading experiences that are not bound by these terms. This approach allows me to add fresh ideas to existing work on adult relationships with children's literature, and has required me to examine sources that can illuminate this field in new ways.

I base my poetics on an interrogation of mostly British experiences. Although *Rereading Childhood Books* is not a social history of British reading, it responds to and reflects a particular sociocultural context, both in terms of the readers discussed and the body of works they have remembered and revisited. This focus has allowed me to make observations about shared childhood conditions and a common pool of reading material that have been valuable for theorizing the practice of rereading. It is not meant to imply that the British experience is necessarily a model for other national reading histories, nor that British children's literature offers the most meaningful paracanonical material (indeed, I am interested, not in a national canon, but in works that have been in some way available to British readers, including those in translation or from other parts of the world). Keeping some loose geographical boundaries in place has also been helpful in terms of selecting sources and managing research for the purposes of this poetics.

In this book, I draw on autobiographical information about childhood reading, remembered reading, and rereading from two main sources. First, I have surveyed childhood memoirs and published autobiographical fragments by British authors, mostly writers of works for children, who so often turn to early literary encounters to position their own readerly identities (a list of these can be found at the top of the Bibliography). Most are individuals who were children in the late-nineteenth or early to mid-twentieth-century Britain or British communities overseas, although I have not attempted a comprehensive sweep of the period. My examination of published writings has tended to highlight the reading experiences of children between 1860 and 1960, a version of a long twentieth century that reflects the fact that literary autobiographies are generally written by older individuals who are already established as authors. I have taken heed of book historian Jonathan

Rose's warning that memoirists are by definition unrepresentative readers, being unusually bookish and articulate (2001, p. 2), an opinion prefigured by Joseph Appleyard, who considers memoirs to 'reflect the attitudes of a specialized group of readers' (1991, p. 197) and more recently echoed by Tully Barnett, who argues that many individuals who write about childhood books in relation to life stories are members – often 'veterans' – of the literary establishment (2013, p. 85). I have also kept in mind Lorna Martens's advice to study literary accounts of childhood memory 'very carefully,' without losing sight of their literariness, or indeed their differing sociohistorical contexts (2011, p. 12). For children's writers reflecting on their own life stories, reading and childhood books naturally often emerge as an important theme. Where history, background, race, or gender may reveal variation, a shared concern to record memories of childhood reading throughout these writers' accounts offers a chance to observe certain principles and patterns in the content, form, and style of recollection.

At the same time, I have wanted to add more voices to my investigation, responding in part to Robert Darnton's call for a new history of reading that takes into consideration real encounters with books and encounters by 'ordinary readers' (1990, p. 174). To enrich my analysis of memoirs, I also examine interview transcripts and written accounts I have gathered myself from participants in a small research project I carried out in the UK between 2009 and 2014, in which approximately 120 adult readers between the ages of eighteen and eighty-five were surveyed about their childhood reading and invited to take part in a remembering and rereading activity (see Appendix for details of the project and these participants). It is worth noting that the individuals I have corresponded with and interviewed for this book do not act as a representative set, nor a comprehensive overview of possible responses, any more than the selected memoirists do, not least because around three quarters of my participants were female and more than half were aged over sixty (although data were not gathered on these identifiers, I would surmise that the majority were white, middle-class and well-educated); but they do have interesting things to say about what it is like to remember books from a childhood long past and what it is like to revisit them, as well as why they might undertake such an activity. Where Jerome Bruner might call upon scholars of narrative to study 'the work of trained and gifted writers' (1986, p. 15),

I suggest that my participants are experienced, as we all are, in remembering. As self-selecting volunteers, most were also gifted as child readers because they enjoyed reading. They are, therefore, authorities in remembering children's fiction and, at my prompting, have also become specialists in rereading and reflecting on their experience.[4]

My methodology for co-producing accounts of remembering and rereading childhood books with these participants is described in more detail elsewhere (2017b). In this essay, I adapt the term 're-memorying' from critic Lynne Pearce,[5] who uses rereading as a feminist method of exploring '*processes* of reading' (1997, p. 2). For the purposes of this research, re-memorying represents a phenomenological approach that allows the researcher and participant to focus on the specific functioning of individual reading acts, while still acknowledging social and shared meanings. It is a form of memory work, one that is less overtly committed to communal narratives of the past than this methodology's origins in feminism and trauma studies.[6] In interview or written responses, adult participants were encouraged to remember as many aspects of a childhood book and initial encounters with it as possible, including: information about narrator, plot, character, setting, episodes, style, and illustration; details about the material object of the book and the conditions in which it was read; emotional responses, both at the point of original encounter and in subsequent memory; and other associations with, or experiences of, the book. A similar set of questions help to shape a second intervention, based on the process of rereading this book, with additional queries about familiarity, forgotten elements, satisfaction, and any broader sense of influence or impact. The answers to these questions form what Pearce calls '*parallel texts*' or 'the "composite" product of text and reader' (2017, p. 29). My broadly exploratory experimental approach encourages participants to review a significant book that they had not read since childhood, but discussion also often covered texts that were objects of repeated rereading throughout childhood and beyond (see Bibliography for a list of those books mentioned or discussed).

Alongside the authors of children's fiction, who can trace their love of making narratives back to remembered stories in youth, this book thus makes use of the accounts, or parallel texts, of everyday readers. It is innovative in combining analysis of textual and oral accounts in this way, bringing together aspects of literary research and book history. I have chosen this approach because it makes it possible to track patterns in the ways that adults build narratives of remembering and rereading around childhood books, and to elicit deeper knowledge of some of the cognitive and emotional processes involved in these practices. In all cases I have chosen to acknowledge the fact that autobiographical writing is an 'intersubjective exchange between narrator and reader' (Smith and Watson, 2010, p. 16) rather than a reporting of historical truths, and that oral histories can be 'well rehearsed in that the narrator has composed a life story that pivots around a particular incident or life choice' (Abrams, 2014, p. 22). The form of these narrative accounts reflects the literary conventions of life writing and the shape adults see in their reading journeys, as well as the act of childhood reading remembered. Nevertheless, as Stanley Fish argues, 'autobiographies cannot lie because anything they say, however mendacious, is the truth about themselves, whether they know it or not' (1999, n.p.). The very attempt to remember and the purposeful act of rereading represent valid approaches to reading studies and are key methods for thinking about children's literature.

Experiments in rereading

This book is the first attempt to systematically examine such processes, but re-memorying as a way of understanding reading experiences from the past has a critical tradition in the field of children's literature. In 1979, literary critic and psychotherapist Hugh Crago asked what literary criticism could do for the discipline, concluding that the primary purpose of such criticism was to make public and comprehensible the extensive range of private responses to works of art. In particular, Crago claimed, the practice of literary criticism could reveal his own doubts, questions and 'private gratifications' when faced with a text and therefore had a special significance for the study of books for young people, because it could help him as critic 'approximate more closely to the response of the child reader [he] once was' (1979, p. 149). His article, published in the then relatively new academic journal for children's literature, *Signal*, came at a high point in debates about the value of children's literature scholarship and the origins of a discussion about what Peter Hunt subsequently called 'childist criticism': the idea that adults should approach children's books by 'read[ing] as children [. . .] ask[ing] what reading as a child actually means' (1991, p. 191). It also marked the beginning of a series of discursive pieces that demonstrate Crago's ongoing interest in the response of the child reader he once was and his attempts to use an understanding of this earlier self to critically examine both the activity of reading and the nature of children's literature.[7] In one exchange titled 'A Signal Conversation', in which he felt able to reflect on his own attempts at childist criticism and cast it within the history of 'ideas about children and their reading matter as they have been explored in the pages of *Signal*' (1986, p. 122), he expresses approval for academics such as Dorothy Butler and Charles Sarland, who had endeavoured to bring accurate data about real readers' responses to the field. (Crago's own work on his infant daughter's interaction with books, published with his wife and co-therapist, Maureen Crago (1983), also falls into this category.) As part of this 'conversation' about the role of child readers, Crago makes a brief appeal to *Signal* contributors not only to talk to real contemporary youth to build such a childist criticism, but also to make use of their own experience of childhood reading and actively remember books from their past. He is aware of the dangers of such an approach, in which 'memory *can* play us false,' (p. 136) and yet subscribes to the philosophy that adults can access something of the reading children they once were if they approach memory with 'discipline and honesty' (p. 139). A few years later Crago took his own advice and set himself the task to 'record in detail [. . .] memories of a book unopened since childhood, and then [sit] down to re-read that book in order to achieve an understanding of how the earlier reading had been mediated by memory' (1990, p. 99). He refers to his exploratory activity as a series of 'experiments in re-reading', testing his own memory against the tangible reality of the text and hypothesizing why certain episodes or characters remained vivid while others were forgotten or misremembered. Crago takes himself seriously as an individual case study, both assessing his ability to accurately recall books from the past, and also providing detailed and honest field notes on his youthful preferences, practices, and circumstances to enrich a picture of childhood reading. The crux of Crago's work is his suggestion that parallel lines of enquiry are required for a fully realized childist criticism to emerge, with critical self-observation designed to sit alongside theoretical models of early reading experiences and empirical studies of child readers.

Crago argued that his 'experiment' would only reach its full value 'if it [could] be set beside other attempts' (p. 99), but claimed to know 'few people' who had undertaken the same kind of rereading experiment, failing to mention Michael Steig who similarly used self-reflective methodology, and who notably also described his work as a critical 'experiment' in an article published in *Victorian Studies* in 1981 (p. 307).[8] While radical in some ways, Crago's work must be put into context, since it reflects a more general shift in literary criticism towards personal and autoethnographic studies, as well as a growing interest in the reader – not just the text – as a repository of meaning. Early essays such as Crago's and Steig's are of interest partly because they openly reveal the private reading habits and aspects of individual critics' psychologies that are usually hidden from view in academic writing; however, they also mark an important shift away from purely personal reflection by opening up a critical form of phenomenological investigation into remembering and rereading childhood books. This approach has recently reached a peak in Margaret Mackey's impressive autoethnographic study, *One Child Reading: My Auto-Bibliography* (2016), in which she attempts to counter the limits of 'retrospective, edited, and reduced accounts of other readers describing inside their own minds' (p. 9) through vivid, comprehensive, and detailed exploration of her remembered response to an extensive range of childhood literature and ephemera. *Rereading Childhood Books* represents the first 'bringing together' of accounts according to Crago's manifesto. Throughout this book I gratefully make use of his and Mackey's findings. I also draw on other existing critical work that has approached children's literature through an interest in remembering and rereading, especially work by critics who have adopted re-memorying strategies.

Accounts might be categorized into 'bibliomemoirs' and 'autobibliographies': the former taking books read over a lifespan as a starting point for exploring a life history narrative and the latter employing autobiographical anecdote to illuminate certain texts or aspects of literature. One of the best known instances of this body of work is Francis Spufford's *The Child That Books Built* (2002), an intellectual journey through a personal paracanon: 'the sequence of books that carried [him] from babyhood to the age of nineteen' (p. 21). Spufford's first chapter hints at a story of individual growth and a young man coping with the chronic illness of his younger sister in the manner of bibliomemoir, but the majority of the book works in a more autobibliographic mode, using the personal as a springboard for discussing a range of topics relevant to childhood reading, from the history of fairy tale and the hero quest narrative to Lewis's theosophy and its manifestation in *The Chronicles of Narnia*, with frequent references to models of child development and educational theory. Spufford aims to tell the story 'of the reading my whole generation of bookworms did' alongside that of his own relationship with books (p. 21), and thus has cultural as well as personal intentions in revisiting childhood reading. Wendy Lesser's *Nothing Remains the Same: Rereading and Remembering* (2002) – published the same year – seemingly offers up a more private project; an enquiry into individual response to literature based on the thesis that 'nothing demonstrates how personal reading is more clearly than rereading does' (p. 4). Where for Spufford rereading provides an entry into the psychosocial and cultural meanings of reading fiction in childhood, for Lesser it is a form of literary criticism, although not necessarily the childist kind that Crago suggested. Lesser's approach is the more obviously autobibliographic, allowing texts to be held up alongside life history and to a degree judged according to the success of the two to coalesce.

Patricia Meyer Spacks has a slightly different objective in *On Rereading* (2011), and one closer to Crago's – indeed, she uses similar experimental terminology to explain her project, noting that she is her 'own guinea pig in these endeavors' (p. 15). Her aim is to produce 'an autobiography of thoughts and feelings elicited by novels' through the act of rereading (p. 18). Like Lesser, she brings critical credentials to the task and similarly judges some childhood books as less suitable for rereading because of their literary flimsiness. Charles E. Carryl's *Davy and the Goblin: Or What Followed Reading 'Alice's Adventures in Wonderland'* (1885) does not live up to Carroll's original, for instance, although Spacks is quick to admit that the failure of her rereading in this case is due to her attempt to explicitly compare the two texts and in a future 'more random' reading when she does not have this purpose in mind she might be able to 'recapture the sheer fun of it' (p. 36). Her interest in the emotional effects of books she has read leads her to posit a 'magical theory about reading – that one mysteriously discovers, at every stage of life, just the books that one really needs at that moment' (p. 151). The dual forces of desire and need shape the books that remain in the memory and that therefore are ripe for rereading, although Spacks also points out that in some cases these needs are 'embarrassing, sometimes almost incomprehensible in retrospect' (p. 263).

The practice of tracing reading histories, personal biographies, or psychological narratives through memories of early reading has flourished so that it now regularly feeds into popular discourses as well as more academic studies: indeed, rereading forms its own sub-genre of writing about children's literature. As autoethnographic work on childhood reading has become established in a number of different strands of critical work, so popular accounts of remembered reading histories or rereading projects have become part of a publishing trend in the twenty-first century. Collections such as Anne Fadiman's *Rereadings: Seventeen Writers Revisit Books They Love* (2005), a collection of musings on rereading first published in the *New York Times*, and Antonia Fraser's *The Pleasure of Reading: 43 Writers on the Discovery of Reading and the Books That Inspired Them* (1992/2015), demonstrate the appetite for material about remembering or rereading, and not surprisingly these personal reports often centre on childhood books. Recent English language bibliomemoirs featuring childhood books include Lucy Mangan's *Bookworm: A Memoir of Childhood Reading* (2018), Bruce Handy's *Wild Things: The Joy of Reading Children's Literature as an Adult* (2017), Damon Young's *The Art of Reading* (2016), Samantha Ellis's *How To Be a Heroine: Or What I've Learned from Reading Too Much* (2014), Karen Swallow Prior's spiritual memoir *Booked: Literature in the Soul of Me* (2012) and Rick Gekoski's *Outside of a Dog: A Bibliomemoir* (2009), while Susan Hill offers a set of autobibliographical essays in *Howards End Is on the Landing: A Year of Reading from Home* (2009).

It is clear that the driving force for many of these undertakings – as for more explicitly scholarly endeavours – is a desire to theorize childhood reading. There is also an important project for many thoughtful bibliomemoirists in attempting to demonstrate the power of literature to soothe and guide young readers through maturation, trauma, or issues pertinent to understanding language, social interactions, and sexual awakening. For Spufford, reading as a child often offered an escape and a comfort in the face of his sister's uncertain health and other personal challenges, such as attending boarding school. Returning to books of his youth not only represents a memento of his inner world at that time, but also acts as a kind of therapeutic journey, one that Kenneth Kidd describes as a 'positive rather than a phobic theory of text-self formation' (2011, p. 16). Other accounts of childhood reading remember acts of resistance and revision that can be understood retrospectively in terms of identity formation. For instance, through a series of rereadings of key paracanonical heroines, Ellis reworks her own gendered and ethnic identity as the daughter of Iraqi-Jewish refugees growing up in the UK in the 1970s and 1980s. The feminist outrage she feels returning to fairy-tale characters she admired as a girl, including the Grimms's Sleeping Beauty and Hans Christian Andersen's Little Mermaid, is tempered by her comparative rereadings of Jewish biblical stories of her youth, as well as a nuanced interweaving of responses to other cultural media and later retellings of European *Märchen* by Disney. While she 'can't quite believe that [she] was so keen on a story about a mermaid who *gives up her voice for legs to get a man*' (Ellis, 2014, p. 21) she finds ways to make links between 'The Little Mermaid' and her own ethnic homesickness, recognizing in both narratives a shared sense of being 'caught between two worlds' (p. 25). Similarly, in 'On Becoming a Lesbian Reader,' Alison Hennegan locates her youthful love for Blyton's *Mallory Towers* school series (1946–51) within the context of her early desire to find her own books, those that gave her a feeling of 'warmth and pleasure' (1988, p. 168). Since the portrayals of authentic lesbian experience that led to such feelings were hard to find in the literature of her 1960s childhood, she found her own way of 'reading *round*' (p. 174) mainstream texts. She remembers creating romantic subtexts for Blyton's schoolgirl characters and admits that she continues this non-textual practice into adulthood, as she rereads and rediscovers single-sex school stories by authors such as Blyton, Antonia Forest, and others.

Autobibliographic work can also make an implicit case for the possibility of direct access to childhood via memory and rereading. Hill draws on Proust's famous token of *mémoire involontaire* from *The Way by Swann's* (1913) to press home the point that certain remembered childhood books have the power to 'catapult' her back sixty years (2009, p. 25). She claims special status for *Alice's Adventures in Wonderland* and describes this and *Enid Blyton's Treasury* (1947) as her 'madeleine[s]', acting as triggers for a rush of childhood reminiscence. Prior also refers to a Proustian memory prompt when she describes finding her 'old friend,' the horse story *King of the Wind* (1949) by Marguerite Henry, on her bookshelf (2012, p. 10). This is the catalyst for an extended thesis about reading for pleasure and religious enlightenment, and in making an argument for their symbiotic relationship Prior casts her childhood library as 'the reliquary of [her] soul' (p. 9). Hill's sense of being 'transported' by the Blyton treasury and Prior's explicitly metaphysical conception of childhood books as constituting her soul demonstrate how the book as Proustian stimulus for reminiscence is a useful trope for writers who want to present childhood reading as a distant and luminous activity,[9] that can, nonetheless, be reached via talismanic objects and the phenomenological practice of remembering.

The ease with which Hill's journey into the past appears to occur (dramatically catapulting her in a backwards direction) belies the rather more effortful process of recovery and reconstruction through which Proust's madeleine moment proceeds, as his narrator begins his task to raise up memory 'from my very depths' again and again (1913/2002, p. 49). Instantaneous flashes of memory are not the same as the laborious undertaking of remembering or rereading to remember that in fact underpin most autobibliographic projects, especially those such as Crago's and Mackey's, which investigate the substantive contents of books, rather than physical manifestations and nostalgic mementos. Crago points to this labour through a topographical metaphor, admitting that the process he undertakes is like wading into a river and 'lay[ing] hold on the rocks of memory, treacherous though they undoubtedly are' (1990, p. 99).[10] The trope is powerful, casting rereading as a dynamic process and memory as an immersive and unstoppable flow of experience, scattered with meaningful but slippery textual and personal details for us to attempt to grasp. It is not the primary metaphor that I use to underpin my own model of remembering and rereading, however, since, as I argue in more detail in Chapter 2, the flow of a river reflects rather too linear a movement to properly represent a lifelong reading act that moves to-and-fro in its imaginative progress. Nor does the madeleine moment offer the best analogy for this study, although I do return to Proust and discuss his commentaries on childhood reading more fully in Chapter 1. Rather, I have turned to Benjamin's fragment on excavation and memory in 'A Berlin Chronicle' (1932), quoted as an epigraph to this Introduction, and to his call to those who want to approach their own buried pasts to conduct themselves 'like a man digging' (1932/1999, p. 611). Excavation requires patience and hard, often repetitive labour. Memories are matter that require turning like earth: 'For the matter itself is merely a deposit, a stratum, which yields only to the most meticulous examination what constitutes the real treasure hidden within the earth' (p. 611). For Benjamin, this treasure constitutes the fragmentary images and shards of recollections that were previously buried and might now, through the process of remembering, be illuminated by the light of 'our later insights' (p. 611). Not only that, the act of bringing these objects to the surface – or even of finding nothing in 'fruitless searching' – is in itself part of the treasure, the 'richest prize' (p. 611). For remembering readers and rereaders, excavation provides the possibility of digging up fragments of childhood books, their materiality and their imaginative content, but also slivers of information about a remembered childhood self: all necessitate puzzling over and evaluating.[11]

Over the course of the following chapters other metaphors emerge momentarily to help describe specific aspects of adult rereading: calendars and journeys, photographs and lenses, black holes and time capsules, as well as the religious and medical concept of 'anamnesis' as an active recollection of things past. I am mindful that Rosenblatt disliked the use of metaphors to describe reading – 'No metaphor or comparison does justice to this unique character of verbal art', as she put it (1985, pp. 36–7) – and, of course, the truth is that there is no single essence to how adults remember and reread childhood books. I am also alert to the fact that, as Alfredo González-Ruibal explains, metaphorical uses of archaeology, such as excavation, often 'simplify a complex reality' (2013, p. 5). Nevertheless, it is useful to begin with some tools, and the excavator's chisel and brush offer subtle approximations of the ways in which we as remembering readers and rereaders establish an 'intimate contact' with the world (p. 9) and how we might unearth material in order to gain some kind of access to childhood time and space.

Rereading Childhood Books: A Poetics

Reading Childhood Books is a *Poetics*: that is, it attempts to examine and describe the way that memories and rereadings of those books are made (from the Greek *poiein*, 'to make'). This making takes place both in terms of the cognitive, subjective, and affective processes involved for each individual reader when they remember or revisit, and in terms of the written and oral accounts they might create to record such actions. And as reading is a creative act of discovery, *lifelong* reading includes the archaeological endeavour of excavating that which has been covered over or buried.

My poetics does not seek to 'name meaning' but, as Tzvetan Todorov suggests, aims at knowledge of 'general laws' (1981, p. 6). It first takes the form of a general model, outlining the systems and codes that can be used to understand and analyse narrative accounts of remembering and rereading childhood books. In Chapter 1, I discuss the *reading scene*, a conceptual space shaped and defined by remembering in which the activities of lifelong reading take place. A reading scene can also be the narrative reproduction of reading events, and Proust's key account of early encounters with books helps me develop a major argument for this poetics: that in remembering and rereading childhood books, conventions of reminiscence framed by nostalgia can be supplemented by other forms of remembering, such as recollection and recognition. Chapter 2 introduces the *life space*, a temporal and spatial zone in which encounters with books take place and are linked to other actors and spaces in real-world contexts. The first part of the chapter maps the autobiographical waymarks of childhood reading through autobiographical accounts, plotting points from early aural experience and learning to read, through to reading for pleasure and reading at school. In the second half, I expand this linear approach by constructing 'autotopographical' accounts of reading histories, particularly focusing on responses to place and space in remembered fiction that reflect spatial conceptions of both memory and life history. Chapter 3 deals with the ways that adult readers retrieve and develop relationships with childhood books over time through *affective traces* and archaeological residue. Lewis's aesthetic, theoretical and autobibliographical writings offer a foundation for this discussion, highlighting ambivalent emotional contexts for remembered reading alongside more commonly recognized frameworks of moral improvement and pleasurable delight.

The second half of *Rereading Childhood Books* presents two thematic explorations of lifelong reading. In Chapter 4, I consider adult rereading as a purposeful act that can be personal or professional. I interrogate the risks and opportunities that come with rereading, as well as questions of disenchantment and re-enchantment. I also explore the *rereading attitudes* displayed in written and oral accounts, which represent a spectrum of adult response. In Chapter 5, I pay attention to adult rereaders who misremember texts, are frustrated by different editions and translations, or who report forgotten elements within their paracanons. I establish the practice of *anamnesis* – an active recovery of forgotten experience – as a crucial part of the lifelong reading act. *Rereading Childhood Books* itself represents a process of cultural anamnesis, recovering autobiographical sources and reading histories that give new insights into childhood reading from the perspective of adult memory.

Throughout the course of the book I present case studies built around the written or oral accounts of adult rememberers and rereaders. These encompass discussions of a wide range of texts, some of which would not be conventionally understood as children's literature or books in their usual form: from *Alice's Adventures in Wonderland* to Noel Streatfeild's *Apple Bough* (1962), from the Ladybird rhyming story *Downy Duckling* (1946) to Thomas Hardy's *Under the Greenwood Tree* (1872), from translated classic such as Johanna Spyri's *Heidi* (1884) to fragments of forgotten poetry and ephemeral material such as the *Ally Sloper's Half Holiday* comics (1884–1916). Remembered childhood books emerge as a catholic and eclectic cultural body of work. Thus my study also offers new ways of constructing a history of children's literature in Britain, shaped primarily by readers and their paracanons rather than by more official narratives.

I conclude my poetics with some thoughts on the value of memory work in the field of children's literature studies, and some suggestions about future research in the context of rereading as a communal and global activity, contemporary technological developments and an ageing population. *Rereading Childhood Books* offers a valuable model for researchers wanting to develop an understanding of the reach of childhood books across these different terrains and tools to help analyse diverse attitudes toward childhood reading selves and remembered – or misremembered – texts from the past.

As in my findings, so too in *Fire and Hemlock*, childhood fiction remains crucial throughout an individual's life journey. Jones catalogues books that shape Polly's identity and structure her heroic development, including classics from American and British children's literature, as well as fairy tales and ballads.[12] The level of intertextuality in the novel is almost overwhelming, in fact, but just as important as the specific literary tradition into which Polly is initiated is the act of reading itself, along with the memories of that reading and the process of rereading. All of these acts are crucial for Polly's final quest. By rereading the book of supernatural stories and then through a process of mindful remembering, as well as through other methods such as revisiting places, meeting old acquaintances, and engaging with prompts in books, Polly remembers a new version of her childhood and is able to recall Tom's existence in her parallel past and recognize what she must do to save him.[13]

Childhood books do not need to be portals to the supernatural in order to be extraordinary forces in our lives. Naming remembering and rereading as ordinary, everyday and ongoing practices with resonance across the life course opens up new avenues for thinking about how adults read children's literature. I hope *Rereading Childhood Books* will go some way to supplement and extend Hunt's longstanding catalogue of 'ways of reading children's literature', which lists '*as if they were peer-texts*', '*on behalf of a child*', '*with an eye to discussing it with other adults*' and '*reading as a child*' (1991, pp. 45–8). This book presents a fifth way – *as a process of 're-memorying'* – that allows for return and integration into a wider autobiographical narrative of a childly reading self. In this respect, my model of a lifelong reading act sets moments of reading, reimagining, and rereading in a continuum and emphasizes the crucial role that memory plays in every stage of engagement with childhood books.

1

The reading scene

What forms of knowledge about childhood reading might be reached through acts of memory? How do autobiographical accounts construct the remembered reading self? To answer these questions it is first necessary to examine the dynamic fulcrum that is the *reading scene*: a conceptual and narrative space, shaped and defined by remembering, in which individual encounters with texts take place. My purpose in this opening chapter is to determine how reminiscence, recollection, recognition, and reconstruction function in this space and how they are accounted for in adult responses to childhood books. A scene implies a fixed and relatively contained setting, in both spatial and temporal terms, whereas any act of remembering is, after all, glancing, momentary, and bound by the constraints of the mind and its ability to conjure the past in a meaningful way. That scene is always enriched by examining the strata of memories underlying it, however; in Walter Benjamin's phrase 'the probing of the spade in the dark loam' (1932/1999, p. 611). One aim in this chapter is to examine the relationship between the surface of remembering in the now and the depths of remembered textual encounters of the past, paying particular attention to how the activity of excavation might be cast as more than nostalgic indulgence. Reader response theory has always acknowledged memory's role in the transactional process of reading. For instance, Louise Rosenblatt notes that there is a complex 'penumbra' of readerly memory effects – a 'mnemonic matrix' – that inflects every act of reading (1978/1994, p. 58). While her concern is primarily with the evocation of a work of art through the literary operation of such features as 'repetitions, echoes, resonances, repercussions, linkages, cumulative effects, contrasts, or surprises' (pp. 57–8), my focus will be on the mental work undertaken by adults to revive such initial evocations through remembering. In some cases, the practice of rereading represents an additional instrument for digging up the past, unearthing substantial, often hidden, aspects of previous childly interactions with books.

My notion of the reading scene as theoretical apparatus for understanding how individuals represent, deal with, and sort the past is partly informed by recent work undertaken by scholars of memory working at the interface of the arts and sciences, particularly those interested in the spatial underpinnings of memory. I have drawn on some of the most salient of these theories to help articulate how elements of narrative accounts of remembering reading intersect with recognized structures of scene and background memory in cognitive terms. Mine is not a scientific enquiry though, and I do not propose to analyse accounts of paracanonical reading for particular truths about memory functions that correspond to scientific discoveries.[1] Instead, this chapter begins the work of integrating and analysing a range of autobiographical sources in order to understand common themes and strategies among adult 'rememberers'. In the course of my discussion, I move between literary accounts, material from bibliomemoirs, and re-memorying parallel texts co-produced in interview, seeking insights into how the workings of readerly memory are translated into common discourses, and recognizing that different aspects of my mnemonic taxonomy will be foregrounded according to variations in motivation and intent across these sources. Memory operates as a narrative tool as well as a cognitive one, allowing memoirists and other remembering adults to shape accounts of their lifelong reading. These individual readers often reflect on what is and what is not easily recalled to memory, and what it means to recover certain readerly memories through the process of returning to books from the past. They recount textual features and also connect significant childhood books to particular ideas of the autobiographical.

To explore the role of readerly reminiscence and its disputed role in the history of children's literature scholarship, I turn to one of the most famous literary accounts of childhood reading. Marcel Proust's detailed interrogation of autobiographical memories of early reading provides some clues, not only to why many readers and critics consider such memories to be dangerously clothed in nostalgia, but also to how hidden fragments can yield other types of memory work in action, particularly processes of reconstruction. Further case studies produced from interviews with real readers and autobibliographical writings provide a more detailed map of the recollection, recognition, and reconstruction of paracanonical childhood books that I hope complicates the terrain. I begin this chapter by setting out the theoretical basis for the reading scene, the first element of my model of lifelong reading.

Memory and the *reading scene*

As a reader ages, his or her life is populated by a wide range of reading matter, as well as literary and non-literary events that inflect reading response. Encounters with books and with co-readers, playful re-enactments of stories and characters, and the development of a readerly identity are all part of lifelong reading and take place across the complex landscape of childhood and adult experience. Dynamic interactions with texts themselves, including those exchanges that take place after the initial encounter in the form of memories or revisitations, represent part of this activity. They occur across the life course and are influenced by its affairs. But such interactions also remain discrete from what I will term the 'life space' in the next chapter by dint of their particular nature as a form of internal, mental undertaking. In my model of remembering and rereading, then, the reading scene acts as a way to identify and contain individual moments of cognitive and emotional engagement with texts.

The relationship between childhood book and reading scene that I suggest reveals my debt to reader response theory, in which the virtual space between text and reader is a site for meaningful interpretation or communication. Rosenblatt suggests that this site, which she calls the 'poem', is a 'coming-together, a compenetration, of reader and text' (1978/1994, p. 12), while Wolfgang Iser argues that the activity of reading is a framework for, or process of, bringing the virtual text into being (1974, pp. 276–9). In each case, the ink on the page is less important than the event of the meeting between reader and text, a fact that seems to me even more pertinent in the lifelong reading act where the page itself may be faded, dog-eared, or torn, and the material book damaged, lent away, or lost, but the virtual space of compenetration continues to be activated through memory.

The reading scene is a theoretical concept – a virtual space in which these encounters and re-encounters, memories of books and memories of readings, are enacted. It also functions as a practical tool for organizing such mental work, in the form of descriptive accounts of remembered reading. Although it may seem rather contrived to combine two different senses in the same term, the overlaying of meanings point to the textual, narrative, and spatial qualities that cognitive reading processes and autobiographical accounts share when it comes to reading. The conflation also allows multiple meanings of the word 'scene' to come into play, referring to a sequence of action in a narrative or to the setting or place of that action, for instance. In her monograph *Architexts of Memory* (2005), Evelyn Endere explores the work of several 'exemplary architects of mnemonic scenes' (p. 3), including Proust, George Eliot, and Virginia Woolf, in order to argue for the crucial link between memory and subjectivity, both in imaginative writings and in real life. These authors, Ender suggests, create coherent and meaningful literary expressions of the phenomenon of remembering, and regularly offer up to readers beautiful or thought-provoking sketches for this complex aspect of human consciousness. The reading scene is a specific form of mnemonic scene, similarly reflecting and constructing inner processes – remembering and reading – that usually remain hidden from view. As we shall see, Proust is particularly skilled at creating both such scenes in relation to his childhood self.

The Modernist authors that Ender analyses often tie remembrance to a spatial context: memory gardens, childhood landscapes, or photographic and filmic visions. In doing so, they anticipate and articulate in imaginative terms aspects of more recent neuropsychological understandings of the cognitive functioning of memory, specifically 'scene construction theory'. The premise of this theory is that individuals mentally generate and maintain complex and coherent visual scenes as part of their everyday processes of remembering and predicting the future. The hippocampus facilitates the construction of these scenes by 'allowing details to be martialled [*sic*], bound, and played out in a coherent spatial context' (Maguire et al., 2016, p. 433).[2] Charles Fernyhough explains that this mechanism for autobiographical memory can be understood as the 'spatial backdrop' against which specific past experiences are placed (2012, p. 154), and in stating this he demonstrates its links to the tradition of medieval architectural mnemonics, which created a 'locus' or imagined environment into which a rich set of memory images and thoughts might be placed (Carruthers, 2008, p. 166). Other psychological and neuroscientific insights also stress visual and spatial elements of autobiographical memory. Daniel Dennett's work on consciousness (1991) highlights the importance of mental images, for example, showing how they create or recreate virtual sensations to help humans process the world around them without needing to be continuously in the act of perceiving or feeling. Ian Hacking (1995) argues that spatial tropes, in particular, can work as valuable metaphors for articulating aspects of autobiographical memory that other frameworks – such as linguistic models or notions of narrative – do not fully express.

The reading scene in its conceptual form presents a kind of cognitive backdrop then, allowing detailed description of specific phenomena and processes that are unique to decoding and responding to text as it is remembered or re-encountered in time and across experience. Reading scenes in their textual manifestations portray the scripts and processes underlying human memory functions in imaginative and structured ways. They need not always be the province of imaginative literature; they can appear in autobiographical accounts, such as the childhood memoirs I explore in this study, and can also be purposefully produced in discursive spaces, such as in interviews and other forms of re-memory work.

Memory is the major cognitive faculty at work here. However, memory is not a simple bridge between the self and the past. 'The memory' in its singular form has a number of symbolic connotations that transform it into either a cultural or metaphysical entity. Like the notion of the soul, it provides clues to the very nature of humanity and can be related to larger systems, such as a community, generation, or nation. It is sometimes represented in lay discourse as an active organ of cognition (the bit of the brain or mind that does our remembering) or as a repository of individual and subsidiary memories (again, often somehow a part of human physiology). Meanings multiply, leading prominent memory researcher Endel Tulving to bemoan the lax employment of terms for different concepts of memory 'in the real world', where, he argued, 'powerful forces of history and tradition' militate against 'rational behaviour' (2000, p. 37).

While I do not pretend to avoid such dangers completely, some attempt at rational definition seems sensible to allow for more precise discussion. The terms 'memory' and 'memories' encompass a range of more discrete cognitive phenomena, including long- and short-term systems and different faculties such as procedural memory for unconscious actions and declarative memory for conscious recall. I am mostly interested in autobiographical memory in this book, although semantic memory or memory for facts – such as remembering the name of an author – does play a role in accounts of childhood reading. This faculty is usually contrasted with what psychologists and philosophers call 'episodic memory', or memory for events. There is some slippage, however. If, for instance, an individual's account relates the moment in which he or she first recognized an author's name as the creator of a particularly significant childhood book, the episode itself is important as is the fact recalled. Since there is a tendency to think of remembered human experience in terms of a sequence of events, autobiographical memory can easily be conflated solely with episodic memory, but the remembering self may also recall information about that self – such as the fact that he or she was a voracious reader – in the form of 'autobiographical semantic memory'. Autobiographical memory can be further broken down into what William F. Brewer terms 'personal memories' and 'generic personal memories' (1986, p. 26), although I prefer the terms 'specific autobiographical memories' and 'generic autobiographical memories'. Both place the rememberer at the centre of his or her autobiographical memory, a characteristic known as 'autonoetic consciousness' (Tulving, 1985, p. 3). Generic memories – such as Jamila Gavin's recollection of 'gobbl[ing] up detective fiction' as a teenager, recounted in her youth memoir *Walking on My Hands: Out of India* (2007, p. 66) – cannot be connected to any particular instant of the rememberer's early life. Specific memories – such as the account Nina Bawden includes in her 'almost' autobiography *In My Own Time* (1994) of reading *Jane Eyre* aged eight and conjuring an imaginary madwoman in the house next door (p. 22) – relate to mental images of discrete episodes from his or her past experience.

Autobiographical memory is clearly at work in the lifelong reading act in a variety of ways. There is a difference between the manner in which childhood books are remembered when a memoirist purposefully narrates his or her youth or an interviewee is asked to consider broadly significant texts from the past and the way specific elements of those texts might be recalled or recognized through the conscious reaching for more detail via memory work or rereading. Other forms of declarative memory are required to specifically recall the titles of paracanonical books as well as the details of plot, character, setting, and language that might be retained over time and revisited in the reading scene. Mnemonic cues prompt remembering adults to recall a favourite character, incident, or turn of phrase. Triggers range from an interviewer's question to a glimpse of an illustration to a real-world event that chimes with a fictional one. It is likely that readers will recall more content, more readily, when there is what Daniel Schacter calls an 'affinity between encoding and retrieval processes' (1996, p. 60). In other words, if some aspect of the backdrop for the original reading experience (a place, a feeling, an image) reappears or perhaps is consciously excavated through discussion with the researcher, then part of that original may be re-experienced vividly and with some success in reliability. It is interesting, then, to interrogate why certain details emerge in any reading scene, and to ask what conditions in the past and present might have encouraged these to surface.

Just as memory is not the only cognitive faculty at work in reading (which also encompasses perception, attention, language skills, and so on), the reading scene is not a direct analogue for the mind in the act of remembering reading. The reading act is only one part of the mental activity that goes on for an individual at any given moment. The virtual zone of exchange that reader response theorists construct does not always encompass unconscious processes, such as the turning of pages, for example, nor the sociocultural context in which such a mind is embedded, although Iser acknowledges (and so does Rosenblatt) the importance of the 'individual mind of the reader with its own particular history of experience, its own consciousness, its own outlook' that undertakes the activity (1974, p. 284). In a model of remembering and rereading, those contexts are similarly mapped in the external life space, feeding into each textual encounter, and I shall explore them in the next chapter; however, they are also more expressly *reproduced* in the reading scene, since a remembering adult may recall the circumstances of reading as readily as the details of the text that was read. A childhood book can be a 'magic object causing memory', as George Shannon puts it (1986, p. 180), leading adults to remember intricate details about their earlier reading lives and experiences.

The actual retrieval of the original text and an encounter with it relies on complex psychosomatic mechanisms, ones that I cannot hope to lay out with any authority here, but many accounts of remembered reading and rereading, from Proust's to the interview responses of my participants, elegantly allude to the processes involved and analysis of these is illuminating in its own right.

Historically, such acts of reminiscence have provoked debate about what exactly produces appropriate forms of knowledge about childhood reading and what constitutes a reliable source. Proust's famous description of childhood reading presents an excellent case of remembrance as a form of reminiscence. Although he was neither a writer for children nor a British child, as a commentator on reading and the workings of memory he is difficult to ignore in any study of remembered reading. He is, as Ender explains, our 'arch-rememberer' (2005, p. 2). It is no wonder that his eloquent insights – predominantly to be found in his semi-autobiographical magnum opus, *À la Recherche du Temps Perdu* (1913–27), and also in essays and criticism – are often used as a starting point for discussing aspects of autobiographical memory.[3] His subtle explorations of the importance of remembrance are well known, but, as Adam Watt has pointed out, Proust is also an authority on the practice of reading, deeming it to be an essential process 'learned in childhood, which, for the rest of our lives, now underpins and now undermines our being in the world' (2009, p. 2). The voices of other memoirists echo some of Proust's insights and in the following section I incorporate them into my investigation into this part of the reading scene.

Childhood reading and reminiscence

One of the most famous mnemonic scenes in literary history dealing with remembered childhood reading was published in 1906, as part of a French translation of John Ruskin's treatise on the role of reading for the common man, *Sesame and Lilies* (1865). In a short essay prefacing this booklet, variously known as 'Days of Reading' or 'On Reading', Proust presents his own philosophy of reading.[4] He claims to have a phenomenological purpose in exploring the 'original psychological act called *Reading*' (1906/2011, p. 18), yet his essay begins by foregrounding the life space instead, describing the various places and circumstances in which he would read as a boy: sunk in an armchair by the fireside, under the hazels and hawthorns of the park, and by candlelight in bed. He provides a portrait of his childhood environment, with a detailed account of all of the activities that might be considered as interruptions and impediments to a child absorbed in fiction: those vulgar obstacles such as a 'bothersome bee' or a boisterous outdoor game or a dinner waiting at home that get in the way of the 'divine pleasure' of reading. He notes that although full engagement with pleasurable reading should have easily kept attention away from such distractions, on the contrary, 'it has graven into us such happy memories of these things (memories much more valuable to us now than what we were reading with such passion at the time) that if, today, we happen to leaf through the pages of these books of the past, it is only because they are the sole calendars we have left of those bygone days' (p. 4).[5]

Proust's seemingly casual dismissal of his childly passion and the texts that inspired it, and particularly the metaphor of the childhood book as a calendar of 'bygone days', represent a contradiction in his task of remembering reading. A calendar is a temporal index that directs the user towards other, more meaningful information rather than being of interest in and of itself. If childhood books act similarly as indices, they are not memorable in themselves but rather point towards the reader of the past and the context in which he or she read. In other words, Proust appears to be creating the backdrop for memories of reading and yet not populating this space with the recollections themselves. The more he attempts to recall the content of the book or the act of reading and its fundamental internal qualities, the more he portrays peripheral information about the external world of his childhood instead, a fact about that process which he terms its 'sorcery' (p. 18). Rachel Falconer summarizes his sense to mean that 'those same books re-encountered as an adult would bring vividly to mind not so much the books' contents, as the material circumstances in which they were read' (2008, p. 158). The backdrop to a reading event, it seems, is often more open to literary description than the literary encounter itself.[6] It can certainly appear to be more stable or tangible than the transaction between reader and text, and therefore more amenable to textual expression. Proust's long diversion from the act of reading itself into an autobiographical account of the social world of his youth, with details about remembered games, places, family members, and traditions, offers a pleasing portrait of life in nineteenth-century rural France and of experiences instantly recognizable even beyond that context and provides an example of the tendency for bibliomemoirists to write 'of everything but books' (Proust, 1906/2011, p. 18). Writers might want to draw attention to the joys of reading by relating specific titles, reading choices and responses, but adult rememberers, particularly authors, are prone to portray books as 'calendars' or as containers of picturesque atmosphere for an autobiographical narrative in this way.

Like Proust, naturalist Denys Watkins-Pitchford, better known as children's author 'B. B.', records a familiar and cosy account of a child reading in an enclosed interior as adults go about their business around him. In his memoir, *A Child Alone* (1978), he writes: 'It was in the long winter evenings that I did most of my reading, or was read to by my father. Soon after four o'clock, the housemaid would bring in the brass oil lamps with their white china shades, the tall shutters would be closed, the curtains drawn, and I was away in another world' (p. 37). B. B. recreates – in the context of Edwardian Northamptonshire rather than Third-Republic Provincial France – a habitual state of absorption akin to Proust's, illuminated literally and figuratively by the material world around him. In his autobiographical writings *Something of Myself* (1937/1991), Rudyard Kipling likewise recalls domestic details related to reading, recounting a period when he lodged with three London ladies as a young teenager. He mentions twice that their house is 'filled with books' with 'walls of bookshelves of anything one liked' (1937/1991, p. 15), without going into detail about any single title lodged therein. In his fictionalized reminiscences, published as *Dream Days* (1898/1929), Kenneth Grahame describes a childhood visit to a grand house in Berkshire where the walls were 'honestly upholstered' with unnamed books, which 'glimmered provokingly through the glass doors of their tall cases' (1898/1929, pp. 136–7). In *Surprised by Joy* (1955/2012), C. S. Lewis describes the plethora of books housed in his family home in Belfast: 'books in the study, books in the drawing room, books in the cloakroom [. . .] In the seemingly endless rainy afternoons I took volume after volume from the shelves' (1955/2012, p. 9). As a poignant contrast to these material excesses, in an article published in the *New York Times* in 1920, Frances Hodgson Burnett reports the 'haunting memory' of rainy days spent as a girl wandering in a large house devoid of books (cited in Tatar, 2009, p. 206), an image that chimes with her own fictional creation Mary Lennox roaming the corridors of Misselthwaite Manor in *The Secret Garden* (1911). As well as acting as indices for childhood experience, these bibliographical details bestow a certain glamour upon the physical reality of reading matter, which has the effect of distancing the child figure from acts of reading themselves and also gives some social context about the relative luxury of book ownership for many pre- and early-twentieth-century children.

There can be a tension in such accounts between literary portrayals of the past and individual memory. Reminiscence is a process of conscious recollection that has a personal, creative, or social impetus: according to Kathleen Woodward, it is 'generative, restorative' (1997, p. 3). It is purposeful in this way, and can be the basis for a rich and intensely felt narrative of the past that avoids the pedantic searching for 'truth' that recollection in its purer form requires. When it is used within the context of clinical practice or social and oral history research, for instance, reminiscence 'depends less on the accurate remembering of the past and more on the process of exchange and listening' (Bornat, 1989, p. 21). One example from my research project illustrates the potential utility of this kind of remembering in more personal contexts. The participant began our interview by naming the title of a childhood favourite but then mentioned nothing more of the book itself throughout the whole discussion. The memory of the book was a springboard for her to move into chronicling some painful details of her own life history that were related to it and the interview acted as a form of therapeutic remembering. This example also reveals some of the potential challenges of re-memory work for the investigator, raising ethical questions about how far researchers into reading memories should be prepared for these kinds of personal revelations and potentially traumatic revisitations.

As a form of therapy or a subset of 'life review', reminiscence is considered in sociological fields to be an 'ecologically valid form of episodic memory' (Webster and Haight, 2002, p. xix), yet in literary terms is often regarded as self-indulgent. For instance, Harold Rosen's opinion is that the 'proliferation' of reminiscence publications among the 'eminent and notorious' often represents 'ephemeral trivia' (1998, p. 177). Indeed, we might ask why Proust should turn from his task of describing the processes and benefits of reading in general to dwell on his childhood milieu. Why must authors assume that the backdrops to their childhood reading are worth relating at length? While I consider such accounts to be an organic element of the reading scene, and do not judge them to be uninteresting in any way for the purposes of understanding what happens when adults remember books from their past, the critical discourse around reminiscence and childhood books has shaped much children's literature scholarship and is worth examining further.

Reminiscence shares territory with nostalgia (which I shall return to in Chapter 4), and Proust's account appears to be a form of nostalgic writing in the sense that it recreates a longed-for childhood through the trope of reading. Moreover, alongside the personal and storytelling aspects of his account, there is also a shared or communal quality that seems to speak nostalgically to all adults across time. This is conveyed in the essay's mixture of idiosyncratic detail and common experience: references to particular family members and servants who interrupted the young Marcel reading featuring alongside appeals to recognize universal conditions for the reading act in childhood. The shift from the personal to the general is marked in Proust's account by narrative frequency and duration, voice and address:

> In the morning [. . .] I would slip into the dining room where, until lunch, still such a long time away, no one would come in except for old Félicie, who was relatively quiet, and where my only companions, very considerate of my reading, were the painted plates hung with hooks on the wall, the calendar whose previous day's page had just been torn off, and the grandfather clock and the fire, both of which talked without asking you to answer them, and whose gentle speech, empty of meaning, never replaced, as people's words do, the meaning of the word you were reading. (1906/2011, p. 5)

The two hours of silent reading take him a page and a half to describe and, ironically, the episode enacts precisely that replacement of 'the word you were reading' by the distracting words of adult speech that Proust complains about. The passage gives a vivid sense of intense time slowly passing, while the calendar on the wall is both an explicit indicator of this temporal progress and a reminder that books are types of almanacs. In referring to 'vacation-time reading', Proust indicates by the use of the past-habitual that he read in the quiet of the dining room not just on one morning, but regularly. Although the amount of detail included implies a specific autobiographical memory, the sense of this being a repeated act also indicates a more generic memory, one that might be shared by other adults who were once children on holiday. The shifts from first person to second person and from informal to formal (the passage slides from '*je*' to '*on*' and finally '*vous*' in the original French) in describing the way adult chatter interfered with meaning of the 'word you were reading' also invites the reader of the account to consider his or her own memories of being interrupted or disturbed when reading as a child.

This is not simply an isolated case of Proust's esoteric style and the nuances of translation from the French, since the same slippage can be seen in other accounts of remembered childhood reading where the memoirist aims to achieve some recognition from his or her reader. For example, the tactic is acknowledged overtly by Spacks in her autobibliography *On Rereading* (2011). Spacks discusses Lewis's *Narnia* sequence, which she has first read as an adult, and reminisces about other series books she enjoyed reading as a child:

> The child reader, I strongly suspect – drawing on my own experience as a child/adult reader – responds positively to predictability of the sort that Lewis's series offers. Remembering older, duller series from my own childhood – the endless Nancy Drew books, the even more innocuous careers of the Bobbsey Twins – I realize that predictability, which marks all these works, constitutes part of their appeal [. . .] You want them to go on forever, precisely because you know ahead of time just what pleasures they will give. (2011, p. 51)

Spacks suggests that readerly reminiscence works to transform the personal, interior experience of reading into a recognizable externalized pattern of activity that others will understand, and thus construct an image of 'the child reader'. That figure has been a troublesome one ever since the publication of Jacqueline Rose's critical work *The Case of Peter Pan: Or the Impossibility of Children's Fiction* (1984), which set out concerns about the lack of a real child behind the category of children's fiction 'other than the one which the category itself sets in place' (p. 10). Her point is that adult desire for the pure state represented by fictional childhood is at the heart of the endeavour of writing for children rather than any simple service to actual young readers. This is an issue I will come back to in Chapter 4, alongside Spacks's reading memoir, when I consider the ways that critics reconstruct childhood reading as a universal act. As I have implied in my discussion of Proust's account here, it is not just a remembered child who might be constructed through reminiscence about reading experiences either; there is also a remembering adult evoked in universal terms. Anxieties about critics speaking for children and colonizing their imaginations can shroud the practice of speaking for all remembering adults, regardless of experience, background, or individual predilections.

While Spacks is upfront about the relationship between her specific set of memories and the theory she extrapolates from it, in other cases this connection not so clearly set out. For instance, in *Enchanted Hunters: The Power of Stories in Childhood* (2010), Maria Tatar aims to build a detailed picture of the lasting influence of children's literature by drawing on the memories of published autobiographical narratives and interviews with students who she calls 'obsolete children' (2009, p. 30), an expression she takes from Dr Seuss's 1986 nonsense book for adults called *You're Only Old Once: A Book for Obsolete Children*. She argues (and I agree) that what sticks in the memory is hugely significant and can provide insights into childhood reading, but she does not always acknowledge the subtle shifts she introduces from personal to universal. She claims 'we can all remember the jolts and shimmer of books we read as children, the moments that sent shivers up and down the spine. This is why we revisit them as adults raising or educating children' (p. 11). She then asks 'who can forget' such key 'wow' moments, such as Iorek Byrnison's bloody triumph over the usurper bear king Iofur Raknison in Philip Pullman's *Northern Lights* (p. 12) and the Snow Queen's luring of Kai into her icy realm in Hans Christian Andersen's 'The Snow Queen' (p. 81). The statement and questions presuppose that all readers encode memories of books in the same way, and that all adults will decode through identical forms of remembering. In fact, as I shall show in Chapter 5, readers frequently forget climatic events or crucial details from their childhood books, so the answer to Tatar's question is not necessarily a foregone conclusion.

David Rudd disputes Tatar's claims for a 'uniform, universal child' (2013, p. 35). Individual remembered reading experiences can also be deployed in order to challenge her claims by 'checking' ideas about universal response against the remembered past. One published example of this form of correction can be found in J. R. R. Tolkien's treatise 'On Fairy Stories', first published in 1947, in which he examines the assumption (still evident in Tatar's book) that children enjoy fairy tales because of their innate desire to believe in marvels.

Tolkien makes a strong case for qualifying this theory by using own childhood reading tastes as a counter-example. He enters into critical debate with Andrew Lang, collector of fairy stories and publisher of the *Fairy Books* published for a young audience in the late nineteenth and early-twentieth centuries (1889–1930), who in introducing these to his readers explains they appeal to children's natural taste for the marvellous. Tolkien makes a rebuttal on this claim based on the authority of memory: 'Lang's description does not fit my own memories [. . .] speaking for myself as a child, I can only say that a liking for fairy-stories was not a dominant characteristic of early taste [. . .] I agreed with Lang's generalized "children" not at all in principle, and only in some points by accident' (1947/1964, pp. 39–40). Children's fiction and non-fiction writer Naomi Mitchison also expresses ambivalence towards fairy tales based on her memory of childhood reading in her book, *Small Talk: Memories of an Edwardian Childhood* (1973). She liked some tales but not the 'romantic' ones edited by Lang: 'Later on when I was eleven or twelve I told him I hadn't like them and he didn't mind at all; these collections had just been a job' (p. 51).

Reminiscing in the style of Proust can therefore be employed, intentionally or not, to support generalized theories of childhood reading by creating recognizable reading scenes, to appeal to others' sense of common ground, and to provide a compelling backdrop of generic autobiographical material to accentuate an individual act of remembrance related to childhood books. In other words, this form of remembering allows the rememberer to go on a journey into the past without worrying too much about the veracity of his or her recollections or the precise details of that distant land. Working with memoirs can be problematic for this very reason and it is why other critics have rejected it as a methodology. Appleyard indicates his intention to avoid first-person accounts of childhood reading experiences written by adults as a way of comprehending the nature of children's reading because these works are likely 'to be filtered through the lens of memory' (1991, p. 198). Perry Nodelman has similarly dismissed the very possibility of valuable evidence about childhood reading emerging from adults (such as himself) recalling their own childly experiences or rereading books encountered in youth:

> The child I remember or imagine still being with me, viewed through inevitable lapses of memory and the filter of later knowledge and experience,

> is not the child I was. It is, inevitably, an adult's nostalgically reimagined version of childhood [. . . and] not, therefore, likely to provide accurate insights into real childhood experiences. (2008, p. 84)

The technical problems Nodelman highlights are indisputable: adult accounts of reading have the potential to be unreliable because of the imaginative force of reminiscence – in this case, featured as adult nostalgia towards their own childhoods and childhood in general – and also because of the inevitable 'lapses of memory' that are an inherent part of the reading scene. However, it is not true to say that all adult memories of childhood reading are 'invariably' nostalgic, as Nodelman implies, nor that they are inevitably marred by the obscuring lens of memory to the point of offering no useful insights into the lifelong reading act. Reminiscence forms a substantial node in the mnemonic matrix: it is a major mode for autobiographical writing about childhood books and naturally emerges from oral history methods of discussing childhood reading with participants. It is the most common starting point for discussion with adults when I explain my project to them and it remains a pleasurable and purposeful part of the reading scene. It is worth paying attention to moments of reminiscence then, not just in terms of their displays of nostalgic urges, but also in terms of how they feed into readers' sense of themselves over time and their remembered interactions with childhood texts.

Adults also produce accounts of remembering that deal in more precise types of recollection and accounts of rereading that offer evidence of recognition. These cognitive functions can in some sense be 'checked' or verified through reference to material objects – the books themselves as 'one kind of reliable data set', as critic Margaret Mackey puts it (2016, p. 12) – should we want to test memory against reality to counter some of the more sceptical opinions about adult memory encountered so far. Interviews and re-memorying accounts co-produced with my project participants represent valuable material for such enquiry. Proust also probes these other forms of remembering in his literary 'reading scene', and I want to briefly return to him to complicate the discourse of nostalgia that has up to now saturated his narrative.

Childhood books and recollection

Proust's account and the way it conjures a picture of 'everything but books' (1906/2011, p. 18) has led Călinescu to gloss the passage by suggesting that children's books are mere 'pretexts for remembering' without much intrinsic value in and of themselves (1993, p. 96). As I implied in my introduction, this is not the complete picture. While 'On Reading' is certainly interested in the context of reading, it is also concerned with the exchange between text and reader as well as the cognitive and imaginary space of the literary work that has been identified by transactional reader response theorists. Watt notes that Proust's essay emphasizes 'the highly subjective, creative nature of the act and the ceaseless, complex interaction between the reader, the text, and the environment in which reading takes place' (2009, p. 3). Memories of a singular childhood book, freed to some degree from nostalgia, do play a part in his writings. A little while after the lengthy discussion of childhood reading habits, and in developing further his ideas about the purpose of reading, Proust draws attention to the specific novel he has portrayed in the hands of his younger self. In doing so, he somewhat undermines his concerns about the 'sorcery' of remembering reading, which leads the rememberer away from 'everything but books', although with great Proustian style the paragraph almost threatens to be magicked away into description of material conditions once more:

> The book you have seen me reading just now by the fireplace in the dining room, in my bedroom deep in the armchair with its crocheted head-rest, and during the beautiful afternoon hours under the hazelnut trees and the hawthorns of the park [. . .] since your eyes, straining toward that book at a distance of twenty years, may not be able to make out its title, my memory, whose vision is better suited to this type of perception, will tell you what it was: *Captain Fracasse* by Théophile Gautier. (1906/2011, p. 21)

Proust plays with notions of nostalgia and memory here, leading his own reader away from conventions of reminiscence and yearning towards a more concrete recollection of the text itself. He remembers factual details about the book – its title and author – and sentences from within its pages, including a 'long, boring description of a castle' (1906/2011, p. 22), which he subsequently recalls with apparent accuracy. He also describes his remembered responses to the sensational novel *Captain Fracasse* (1863), which excited him and led him to think of other childhood reading of a less thrilling kind that he had undertaken 'during an unusually cold March' (p. 22), moving from the past-habitual of generic reminiscence to the temporally specific past-continuous to mark the process of recollection. He relates the feelings of curiosity provoked by what he considered one of the more philosophical moments in the novel and the sense of disappointment he experienced when the text followed it with an 'insignificant' realist description of 'a table "covered with a layer of dust"' (p. 23). Proust remembers *Captain Fracasse* from the inside out, recalling the sentences that he considered the most 'original and beautiful in the book' (p. 21) and explaining how these brought him to a state of 'intoxication' as a boy (p. 22). He uses these particular recollected details drawn from memories of his transaction with Gautier's work to develop his thesis (disagreeing in part with Ruskin in *Sesame and Lilies*) that books do not provide complete or final answers to the questions a reader might bring to them, but are instead essential stimuli that prompt the desire for knowledge and understanding, especially for young readers.

In the early part of the essay, the identified novel *Captain Fracasse* is nameless and apparently irrelevant. Once named, the book is no longer a mere pretext for reminiscence about the self nor simply a cherished love object, but rather very much a distinct recalled entity which helps the essayist Proust reconstruct something of the reading act to further his argument. He writes of remembering his younger self experiencing a yearning to derive intellectual and existential insights from reading Gautier's swashbuckling story. As a boy he wanted to learn from his encounter with *Captain Fracasse* (particularly how to derive the correct opinion of Shakespeare and the classics) and he also wished Gautier himself could advise him on what career to pursue. The tongue-in-cheek tone of this exchange between reader and text, which exposes an ironic mismatch between earnest desire for improvement and the lowbrow nature of the source of that improvement, does not completely obliterate the vivid recreation of *Captain Fracasse* made possible by specific memory of the text. Proust's reading scene is formed not just of the backdrop of reminiscence against which an appeal to shared experiences or common contexts can be made; it also features foregrounded instances of textual recollection.

In this way Proust moves away from nostalgic description of bygone days and points towards a memory enactment of the phenomenological act of reading, even if he does not perform it in totality himself. This primary act is what Roman Ingarden describes in *The Cognition of the Literary Work of Art* (1937) as the 'unfolding continuum of phenomena of temporal perspective' (1973, p. 143). Ingarden borrows the term 'presentification' (*Vergegenwärtigung*) from phenomenologist Edmund Husserl to identify the way in which textual features are encountered by the reader in the present moment and then sink 'slowly into the horizon of the past' to be recovered as traces in the reader's memory (p. 98). On a sentence-by-sentence or part-by-part basis, the reader's job is to use these images to remove or fill in indeterminacies in the text, in a process called 'concretization'. On a grander scale, 'concretion' occurs when all of the mental images held within this temporal scheme are concretized and the full potential of the text is realized. In remembering reading, these are the mental images that may be retrieved from their encoded form within the reading scene.

Other published accounts of reading scenes also gesture towards phenomenological experience, although the *autonoetic* quality of the experience related – the sense of the rememberer being at the centre of recalled experience – can displace memories of the text itself in favour of memories of readerly identity. In her memoir *Ambush of Young Days* (1937), Alison Uttley compares two early encounters with a standalone edition of Andersen's 'The Ugly Duckling' (1843). The first is rich in material and topographical detail, from the remembered 'mouldy smell' of the book's pages to the garden setting for reading (1937, p. 204). The scene is vividly constructed and the memory of reading is then easily set against this backdrop. It has a dramatic quality: Uttley models the process of presentification, recalling the action of turning pages and the 'wretched' feelings evoked by the story, which the young Alison took 'to heart' as a tale reflecting her own ugly and naughty status (p. 204). As a narrative, the account falls within the pattern of a mini epiphany (to be discussed further in the next chapter), conveying a specific transformational autobiographical moment leading to Alison's 'transports of joy, at the miracle of the duckling!' (p. 204). In doing this, it creates a sense of authenticity through its use of particular rather than generalized imagery as well as through the temporal build up to the child's revelation about the duckling and the comfort its transformation provided for her. A tiny sleight of hand disrupts the purity of the memory, as Uttley slips in the fact that she read 'at intervals' and that the narrative revelation happened on an unspecified 'one day', rather than the single momentous day the text was discovered. In remembering a second encounter with the story a little later in childhood, Uttley further destabilizes some of the certainty of the reading scene by revealing that as an older girl she was 'astonished to find my old friend *The Ugly Duckling*' in a collection of Andersen's fairy tales because in her original set of memories she assumed the story was true natural history and not fantasy at all (p. 204). Although no rereading of the story in adulthood is reported, which might have allowed Uttley to explicitly check recollections against the text itself, this account demonstrates the complex ways that the mental, cognitive processes of the reading scene are in dynamic conversation with life experience (including reader identity) and reoccurring encounters with the text over time.

It is worth recognizing that presentification is related to the more common 'presentifying' (*Gegenwärtigung*), of perceiving objects in the world. Remembering can also be conceptualized as a form of seeing, so that the mental images we form as we move through the world are also the images we refer to in order to gain a sense of the past. When Proust claims that his memory is well suited to *perceiving* this childhood book, he points to how intertwined the two cognitive faculties are. Before returning to Proust one final time, I want to go on examine the qualities of recollection as they feature in the reading scene through case studies drawn from my work with adult rereaders, with a particular focus on autobiographical memory and the visual flavour of remembering. Working with parallel texts of rereading as well as remembering is a good chance to distinguish recollection from recognition in this part of the lifelong reading model.

Rereading and recognition

Joanna was born in the late 1960s and was a prolific reader and rereader when she was younger. She continues to read and reread children's literature regularly, having a personal interest in collecting school stories and ambitions to write her own fiction for children. She chose Noel Streatfeild's *Apple Bough*

(1962) to discuss with me. It is a novel she read as a child and which she has tangible memories of 'really enjoying', but it also represents one of the rare texts she did not read multiple times in youth or return to in adulthood. She begins our conversation by stating that there is 'very little' she can remember about *Apple Bough* at all. She certainly cannot produce a working summary that accurately reflects the plot, which involves a family of talented children trying to find a way to bring their family together in a proper home again, after they are separated by the demands of their youngest brother's commitment to a musical career. When prompted further, however, Joanna deploys semantic memory in recalling details about characters – she recalls that the children are musical and that there is some kind of 'factotum' who features in the story – and some limited information about plot – for instance, that one of the children is learning the violin and that the big house, which she thinks might be a rectory, is central to the story.

In addition, Joanna relates some germane autobiographical information through generic and specific memory. She relates how she read and reread other work by Streatfeild as a girl, remembering *Ballet Shoes* (1936) and the *Gemma* series (1968–9) in particular. She claims she was 'addicted to series', and this fact is supported by the list of books she included in the initial survey as provoking the strongest memories from childhood, which range from Laura Ingalls Wilder *Little House* books (1932–43) to Lewis's *Chronicles of Narnia* and the *Sadler's Wells* series by Lorna Hill (1950–63). *Apple Bough* stands apart in Joanna's paracanon then, as a standalone text, or what she calls a 'singleton novel'. Joanna kept precise records of her childhood reading, but *Apple Bough* does not feature in her journal and she can only state that she was twelve or thirteen when she read the novel through deduction, based on the fact she cannot remember borrowing it from the library and the copy she still owns is priced at 40p (which means it was bought after the age of eleven when she had a spate of buying up 10p books at the local second-hand bookshop). On the whole, singleton novels did not appeal to her tastes as a child. Now, as then, she explains, 'I enjoy books where I know that there is more to come when I have reached the last page'. Nevertheless, on rereading *Apple Bough*, Joanna realizes that, as a narrative, it is enriched through the network of connections that can be made to other texts in Streatfeild's *oeuvre*, and that these intertexts offer enough of a sense of it being part of the wider Streatfeild world that she finds it satisfying in new ways as an adult reader.

The role of remembering in Joanna's account is multilayered, therefore, since her experience in reading series novels and her acquaintance with Streatfeild's work (both as a child and into adulthood) means that she draws on general and literary knowledge as well as particular memories of this novel in her attempts to reconstruct the childhood book. She acknowledges this mechanism when she returns to reread *Apple Bough*. She admits she had not remembered the 'film aspect' to it. When, in her rereading, she reached an episode when the youngest boy Wolfgang is on a train she guessed that the person sitting opposite was a film director: 'Now I don't know whether that's just because [. . .] I know how Noel Streatfeild works in her writing, um, or because somewhere in my subconscious [. . .] the memories were starting to percolate through.' Mackey, drawing on her own memories of girlhood reading, suggests that series books and genre fiction act as 'bridges' to help young readers internalize important literary and general stereotypes that can then be used as the foundation for deeper understanding of more complex literature (2013, p. 89). Joanna's self-aware rereading account suggests that both her childly and adult understanding of generic codes and author-specific tropes have aided her in understanding and remembering the moment of *deus ex machina*, in which a rich and sympathetic older character offers a young protagonist approval of their talent and opportunity to exploit it. Yet there seems to be more to this moment of recognition and recollection than informed guesswork and further memories that appear to 'percolate through' in her remembering and rereading accounts add to a richer overall scene.

During the course of our interactions, Joanna found her old 1967 Puffin edition of *Apple Bough* and some of her memories of the content of the book and its importance to moments in her life course are in part cued by the illustration on the back cover by Margery Gill, depicting the child protagonists and their housekeeper-governess Miss Popple making a Christmas pudding. Joanna recollects a personal autobiographical episode relating to this illustration: 'I looked at the back cover, briefly, and I saw this picture of them all stirring a bowl, and it suddenly made me remember that [reading *Apple Bough* as a child] was the first time I had heard of people making wishes when they stirred the Christmas pudding.' Her memory of this moment of securing a new piece of cultural information during childhood chimes with Mackey's experience as a young Canadian girl encountering a description of American Thanksgiving in *'B' Is for Betsy* by Carolyn Haywood (1939), which acted as 'a kind of Rosetta Stone to help translate American school customs into something I could process' (2013, p. 94).

Joanna carefully unpicks her memory, wondering if she had in fact first come across the tradition of 'Stir Up Sunday' reading the novel or in another later context which then 'locked onto that memory that I'd had from the book'. On re-encountering the scene during her adult rereading of *Apple Bough*, it triggers a further memory from her university years, when the concept of Stir Up Sunday was referred to one evening at the Evensong service she attended and when, she reports, the connection with the memory of Streatfeild's story 'crystallized'. There are layers of memory at work here: initial memory images of the fictional scene (of the children stirring a pudding) cued through the visual representation of the back-cover illustration and created through the process of presentification; specific autobiographical memory of Joanna's twelve-year-old reading self registering the concept of 'Stir Up Sunday' and the later young adult self hearing about it again at Chapel; and semantic memory only tangentially connected to the book itself, of an understanding of Anglican liturgy in which the phrase 'stir up' originates.[7] In the novel, the rite is focused around wish-making and is only obliquely linked to doctrine at the point when Wolfgang makes a reference to the 'stir up collect' (Streatfeild, 1962/1986, p. 155). Details of Joanna's own biography, particularly her interest in Christian ritual, contribute to the significance of this textual moment and further demonstrate the intricate mnemonic matrix acting on even the slightest remembered experience of childhood reading.

In particular, there is a powerful dialogic exchange between the cue (in this case the back-cover art and then the episode being reread) and specific autobiographical memory across the life course, which then returns the reading self back to original experience of the textual content. Rereading thus offers a multidimensional 'recollective experience', to use Schacter's term (1996, p. 70). It is one that mirrors other everyday forms of remembering where stored fragments of an episode, also known as engrams, combine with retrieval cues to produce memory itself: 'the subjective experience of recollecting a past event' (p. 70). It is not surprising that illustrations work so powerfully as cues in this way, considering the way memory is understood by so many experts to function through spatial and visual structures. Fernyhough explains that 'vivid visual details are among the most prominent of the sensory-perceptual experiences that form the raw material of memory-making' (2012, p. 85) and points to examples of very early infant memories reported by Woolf and A. S. Byatt, which deal in 'bright shards' (p. 85). Benjamin's notion of the 'pure imaginative contemplation' of the child and his inventory of objects that infants enjoy observing – including bubbles, magic lanterns, and items with 'colored [*sic*] glow' – proffers a complementary view about the importance of images in cementing early memories (1926/1996, p. 443). Children's author and illustrator Shirley Hughes puts it another way in her *A Life Drawing: Recollections of an Illustrator*, musing that imagery 'does get to you deep down' (2002, p. 46).

When Joanna discusses visual imagery in her account of remembered reading, she refers to two different elements: first, the illustrations and cover art from her original edition – as with the picture of characters stirring the Christmas cake, she claims she can still 'see the front cover in [her] head' – and second the visual memory images that she conjured herself as a child through the process of presentification. Both of these elements are doubly 'presentified' via recollection, an activity that is not always a transparent route to the original image. Joanna remarks that a picture of the house from *Apple Bough* she has in mind is 'not necessarily from the book'. That is, it is not necessarily an illustration she has memorized, but a creation of her own, constructed from description in the text as well as personal references to buildings she admired or desired as a girl. Another participant in my study, Fiona, also born in the late 1960s, reveals a purer form of presentification that is not inflected by textual illustration at all. Fiona thinks she probably read Paul Gallico's animal fantasy *Jennie* (1950) when she was about twelve years old. She writes in her initial parallel text that she remembers the novel, in which a young boy is magically transformed into a cat after a near-fatal car accident, as 'a visual image of scenes which I see as my own memory' or 'like a dream'. She recalls a visual atmosphere of 'darkness and rain', a detail that is verified in her rereading of the opening chapter, and describes her way of remembering the book overall in autonoetic terms: 'rather than seeing Peter the cat – as if *I* was the protagonist'. Fiona reports what Ellen Esrock terms a strong 'visual epistemology' (1998, p. 159), encapsulating the interplay between presentification and memory in terms of perspective. Her reading scene also potentially demonstrates her preferred style of childly reading strategy and the nature of Gallico's narrative. The prose in *Jennie* has a nightmarish quality at times:

> He ran. He stopped. He started again. He faltered and kept on. He thought his eyes would burst from his head, and his chest was burning from his effort to draw breath. But ever when he came to pause, something happened to drive him on – a door banging, a shout, a sign waiving in the wind, some new noise assaulting his sensitive ears, dark, threatening shapes of buildings [. . .] A bottle thrown that crashed into a hundred pieces on the pavement close to him and showered him with glass. (1950/1973, p. 23)

Such descriptive passages could easily tap into a child's own anxieties about getting lost and the highly focalized text could thus be encoded as an autonoetic experience that retains atmosphere over plot in future recollection.

Jack's experiences of remembering and rereading Andre Norton's *Star Man's Son: 2250 AD* (1952)[8] further reveal the extent of the mnemonic influence of scenes in the mind. Seventy-two-year-old Jack first read this science fiction adventure when he was fourteen, growing up in a working-class family in north London. The story itself represents his favourite genre as a young man and into adulthood: 'As a child I liked the idea of the deserted post-apocalyptic world, the freedom to forage and do whatever you wanted.' Jack's initial, reasonably accurate semantic memories for plot and episodes indicate his interest in the heroic aspects of the text. He recalls details such as the young protagonist deciding to leave his community at the beginning of the story and narrative episodes, such as when he 'fights a tribe of intelligent rats or lizards', indicating reasonably good recall overall (the tribe are beasts mutated from rats, in fact, and the intelligent lizards are their prey). In addition to these plot-based memories, Jack's recollections are often visual in nature, having an immediacy and potency that implies he still 'sees' some of the scenes in the novel in a way that highlights the close relationship between presentification and presentifying; that is, between the mental work required to transform text into memory trace and the mental work of interpreting the real world of experience. For instance, his recollection of the opening scene specifically places Fors, the nominal hero, standing outside a building, and Jack goes on to suggest that the real hero is actually 'the empty world, the deserted cities and rusting cars [. . .] conjured up in graphic detail'. Jack's memories of the illustrations in his original hardback copy of *Star Man's Son* also permeate his account of remembering and his reflections after rereading the book. He first remembers the front cover, illustrated with a black and white picture of a 'tower or broken building', and on rereading the novel he notes the moments where he recognizes unfolding events and anticipates the picture that goes with them, explaining that the 'remembrance of some of the illustrations surfaced'. The illustrations are probably Nicolas Mordvinoff's striking original images, which add a stark and nightmarish atmosphere to the apocalyptic storyline, and seem very likely to combine with mental images constructed through reading the text to produce new, and perhaps stronger, memory traces. As with Joanna's account of the Stir Up Sunday picture and the image of the house Apple Bough, illustrations consolidate a form of remembering that is deeply embedded in the reading scene.

Accounts of rereading illustrate how reading memory works through recognition as well as recollection. In other words, certain knowledge about the text and the reading self emerges when the original object is re-encountered and is marked by the mind as familiar rather than new. This process seems to work in multiple ways. At the end of the first chapter of *Star Man's Son*, Jack records in his notes that the story is coming back to him and that the mind is a 'remarkable instrument'. For Fiona, the quality of familiarity is less reliable. She reports, 'I'm employing a strategy of "prediction" and this is mixed with vague memories [. . .] I'm finding I keep reworking the endings, particularly at one point where I wanted an outcome but it didn't happen.' Where Jack's recognition of the text seems easy and steadfast, Fiona's memory appears to be building new material based on prediction and expectation rather than recollection, and thus feels more unstable. Joanna also has a mixed experience. She describes how during the rereading process she tended to remember some events in *Apple Bough* just before she read them and that this was satisfying, yet some parts of the novel remained completely unfamiliar: 'You've got the memories you've got before you read them and then as you read it clicks and you remember knowing it, and then there are aspects that you're reading a passage and you can't remember it at all.' Nevertheless, her evaluation of the rereading activity is positive overall and relates an experience that is contrary to Nodelman's concerns and quite different from Proust's description of his re-encounter with *Captain Fracasse*. She explains: 'I had such vague memories to begin with. I had just images really. Faint images, like a faded photograph that's so faded you can only just see the shadows. And it was just really exciting to have those brought back to life again.'

The notion of reading memories being like faded photographs being brought back to life by revisiting offers an interesting metaphor for thinking about the reading scene, not dissimilar to the excavation of relics. Like Ingarden's theory of concretization, it suggests that elements that have sunk into the past can re-emerge in the present in a temporal process. The trope of the fully developed photograph is both intimate in its association with family history or the recording of significant life events, and represents a complete snapshot of a past scene. It implies a form of interaction with a remembered text that is spatially shaped and made meaningful through personal knowledge. Moreover, the faded family photograph exists on the borderline of representation and creation, offering up 'material for interpretation – evidence [. . .] to be solved, like a riddle, read and decoded, like clues' (Kuhn, 1995/2002, p. 13). The reading scene certainly encompasses much of this interpretative quality through forms of reconstructive memory. Not all adult accounts acknowledge this aspect of the mnemonic matrix, but, when they do, they enrich our understanding of the lifelong reading act.

Reconstructing through rereading

Proust's essay demonstrates how the self interacts with the past through books in different ways. These books can act as 'cues', which when 'we happen to leaf through [their] pages' (Proust, 1906/2011, p. 4) stimulate memories of other activities, circumstances, and surroundings from the same time (or linked in other ways); alternatively, they are artefacts which can themselves be remembered or used as an *aide mémoire* for remembering specific events of reading. Case studies from my rereading project bring to light the importance of recognition across multiple cognitive and autobiographical activities: as a way of checking memory or verifying knowledge from the real world. The activity of rereading as an adult also features in Proust's account, albeit in a footnote.[9] Having quoted the remembered lines from *Captain Fracasse* on Homer's *Odyssey* which seemed to him 'most original and beautiful', Proust then notes as an aside that, 'in truth, this sentence will not be found in *Captain Fracasse*, at least not in this form. Instead of "as stands written in the Odyssey of the Grecian Poet," the text has simply "as Homerus says" ' (p. 22). The act of rereading the actual text brings into question the veracity of Proust's memories of it from his youth, and he admits that he has permitted himself to 'fuse' together various sentences from Gautier's original in a bathetic moment of reconstruction,

> to make the example more striking for the reader, especially since, truth to tell, I no longer have for them the same pious reverence [. . .] In any case, I can no longer recapture these forgotten pleasures precisely enough to be sure that I have not overstepped the mark, have not gone too far in piling all of these marvels into a single sentence. I don't believe that I have, though. And it pains me to think that my ecstatic recital of a sentence from *Captain Fracasse* to the irises and periwinkles bent over the riverbanks with the path's pebbles under my feet would have been even more pleasurable if I had been able to find in a single sentence of Gautier's all the charms I have artificially brought together today without, alas, it giving me any pleasure at all. (1906/2011, p. 22)

In a sharp observation about his younger reading self, Proust playfully undercuts his recorded memory of Gautier's sentences on Homer by explaining that his childly response to the work was wildly out of proportion with the quality of the content. His main point is concerned with developing literary taste, but there is a hint in this passage that he also recognizes the process of reshaping that may have gone on in memory. Although he remembers that *Captain Fracasse* gave him pleasure once, the precise lived experience of this sensation has been forgotten, and cannot seemingly be recaptured by returning to the book as an adult. Even those readers like Joanna who kept a diary of their childhood encounters with books cannot trust the written record to provide meticulous accounts of books or responses to them. Children's authors have struck upon the same rocky ground in their excavations. Former Children's Laureate Jacqueline Wilson was also a prolific diarist as a child, who uses diary entries to support an account of her reading history in *My Secret Diary: Dating Dancing, Dreams and Dilemmas*, although she admits that 'sadly I didn't record every book I read' (2009/2010, p. 86). Mitchison is more frank about the limitations of this method in her autobiography, wondering if she can 'fairly use these for checking' her own memories or if the contents should just be 'set down straight without passing through the memory sieve' (1973, p. 26). (In fact, she only uses them to check at what age her brother read Jonathan Swift's *Gulliver's Travels* (1726) to her: she was five, and she does not think she 'got much out of it'; p. 70.)

Recent theorists of memory support a stance that suggests that the notion of matching individual memories to past events as they really happened is mostly an irrelevant endeavour. Unlike realist philosophies, which consider memory to constitute a direct, if mysterious, awareness of past events – and unlike the representational view, which proposes that memories are experiences of memory images that exist for us in the present – the reconstructive approach proffers a model that is more fluid. Schacter explains the thinking about memory and mind behind his research: 'We extract key elements from our experiences and store them. We then recreate or reconstruct our experiences rather than retrieve copies of them. Sometimes, in the process of reconstructing we add on feelings, beliefs, or even knowledge we obtained after the experience' (2001/2002, p. 9). Memories can therefore be understood as active reconstructions of past experience created in the present, rather than simple representations filed away and retrieved; they are also 'changed by the very process of reconstructing them', as Fernyhough puts it: 'every memory that an experimental participant reports is likely to have been contaminated by previous acts of remembering' (2012, p. 13).

If this premise is taken as the basis for my reading scene, then memory is never an accurate record of events and, as Nodelman suggests, cannot be used to reconstruct an earlier version of the self; however, it can provide some important, and indeed accurate, insights into the past. After all, many grown-up individuals would claim they could say something concrete about the experience of reading a book last week, and others could confidently extend their reflections back a month, a year, or to their early adulthoods. Even if these memories are creative acts rather than true histories, as examples of how individuals remember and choose to present their memories, they can still offer interesting narratives about childhood reading.

Conclusion

In this chapter, I have introduced the concept of the reading scene to my model of lifelong reading, and explored the forms of memory that shape this virtual space. Reminiscence plays the greatest part in autobiographical writings about childhood reading. Although much of this writing deflects attention away from specific remembered texts and the phenomenological experience of reading, it is not true to say that the accounts are always indulgent, nostalgic, or unreliable in relating the workings of the reading scene. The generic autobiographical memories that shape reminiscence create the rich backdrops of context necessary for remembering to take place. Proust's 'calendars [. . .] of bygone days' mark the passing of time against consistent scenes of childhood hobbies and activities, but also appear as discretely recalled texts that have shaped the young Marcel from youth into adulthood.

The specific mechanisms of recollection and recognition appear less often in memoirs and other published accounts of remembered reading. However, they can be interrogated in more depth through interview using methods of probing that aim to draw out particular aspects of a phenomenological experience.[10] As a form of excavation, these types of purposeful remembering reveal something of the structures of memory as it pertains to the reading act. Adult re-memorying traces those elements of texts that are most vividly encoded in childhood and subsequently retrieved later in life, and the perceptual nature of reading itself as a form of presentification is reproduced in memory images that surface in narrative accounts.

The reading scene incorporates memories of a first encounter with a childhood book, as well as re-enactments of that encounter over time, through childly imaginative play and also in adult versions of such play (in the form of connecting a favourite childhood book to later reading, or in the act of constructing identity in relation to remembered characters or fictional events). Rereading represents a further part of the reading scene. It produces some active repetition of the original reading of a book, but also invites recognition, as familiar textual features that were not initially retained in recall are encountered once more. Joanna used the metaphor of a faded photograph to describe her initial adult memories of *Apple Bough*, explaining how the rereading process allowed these faint images to 'come back to life again'. Ender also deploys a photographic metaphor in describing the functioning of Proustian memory scenes more generally. She explains that the stored fragments of a memory are like a child's 'snapshots of certain ephemeral details' that are not fully processed until the adult photographer is prompted by some kind of trigger to 'go back to his lab': 'Only the fully developed photograph, with its touches of colour and specific composition, will bring the picture to life' (Ender, 2005, p. 117). The reading scene is the lab in which memories of childhood books can be sorted, developed and retouched. Mental images are its fragmentary material. Set against the backdrop of the life space, these faded images can be brought back to life in the fresh phenomenological experience of remembering. It is to the backdrop, in its rich evocation of a reading life journeyed through, that I now turn.

2

The life space

All reading activity takes place in time and space. In addition to the interior reading scene, any model of lifelong reading therefore needs to consider the reader and text as temporal entities that exist within certain sociocultural and geographical contexts. Louise Rosenblatt observes that the reader and text come together in 'an event in time', to which the reader brings 'past experience and present personality' (1978/1994, p. 12). She goes on to state that the reading event, in turn, becomes 'part of the ongoing stream of [the reader's] life experience' (p. 12). This chapter is concerned with the relationships that British readers have had with books as part of childhood and adult life experience throughout a long twentieth century and attempts to expose patterns in the ways that aspects of identity, particularly class and gender, may have inflected textual encounters. In the first part, I illustrate the trajectory of Rosenblatt's ongoing 'stream' of experience in terms of childhood books, using mostly published autobiographical accounts to help map out common waymarks in early reading journeys, from early aural experience and learning to read through to reading for pleasure and at school. The influence of familial and educational environments is crucial in formulating these journeys, while moments of personal epiphany also often shape their trajectories.

Individual autobiographical accounts provide some of the richest data about encounters with childhood books.[1] These accounts can provide insights into the mental and imaginative experience of reading as well as contextual information about the influence of books and reading over time. This is Margaret Mackey's declared enterprise in *One Child Reading*, for instance, in which she investigates her 'childish reading self' by revisiting the materials she 'read, viewed, heard, and played' (2016, p. 4). Other memoirists mention reading in passing as part of a larger narrative of their life course, with books often playing a large part in the autobiographical musings of writers. Such reading histories are regularly conceptualized as journeys, sometimes mythical ones: take, for instance, children's literature librarian and critic Elaine Moss's reminiscence in which she describes opening the 'appallingly produced books' available in her childhood being like 'taking the first step into a mysterious forest' (1974/1977, p. 335). Her fairy-tale-esque quest is echoed by Francis Spufford in the first chapter of *The Child That Books Built*, which deals with 'the forest at the beginning of fiction' (2002, p. 25), and by other memoirists, such as Rebecca Solnit, who claims that she disappeared into books when she was a child 'like someone running into the woods' (2013, p. 60).[2] Tully Barnett has traced patterns of transformation in a number of bibliomemoirs in more culturally structured terms, arguing that for certain bookish individuals childhood books appear to be 'the magic that set them on the path to becoming lovers of, and contributors to, and gatekeepers of, literature' (2013, p. 85).

While the idea of a reading journey is helpful, it does not tell the full story of lifelong reading, partly because it avoids Water Benjamin's call to 'return again and again to the same matter' through the strata of memory (1932/1999, p. 611). To fully understand lifelong reading and its attendant labour of excavation, then, I find I have needed to rework Rosenblatt's metaphor of the stream flowing in one direction, conceptualizing reading, remembering and rereading in a more flexible topography, within what I call the *life space*. This might be understood as the lived version of the cognitive process of scene construction, discussed in the last chapter. The life space represents the 'set of connections that links the immediate scene to other spaces and actors' (Reavey, 2017, p. 109; also see Lewin, 1936). In other words, it models the way that each individual reader and his or her ongoing experience of a childhood book is framed by both sociocultural contexts and material and geographical contexts. By plotting individual experiences of childhood books across the life course according to an 'autotopographical' method (González, 1995; Heddon, 2002) rather than by following a straightforward chronology, existing reading histories can be both complicated and enriched. In particular, interrogation of different types of spatial encounters with childhood books helps to reveal the complexity of reading within the life space and shape new types of narrative. In the second part of this chapter, I therefore analyse the 'first spaces' of engagement with texts in the real world, interaction with virtual worlds created through fictional spaces portrayed within texts themselves, and representational spaces in which readers re-enact or respond to stories they have read in order to map these autotopographies. Daniel Defoe's *Robinson Crusoe* (1719) and subsequent desert-island narratives or 'robinsonades' (children's books inspired by Defoe's tale) provide a focus for a discussion, not only because they represent common material for autobiographical musing among memoirists and participants of my rereading study, but also because they play out in salient ways forms of spatial engagement with remembered books.

The *life space* and autotopography

A single text can work meaningfully as a landmark on the reading journey. It can, as American children's librarian Anne Carroll Moore described in the early part of the twentieth century, provide 'assured companionship' along the 'roads of childhood' towards the rest of mature life (1920, p. 61). It can also symbolize a significant shift or moment of transition and revelation in an individual's life story. Hugh Lofting's *Dr Doolittle* books (1920–52) provided a 'eureka' moment for Richard Adams as a boy, locating him within a tradition of writing that then directed both his continuing passion for animal welfare into adulthood and his interest in nature writing, which culminated in the novels *Watership Down* (1972) and *The Plague Dogs* (1977). As he wrote in his autobiography, *The Day Gone By* (1990), 'If I am up to the neck in the animal rights movement today, Dr Doolittle must answer for it' (p. 22). For Penelope Lively it was a natural history textbook called *Eyes and No Eyes* first published in 1901 that represents a turning point. In her memoir, *Oleander, Jacaranda: A Childhood Perceived*, Lively connects the author Arabella Buckley's 'scholarly' approach to the flora and fauna of English waterways (particularly her labelling of the various botanical objects illustrated with letters '*a*, *b*, *c*, *d*') with her own fledgling attempts to gather and identify natural phenomenon in her childhood garden, and she is clearly grateful for being introduced to the idea of accessible, practical science and successful women scientists early in her education (Buckley was secretary to geologist Charles Lyell and a respected writer and educator). Importantly, Lively reveals the influence that this text had upon her young self and into adult maturity as a writer, since *Eyes and No Eyes* inspired her first creative output at the age of seven and encouraged a serious approach to the practice of observing and telling. Mable Dearmer's *The Cockyolly Bird* (1914) is similarly located at the centre of Elizabeth Goudge's reading history. In her autobiography, *The Joy of Snow* (1974), Goudge claims that it contains 'the original of a bird who seems to fly in and out of my mind whenever I am writing' (p. 29) and that it has shaped her own sense of narrative voice as an author later in life (writing successful children's books such as *The Little White Horse* [1946]). She remembers her paracanonical text erroneously as *The Cocky Olly Bird* (possibly the play version, the picture book, or simply a reference to Dearmer's reoccurring avian character) and yet, despite its relatively ephemeral nature, it is closely tied to a concept of 'serenity' that has followed her throughout her career.

Books or reading experiences often work as emblematic waymarks on a journey to adulthood in this way, representing a threshold between past and present. In the memoirs I explore, moments related to reading in childhood can also be epiphanic, alterning 'the fundamental meaning-structures in a person's life' (Denzin, 2013, p. 70), either through personal and professional forms of enlightenment, or through radical awakening or revelation. In his influential study of working-class autodidacticism, Jonathan Rose recounts several examples of adults remembering reading a particular text in their youth as a significant turning point in their public lives. For many, the significant book was *Robinson Crusoe*, which as Rose notes is one of the English classics that could produce a 'kind of epiphany' among autodidacts (2001, p. 406). For instance, he introduces Thomas Jordan, a working-class boy who read Defoe's novel of solitude and survival in 1903 at the age of eleven and who, in his unpublished autobiography, claims that the book's dealings with 'far away places fired his imagination' (cited in Rose, 2001, p. 109). Twelve-year-old ploughboy John Ward had also 'devoured' the novel in 1878 and as an adult wrote that it had given him his 'spirit of adventure' (p. 109). Rose argues that this classic tale of individualist adventure made 'innumerable plebeian readers discontented with their station in life and eager to explore' (p. 108), to transcend their working-class origins, and turn to military or political careers. In this way, *Robinson Crusoe* acts as a crucial marker for change in the life journey of the memoirists he studies.

Important as this narrative of transformation and progression is, it can be complicated by seeking out other patterns of journeying that emerge in accounts of remembered reading. Peter Hollindale's critique of the journey paradigm as a way of understanding human development provides some clues about how voyaging tropes must be carefully deployed. Suggesting that human development is a convoluted process, involving scrabbling and sliding as well as striding, in addition to pauses to picnic or survey the surroundings, Hollindale also argues that any journey is necessarily complicated by the details of authentic topography:

> To understand the adult's plateau we must see that it undulates, has knolls and dips and sometimes chasms, that you must fight against a gale to keep your footing. (Some people find a hollow and just sit there.) Occasionally you climb back the way you came, either to shelter from the wind or to see the lower slopes again more closely, although they will not look the same as they did the first time, for you bring down with you your knowledge of invisible horizons. (1997, p. 38)

As a metaphor of human life, Hollindale's landscape usefully punctures the idea that adulthood is a fixed and 'finished' state representing the high point of a child's development. It also helps us recognize, via the concept of 'childness', that children and adult selves can sometimes co-exist within a shared world, as adults look back at the 'lower slopes' through memory and children look forward to the 'plateau' through anticipation, hopes, and fears. Applying Hollindale's insights to the specific phenomenon of childhood reading can, therefore, add nuance to teleological reading histories. Considering lifelong reading in these terms, it becomes possible for any linear, temporal sequence of reading events from childhood to adulthood to be disrupted by the potentially meandering shape of an individual's navigation through the terrain. Response to a single text over time, through reading, remembering, rereading, and other imaginative activities, suggests less the journey of a traveller from A to B, or of the flow of a river to the sea, and more a process of 'getting my bearings', as one participant in an oral history project on reading astutely puts it.[3] The idea of a varied landscape, and flexible movement through it, supports a model of lifelong reading in which some topographical features can be revisited (favourite books, for example), although others remain inaccessible (it is not always possible to recall the process of learning to read).

Hollindale's discussion reflects a general move in autobiographical research to critique linear timeframes. For instance, it reflects a phenomenological model of time that decouples common categories of experience such as childhood (past) and adulthood (present) and instead works to illuminate the way that human experience functions via a network of '*before* and *after*' conditions (Currie, 2006, p. 17). Similar moves are made within lifespan studies, which suggest that a sense of ageing identity is formed through a non-linear perception of remembered, lived, and anticipated events (Brannen and Nilsen, 2002; Rathbone, Conway and Moulin, 2011). Drawing on the work of Kurt Lewin and his theories of topological psychology, Paula Reavey points out that although humans generally narrate memories as situated in particular time periods, 'we do not necessarily experience them this way, as we recall' (2017, p. 107). Instead, remembered episodes and events are made meaningful according to their 'degree of connectedness between past and present events' and to the way that the experience 'in the head' is 'threaded entirely into the spatial distribution of activities' (Brown and Reavey, 2015, p. 49). If this life space can usefully describe the interrelation between a psychological event and the 'scenes and settings' – both real and cognitive – in which it is made manifest, then it is possible to adopt elements of the temporal journey with its starting point and waymarks, but expand beyond the linear to include more dispersed and ambient aspects of the reading act, such as references to places related to the reading scene, the reading object or other resonant material items, and other actors involved in co-reading, remembering or re-enacting the text in question. The life space in my model represents a complete environment in which the activities of the reading scene – reading, remembering reading, and rereading – take place and in which they are connected to other phenomena, often through the affective traces I shall discuss in Chapter 3. Connections with space and place help provide a fuller picture of a reading act over time, showing in some detail how texts integrate with lived experience both at the time of reading and in subsequent rereadings and rememberings. Moreover, the act of excavation, which is central to this poetics of remembering and rereading, forces us to consider the importance of digging 'down' into the strata of past reading experience as well as traversing or mapping a landscape on the surface.

The life space is an analytical and descriptive concept: its methodological counterpart can be identified as 'autotopography' and as a method this practice helps to tease out further connections between the remembering reader, past reading self, and the social and spatial contexts in which childhood books are encountered through the life space. Autotopography is the term cultural critics have used to describe both the crossover of identity with real and social space (Heddon, 2002) and the recording of self through a collection of objects from the past that represent 'a coherent series of relations' (González, 1995, p. 144), specifically to other times, environments, and individuals. Autotopography provides a method for understanding a single life through multifaceted reading acts and books that have been read, in the manner of Mackey's autobibliography. Mackey describes her project as a form of mapping, offering 'varied sweeps across the same territory' to provide 'important perspectives on a highly complex intellectual challenge' (2016, p. 44). Hers is thus a process of 'thick mapping', a practice associated with ethnographic methodologies of 'thick description': that is, it is an attempt to get at the complex strata of context and meaning that go beyond the immediate surface facts of any cultural phenomenon (Geertz, 1973). Thick map cartographers construct layered, interactive and evolving representations of place that indicate multiple dimensions of human activity and relationships (Presner, Shepard and Kawano, 2014). By deploying the same approach in examining reading histories, it is possible to incorporate various aspects of the life space into analysis and interpretation and show connections between places, people, and literary objects with an added dimension of shifts and changes over time. Reading histories are complex sites of meaning. Autotopography works to map a conceptual terrain that encompasses real and fictional geographies involved in adult memories of childhood books and their relationships with them, at the same time encouraging the reader and critic to excavate meaning over the course of the life span.

The memoirist and reading historian both benefit from troubling the assumption that time can only be understood as a single sequence of past-present-future events. They can also find productive ground in the notion that reading as a phenomenon is embedded in space as well as time. Although Hollindale relies on figurative language, the passage also speaks to a broader and more literal 'spatial turn' in the arts and humanities (Tally, 2013). Scholars of reading have embraced this move, examining ways that childhood reading works as an embodied practice (Harde and Kokkola, 2017), asking how geographical locations inflect access to books and literary tastes (Fuller and Rehberg Sedo, 2013), and exploring the influence of imaginative and real landscapes on readers' encounters with books (Cliff-Hodges, Nikolajeva and Taylor, 2010). For instance, remembering readers may recall occasions of reading, not purely because of the life-changing properties of the book or reading experience, but because of the physical and geographical spaces – 'actual space' or 'geospace' – in which these were embedded. Before examining reading histories in more detail from this topographical perspective, I have attempted a thick mapping of common waymarks in the more conventional reading journey, recognizing that autotopographical identity can be revised or shaped through dialogue with other individuals who may have moved through similar time and space, reading similar books.

Co-reading

Arthur Ransome makes a striking claim in his autobiography: 'I do not think that there was anything in my childhood for which I have more reason to be grateful than my mother's regular reading aloud, and the habit of eager reading to myself that her reading encouraged' (1976/1985, p. 37). As a starting point for an autobiographical account of a reading (and writing) life, this statement locates the remembered child self firmly in the context of a supportive family sphere and a landscape of aural and written texts. It also reflects a broader point about the plurality of children's experience of fiction: they are read to, they regularly interact with books in a social context, and they are also encouraged to read silently on their own. The case of children's reading provides a clear refutation of the tendency among some book historians to think of modern reading practices purely in terms of 'silent novel reading' (Littau, 2006, p. 37). The regular occurrence of memories of sound and voice in published accounts of early reading like Ransome's testifies that reading aloud is, in fact, the 'dominant practice' in this context (p. 37). Many books deemed suitable for the youngest of children are picture books, rhyming stories, or collections of poems that invite dramatic co-reading. As Appleyard points out, 'long before children can read a page of print by themselves, reading is apt to be an intensely participatory initiation into a world beyond their own immediate experience, with the most trusted persons in their lives as guides and interpreters' (1991, p. 22; see also Meek, 1988). Examples of this participatory initiation abound in written accounts: for instance, in their respective autobiographies, both Adams and Kevin Crossley-Holland remember their mothers reading popular poetry anthologies or collections to them at bedtime, such as those by Robert Louis Stevenson and Water de la Mare.

Ransome's sense of gratitude towards his mother's routine of reading aloud to him chimes with a growing philosophy in the latter part of the nineteenth century and into the twentieth of the value of reading directly to young children, not simply as a way of controlling and disciplining young people, or of imparting quality literature as early as possible, but as a bestowing of gifts. These offerings could be represented both by specific texts and through the literary experience more generally. Women and mothers are especially implicated in this form of cultural work, most often because of their perceived natural skill and grace in oral storytelling or recitation. Goudge makes this point explicitly in her autobiography, investing much in the act of reading aloud as an aesthetic and moral undertaking. She equates storytellers, readers-aloud, and writers with equal high value in a child's world, explaining that her mother had no need to read published works to her children because she was a born storyteller and could recite made-up tales efficiently instead. Instead, it was a mother *figure* – a family friend called Mrs Hollis – who *read* to the young Elizabeth. Goudge remembers this woman as both beautiful and calm, noting that 'a good reader aloud should always have serenity: it casts a spell' (1974, p. 28). Mrs Hollis is ascribed transcendental qualities in her ability to convey texts to the young recipient and to fix them in memory through this almost magical gift of a beautiful voice and serene delivery. Children's authors Joan Aiken (1974), Roger McGough (1992/2015), Naomi Mitchison (1973), the Pullein-Thomson sisters (Josephine, Diana and Christine) (1996), and Rosemary Sutcliff (1983), also stress their own mothers' flair for reading to them. Sutcliff recalls that her mother 'read aloud beautifully and never got tired' (p. 53) and poet McGough stresses the importance of the regular nightly maternal practice, admitting 'it was she who would put me on to a merry-go-round of nursery rhymes and simple prayers, then take me off, dizzy with words' (p. 138). All chime, to some degree, with the philosopher Jean-Paul Sartre's compelling account of being read to by his mother, when 'all [he] wanted to do was hear her voice' (1967, p. 31).

Although less serene in their delivery, fathers have also traditionally read aloud, particularly in literary families. Eleanor Farjeon, who grew up to write poems, stories and plays for children, recalls her novelist father reading aloud to her and her siblings every night, and remembers liking his practice more than her mother's transmission of texts because it was more 'exciting' (1935/1960, p. 328). She reports that he made her scream in bed one night when he read a particularly thrilling chapter from Alexandre Dumas's *The Count of Monte Cristo* (1845, p. 227). However, fathers are more often connected to the idea of transmitting the gift of a particular transformational text rather than the aesthetic practice of reading itself. As the principal of a theological college, Goudge's father read her New Testament picture books, bringing the characters – particularly the figure of Christ – alive for the young Elizabeth, influencing her own religious certainty and resulting in an adult belief in the importance of 'theophanies of children' (1974, p. 73). Both Adams and B. B. relate memories of their fathers reading inspirational books that later shaped their own writing interests. For Adams, as I have already noted, it was the Dr Doolittle books, and for B. B., who went on to write and illustrate stories for children set squarely in the English countryside (most famously *The Little Grey Men* [1942] and *Brendon Chase* [1944]), it was Richard Jefferies's *Wild Life in a Southern Country* (1879), *The Amateur Poacher* (1879), *Bevis* (1882) and *Life of the Fields* (1884).

In all of these accounts, individuals look back from the position of their own adulthood and see the older generation's literary recommendations as a form of generosity and the valuable passing on of texts or words. Reading aloud is recalled by adult memoirists in terms of a gift that grounds them as a developing child reader in time and space as well as a crucial preparation for later journeys into books and reading. Attention, time, quality oral transmission, and meaningful books are represented as positive endowments that help to instil comparable good habits in the young reader. Memory appears to produce the shared context of being read to as a distinct landmark that secured the remembered child reader to their familial sphere and pointed him or her in the right direction for future travel. In this sense, adults and children occupy a communal literary landscape traversed with more and less skill.

In contrast with narratives of positive influence and exchange, of safe and nurturing spaces where child and mother encounter books together and where, as Diana Pullein-Thompson puts it, a 'much-loved' parent (1996, p. 7) might also nurture 'the germ of a vocation' (p. 8), Tatar has described the participatory co-reading situation as a 'contact zone' (2010, p. 4), making use of Mary Louise Pratt's postcolonial terminology to point out that this apparently safe locale is also a zone of potential conflict. From the sheltered harbours of oral co-reading, most readers move into a potentially hazardous terrain of coming into textual literacy, where narratives of conflict and overcoming adversity do emerge. It is notable that while the mother figures recalled in memoirs are nearly always particularly adept and generous in reading aloud, in remembered encounters with fathers in learning to read, a more troubled landscape is mapped. It is in this part of the journey that memoirists are most likely to write within the convention of a transformative moment or turning point.

Learning to read

Ransome's famous statement – 'Any book worth reading by children is also worth reading by grown-up persons' (1976/1985, p. 35) – is a critical judgment drawn from memories of his own mother's practice of choosing books she herself would enjoy hearing when reading aloud to her children; he writes that 'she was as impatient as we were for the next chapter' (p. 36). The didactic point about 'quality' children's literature, later expressed in parallel terms by C. S. Lewis[4] in a comment that Peter Hunt calls 'one of the worst critical dicta' (2001, p. 200) needs to be understood in the context of this broader philosophy about the natural influence of maternal reading practices, which Ransome understands through reference to his own memories. Sutcliff also makes the case for maternal taste and influence in her memoir, *Blue Remembered Hills* (1983), explaining that her mother 'would never, from the first, read anything that she could not enjoy herself', meaning a 'fine mixed diet of Beatrix Potter, A. A. Milne, Dickens, Stevenson, Hans Anderson, Kenneth Grahame and Kipling' (1983, p. 53). However, her account subverts the discourse of nurturing reading parent by arguing that her mother's willingness and skill in reading aloud was also the reason that the young Rosemary did not learn to read for herself until the age of nine. For Sutcliff, it was not mere laziness, but an unwillingness to be subjected to the kinds of texts considered suitable for early readers to cut their teeth on (I shall return to this point shortly. I will also return to the parent's perspective on co-reading as a form of rereading, in Chapter 4).

Learning-to-read narratives obviously represent a major feature on any map of reading experience, one that is often tackled early on in memoirists' accounts. The momentous shift from non-literate to literate – the move from sentences appearing as 'centipedes [. . .] swarm[ing] with syllables and letters' as Sartre puts it (1967, p. 31) – is important enough to be recognized both as a starting place and as a moment of major epiphany, both at the initial instance for the child and in retrospect for the adult (particularly the adult who has gone on to find reading to be a significant part of his or her existence). First, independent reading may well touch 'every fabric of a person's life', to use Denzin's formulation (2013, p. 52), meaning that autobiographers are likely to gravitate towards the transition into reading as a central shaping event in a life narrative. For some adults immersed in words and stories, learning to read is taken for granted: Robert Westall states he 'read easily' (2006, p. 60) and, for Adams, becoming literate was just 'part of growing up' (1990, p. 99). Not all such readers are as precocious as Ransome, who claims to have read Defoe's *Robinson Crusoe* 'from end to end' before the age of four (1937/1991, p. 34),[5] but there are plenty of examples of early reading abilities in other autobiographical accounts: Crossley-Holland got off to a 'quick start' and 'was able to say [his] alphabet at the age of two and a quarter' (2009, p. 62), and Spacks had apparently been reading 'since before [she] was three' (2011, p. 24).

Although these accounts can appear self-congratulatory, in fact, they represent a discourse of *naturalness* in which learning to read and reading itself is a transparent part of the individual's essence and identity from a very early age. By sampling children's writers I am of course privileging individuals who may consciously or unconsciously value the skill of reading more than other adults looking back at their lives. In some cases these particular memoirists may wish to present themselves as gifted in this respect in order to demonstrate a lineage between bookish youth and adulthood in their own life histories, although such phrasing is also reflected by one of my participants – Lynne, a children's librarian, born in the early 1950s – who says 'I think I was born reading. I don't ever remember a struggle to learn to read'. It is also worth mentioning that most adults do not retain memories prior to the age of three and have relatively fewer memories of the period from three to seven or eight (Bauer, 2014/2007; see also Fernyhough, 2012) and, therefore, any accounts of learning to read, especially in the very young age span, might be considered extraordinary in nature. They are part of the structural conventions of a literary memoir as much as an accurate record of fact.

The nascent child readers in these narratives are not alone on this part of their journey and parental help and guidance is often remembered as a part of the process. As I have implied already, mothers often appear in autobiographical accounts as nurturing figures who respond to the child's natural urge to learn. For example, Judith Kerr remembers her mother patiently responding to her endless demands to know what shop signs and posters said on their tram journeys around 1920s Berlin: 'She always told me, and one day something must have clicked and I found I could read' (1992/2015, p. 50). Sue Townsend also experienced the click of realization when she found that 'black squiggles turned into words which turned into sentences, which turned into stories' through the mild intervention of her mother, who helped her decipher the captions underneath Richmal Crompton's *Just William* illustrations during a period of convalescence in 1954 (1992/2015, p. 219).

Accounts of paternal influence are perhaps more fraught, if no less transformational. Ransome's feat in reading Defoe's novel from cover to cover before the age of five is given context by the relationship he had with his father, who gave him his own copy of the book as a reward on his fourth birthday. In his chapter on 'Various Educators', learning to read is juxtaposed with learning to swim – another rite of passage for a life like Ransome's shaped as much by sailing as by writing – and both forge a sense of the boy Arthur in opposition to his scholarly father. The account will be quoted at length, since it provides a model for learning relevant to memories of reading:

> Observing that men and frogs swim in the same way and that tadpoles do not have swimming lessons, it occurred to [my father] that the young human finding itself in water and out of its depth would probably swim by nature. So one day, my mother not being present, he dropped me naked over the side of the boat. The water was not very deep but more than deep

> enough for me. I went under at once in an agony of terror [. . .] I brooded over my disgrace and secretly spent money given me by an aunt on visits to the swimming baths by myself. Alone in the shallow end, and with nobody urging me to take my feet off the bottom, I was soon gingerly lifting them, copying the motions of the little frogs I had grown from spawn, and at the end of three visits was able to announce at the dinner-table, 'I can swim'. (1976/1985, p. 34)

The notion of a natural ability to swim is debunked through the young Arthur's terrifying experience of being thrown overboard by his father, only to be reinstated in a gentler format in Ransome's memories of teaching himself how to float and finally move through the water with confidence. The key feature of this memory relevant to reading is the child's independence in mastering a skill that is in some ways instinctive, along with the adult's role in motivating if not necessarily facilitating the leap into the new and unknown world.

Ransome's experience is a late-nineteenth-century, middle-class one and reflects Victorian demands for boys in particular to absorb knowledge and accrue faculties under bracing conditions, not to mention a belief that they would naturally 'recognise and appreciate the best in literature', as Edward Salmon put it in his 1888 report on boys' and girls' reading.[6] Ransome, in accord with his father's education on literary taste, officially remembers reading only one comic (*Ally Sloper's Half Holiday*, 1884–1916), which he claims to have found suitably disappointing because there was nothing to read in it beside 'silly pictures' (1976/1985, p. 37). Rudyard Kipling's account of learning to read chimes a similar note, displaying the same qualities of innate ability through perseverance in the right circumstances that is apparent in Ransome's autobiography: 'I was made to read without explanation, under the usual fear of punishment. And on a day that I remember it came to me that "reading" was not "the Cat lay on the Mat", but a means to everything that would make me happy' (1937/1991, p. 6). In Kipling's case it was books such as *Robinson Crusoe*, as well as works by Walter Scott, Alfred Tennyson and other sanctioned literature deemed appropriate for boys.

Other memoirists recall learning to read with adults in terms that expose alternative expectations of gender, class, or historical situation. Like Ransome, Westall reports learning to read with the help of his father, but young Robert's experience took place almost half a century later than Arthur's and it is perhaps not surprising that his coming to literacy is mapped rather differently. Westall's father was also no academic, and, in this account, there is little sense of any paternal pressure or the promotion of quick advancement in reading. Crucially, the central text marking this moment is neither a classic nor what might be understood as quality children's literature: instead, it is the comic *Puck* (1904–40), a staple for many children, especially during what might be called the interwar golden age of comics. Where Ransome's father clearly influenced his son's distaste for comics and checked his swift progress through the works of Scott by examining him on each book before he was allowed to move to the next, Westall remembers his father simply reading comics to him for pleasure. This practice subsequently led to a sudden ability to read. Westall explains: 'in a fashion typical of the Board School child that he was, my father ran his finger along under the words as he read' until the young Robert found himself successfully reading silently 'half a page ahead of him' (2006, p. 60). As a strategy for developing independent reading, Westall's father's approach seems to a modern eye rather more sensitive and less shaped by the constraints of masculine codes, not to mention psychologically sound, than Ransome Senior's method of forcing his son to 'leap' into knowledge. It is not always wise to map such encounters in purely historical terms, though, or as bound tightly by gender. Among my own group of remembering and rereading participants, Izzy remembers her father's involvement in her early literary development in the 1960s in terms that echo something of the Victorian childhoods of Ransome and Kipling as well as Westall's more comprehensive educational context. She explains, 'I have painful memories of my father pointing at the two words "spot" and "stop", stabbing at them with his finger and getting frustrated with me for not being able to read the difference. That's my only memory of him reading with me.' Izzy's father takes on a pedagogical role, albeit briefly, that also enacts something of the nurturing zone that places parent and child in contact with a shared text. Despite the negative connotations of this early moment in her reading journey, a residue of influence also persists as Izzy reflects that this single vivid memory might have contributed to her decision later in life to become a lecturer in early years education, so that her difficult experience might be avoided by other children. Yet this particular encounter in the paternal contact zone, related in precise detail, surely also mirrors the frustrating experiences of numerous children and adults across the long twentieth century – experiences not always accounted for in autobiographical publications that instead regularly stress a positive, shared journey into literacy.

The conflicts apparent in accounts of remembered reading do not quite tally with Tatar's notion of the contact zone, then, which stresses a division that arises because a shared book acts to direct adult and child reader in different directions: 'children want to light out for new territory' and use books as 'road maps for navigating the real world', while adults are looking for ways back to the pleasures of childhood (2010, p. 4). Her perception of the contact zone is thus one that formulates childhood reading in terms of a journey in one direction and adult co-reading in another due to the forces of nostalgia. My analysis does not reveal evidence of the remembered child being aware of such nostalgic division between themselves and their adult co-readers, but other forms of friction are certainly apparent. A further conflict can be found in debates about reading matter appropriate for learning to read, as recalled by admittedly readerly memoirists. For instance, Sutcliff remembers feeling outraged at being told by teachers that she should try to learn to read from a 'dreadful book about a Rosy-Faced Family who Lived Next Door and Had Cats that Sat on Mats' after she had 'walked the boards with the Crummles, and fought beside Beowulf in the darkened Hall of Heriot' (1983, p. 54). Alison Uttley explains the 'torture' of having to study a story about plum stones that she and her classmates were given at school to learn their letters when she could already read and knew very well that the book in which the story appeared contained 'a galaxy of tales' that she could have enjoyed by herself (1937, p. 214). Beatrix Potter, too, recalls with disgust the 'horrid large-print primer' and 'stodgy fat book' she was given to learn to read (Sarah Trimmer's *The History of the Robins* or *Fabulous Histories* [1786]), claiming in an article on the 'roots' of her writing that she instead picked up the skill by working her own way through Scott's *Rob Roy* (1817) (1929/1977, p. 189). By stubbornly not learning to read, the young Sutcliff could avoid ever meeting the Rosy-Faced Family 'or any of their unspeakable kind', and the rich quality fiction read by her mother would continue to flow. Traditional controlled vocabulary primers are also mentioned by Eve Garnett in her 'autobiographical chapters', *First Affections* (1982/1985), who reflects on the tedious reading lessons she endured encountering 'the doings of one Dan, who had a pan or a bun, and who spent his time putting a cat, and sometimes a hen, on a mat' (p. 103). She comments ironically that 'poor Dan' was unable to 'quire [*sic*] anything or follow any occupation requiring more than three letters' and admits that she 'detested him' for it (p. 103). These experiences contrast sharply with those of Lucy Boston who writes in her memoir, *Perverse and Foolish*, that she is grateful that as a beginner reader she was not given 'The cat sat on the mat' but rather 'plunged straight into the deep end of literature' (1979, p. 44).

In an essay on learning to be literate, Lissa Paul (2009) celebrates the texts that became available to British children from the mid-twentieth century onwards (such as the work of Dr Seuss, Allan Ahlberg and Maurice Sendak) which assume an intelligent child audience with a desire to learn and allowed some respite from primers and reading schemes in home reading; it is possible that many children's writers growing up in the preceding decades would have found a happy medium in such child-focused titles, if they had been available. Yet, in the more private survey responses and interviews I undertook, readers who grew up in this later period also refer frequently and with varying degrees of fondness to series such as the Ladybird *Key Words Reading Scheme* (launched in 1964) and individual titles such as *Downy Duckling* (1946), which represent 'a safe and familiar world'. Jillie recalls her mother reading *Downy Duckling* to her so many times during her infancy in the 1960s that she memorized it, so that by the time she was four she could 'read' it all by herself by turning the pages and recalling the words in the right order. Jillie was a reluctant reader elsewhere, having 'very little recollection of reading at school' outside of the *Happy Ventures* reading scheme books by Fred Schonell featuring 'Dick' and 'Dora' (1939), which she was forced to read and which she 'loathed'. However, she reports enjoying the confidence boost the feat of memorizing *Downy Duckling* gave her as well as the gentle rhymes and illustrations that support the text (a comparable experience is recounted by Pullein-Thompson, who learnt the stories in the *Crown Readers* scheme [Rogerson, 1980] by heart so she could pretend to read fluently at an early age; 1996, pp. 6–7). It is possible that for some individuals (particularly those less concerned with the nuances of children's literature than authors may be) each and every text encountered in youth has the potential to be meaningful. Where matters of judgement about literary quality are put aside, and the function that books have is brought to the fore, these reading-scheme texts can occupy an important starting place in a topography of reading history that moves from private pleasures to institutional practices.

School and home

When prompted for memories of childhood reading, many of my participants begin by recalling books they enjoyed. Cultural critic Jack Zipes reminds us that while scholars may know children's literature as a 'vast historical complex' (2001, p. 70), children encounter books as single commodities designed to give pleasure. C. S. Lewis (1945/1970, 1966/1982) considers pleasure in its most transcendental sense to be the basis for interaction with texts by even the youngest of readers, a position I explore in more detail in the next chapter along with more unsettling ideas of reading as thrilling gratification or a kind of frantic 'vertical din' as Roland Barthes puts it (1975a, p. 12). Since the creation of the earliest commercial books for children – John Newbery's 1744 publication *A Little Pretty Pocket-Book* is the best known – pleasure and fun have been considered important ways to maintain the attention of young readers. As Mathew Grenby (2009) has pointed out, very often the urge to provide pleasure to child readers is yoked to a need to edify, so that Newbery's ABC of games and delights appeared alongside moral messages in a whole that was intended for the 'Instruction and Amusement' of its readers. Such Lockean philosophy can still be identified in more modern studies on education, and particularly literacy. Directing his comments to teachers in schools and colleges in an edited collection called *Readers, Texts, Teachers* published in 1987, Emrys Evans asserts that the very first need for the teaching of literacy is that children and young people should be 'able and happy to read for their own satisfaction and enjoyment in the present time' (p. 22), and in a chapter from the third edition of the *Handbook of Reading Research* (2000), John Guthrie and Allan Wigfield plot the importance of engagement and motivation in reading, arguing that young readers who enjoy the activity read more, for longer, and with greater cognitive benefits ('Engagement and Motivation in Reading'). Their theory both reflects and promotes studies into children's reading for pleasure undertaken recently by Maynard, Mackay, Smyth and Reynolds (2007) and Clark and Teravainen for the National Literacy

Trust (2017) in which enjoyment of books is promoted alongside educational concerns.[7]

The majority of my participants were educated in the early and mid-twentieth century, and for many of them school represented an official, public space where 'reading for pleasure' was not a key part of everyday activities. However, for certain fortunate individuals, such as Dorothy, who is aged in her sixties when I speak to her, school is recalled as a site for reading experiences in a way that can be understood in the context of a pedagogical philosophy of enjoyment or, at times, in ways that cross over into more sensual and affective terms. Dorothy strongly recollects a Hardy novel introduced to her at the age of fifteen by her schoolteacher, who read it aloud in class. It is a powerful marker of the past, bringing back feelings of anticipation and curiosity as well as the material qualities of the novel, which was hard-backed and smelled 'schooly'. On the whole, positive memories of reading in school emerge from intimate moments such as these, where schoolteachers adopt some of the gentle storytelling or gifting role more usually to be found in maternal figures. Small schools and home schooling provide context for such encounters, especially in early-twentieth-century examples or alternatively in accounts of expatriate experience. For instance, Claribel attended a liberal English Dame School in the 1930s, where reading was encouraged rather than taught – 'you just did it if you wanted to' and there was 'half an hour after lunch' provided for private reading. Thus, some of the most vividly remembered childhood books mapped for her are ones that were suggested to her by friendly teachers or from the selection on the shelves of the school bookcase. Lauren recalls hearing *Children of the Dark People* by Frank Dalby Davison (1936) as a five-year-old in a tiny Australian bush school in the mid-1940s, recognizing the impact that the skilled teacher had in drawing together children of different ages in a small class to work on this text. She enjoys rereading the book as an adult living in England as a way of accessing through memory 'a world that has vanished for ever'. As with Dorothy, Lauren finds that the reading situation creates a vivid sensory backdrop for remembering: her main memory of the text is the 'musical sound' of the names of the Aboriginal characters, for instance, but she also recalls the envy she felt towards the girl who sat next to her wearing 'a dress made from old lace curtains dyed green' in contrast to her own 'faded navy shorts'. Emotions are foregrounded in both memory of specific naming words ('I still found them beautiful') and the reading context, which is shaded with the wish that her mother had found her better clothes to wear; however, the educational impact of *Children of the Dark People* is not mentioned in this extract.

Memoirists tend to discuss books in institutional situations less frequently than those adults I spoke to in interview. Even the most imaginative rememberer is likely to move away from extended discussions of interior life and instead turn to sketches of social interactions and academic progress when schooldays are being recounted. Lively's account of the disparity between her early experience of expatriate home schooling and later inculcation into an English boarding school explains one of the possible reasons for this shift. From descriptions of an environment where reading formed the core of her everyday learning, Lively's experience of school is recounted mostly through the increasing awkwardness of social interactions with girls embarrassed to admit liking books. Tellingly, Lively remembers that one of the official punishments for bad behaviour at the school was to be sent to the library to read for an hour, demonstrating a not-so-subtle shift between the liberal pleasures of an open attitude towards books as a nurturing force and a delight for children, and an institutionalized disconnection between reading and pleasure.[8] Lively's autobiographical reflection on her early non-institutional education is therefore a familiar mapping of remembered books that links reading to a homely environment, which nevertheless offers a useful insight into how specific books and practices of reading can be embedded in an educational space, even if it is a domestic one. Lively's tutoring was undertaken by her nurse and untrained governess, Lucy, using the syllabus created for international and expatriate children by the Parents National Education Union (PNEU); the experience was rich in 'one-to-one attention' (1994/1995, p. 98). The primary pedagogic method encouraged by the PNEU in this curriculum was reading, memorizing and talking back. Lively's recollections reveal both the intimacy and the intensity of her childhood experience with books in this context, as she and Lucy 'read *Nicholas Nickleby* together, on the pansy-strewn sofa in the nursery, taking a paragraph each, Lucy resuming sewing when it was my turn to read, both of us openly weeping at the sad bits' (p. 108). Where the syllabus dictated a range of texts from mythology to Chaucer for the 'Reading' aspect of its pupils' education, Lively and her governess were forced by circumstances to make use of many of the books on her father's shelves as well as children's books available from the Cairo international bookshop instead. Lively's delight in myths, in particular, is evident in her description of the act of reading as a child, when she could become 'the heroine and the creator all at once' (p. 107), which has continued into her writing life in retellings of fairy tales, classical tales, and local legends as well as supernatural novels for children.

Lively describes how, on returning to England in 1945, she would 'retreat' to her bedroom to 'find solace in a bar of Fry's chocolate and a book' (1994/1995, p. 177). For many children growing up in the twentieth century, the home, rather than school, is the major space for reading and represents a meaningful aspect of remembering childhood books. The bedroom and the bed in particular are central sites of leisure, offering privacy and autonomy. Mackey refers to her childhood bedroom as the 'first space' of her reading history, and crucial to her identity as reader: 'I learned my first powers of reading in processing the details and functions of that room and its view of the outside environment. It gave me a core set of physical and ontological understandings of the world that would be essential in learning to make sense of the virtual universes of the different texts I encountered' (2016, p. 59). Townsend remembers that her favourite place for reading as a child in the 1950s was 'on [h]er bed, lying on a pink cotton counterpane' (1992/2015, p. 220), ideally accompanied by a bag of sweets, an image that indicates certain notions of scant post-war luxury and an increasing child-centred orientation of space as much as it reflects the young Sue's particular tastes. In contrast, Goudge learnt to read not in bed but by spending many hours with books in her sun-filled schoolroom 'flat on [her] stomach [. . .] and later in an upright position' (1974, p. 107). She recalls that books were read 'by suction' yet matched to the reading position in terms of seriousness. The pleasures of reading in bed link remembered books to intimate spaces of comfort or illness and to a prone position of seeming passive consumption. Childhood diseases and infections often led to extended periods of confinement and reading, particularly during the first half of the twentieth century before the National Health System was founded, and the combination of serious illness and new childhood books could be revolutionary for the remembered child self. Boston uses her early experience of hospitalization as a young girl suffering from measles and scarlet fever to pinpoint the moment that she discovered what she calls her first 'non-pi[ous]' book: Lewis Carroll's *Alice in Wonderland* (1979, p. 43); while Alan Garner similarly ties his first experience of properly reading a comic to a bout of meningitis, followed by convalescence in his bed at home, during which he got through 'a whole wall of Nelson's Illustrated Classics [. . .] straight through them like a termite' (1974, p. 224). For Kerr, the sick-bed is the site of an invigorating encounter with Jack London's *Call of the Wild* (1903), which she recalls as so exciting that it unfortunately made her temperature rise again (1992/2015, p. 50).[9] Danielle Fuller and DeNel Rehberg Sedo argue that 'the action of reading always takes place somewhere, whether in [. . .] a domestic and private space such as the home, or in a public space like a library or on a bus' (2013, p. 27). This assertion can be pushed even further as many memoirists build additional landscapes of remembered reading from the combination of their real worlds and the imaginative spaces constructed from and around childhood books.

Reading spaces

The first space of reading is a material starting point for plotting lifelong reading; other spaces are virtual. To explore this topographical approach to understanding reading histories further, it can be useful to track movement of individual texts or types of reading through the life space with an eye to alternative patterns to the journey marked by improvement. Where memoirists discuss the books they chose for themselves, for instance, they often refer to texts that, in Peter Dickinson's terms, may 'contain to the adult eye no visible value, either aesthetic or educational' (1970, p. 8). Some honest autobiographers revel in the eclectic piles of unsanctioned books they recall as part of their childhood reading histories. For Adams, for instance, relatively unknown titles such as Brown Linnet's *Why-Why and Tom-Cat* (1906) and W. M. Letts's *The Story Spinner* (1907) – what he calls 'honest tripe' (1990, p. 105) – map out his early reading experience as significantly as his mother's choices of respected children's poetry, and move beyond the notion of 'good for' into freer aspects of subjective delight. Other memoirists conversely remember books that seemed important or aesthetically compelling because of their perceived difficulty. Vladimir Nabokov's *Lolita* (1950) opened Jacqueline

Wilson's teenage self up to the possibilities of 'rich and elegant' language and taught her what was and was not suitable for young readers.

Not all adults who remember reading *Robinson Crusoe* explicitly position it as a threshold text between past and present, either, as Rose argues his memoirists do. Although the novel was not explicitly aimed at children, following Jean-Jacques Rousseau's recommendation in his treatise on education that Defoe's should be the first book read by a growing boy such as Emile (from *Émile: Or, Treatise on Education* [1762]), the story of the shipwrecked hero became a firm favourite among young readers. Charles Dickens famously wrote about his memories of reading of *Robinson Crusoe* in childhood in an essay called 'Nurse's Stories' (first published as part of his 'Uncommercial Traveller' sketches in *All the Year Round* on 8 September 1860) and it may have inflected some of his later writings: it appears in cameo in *A Christmas Carol* (1843/2006) as the young Ebenezer Scrooge's reading matter, for example (1843/2006, pp. 31–2). The accounts provided in Rose's survey of nineteenth- and twentieth-century working-class readers also attest to this popularity and, by the end of the nineteenth century, the novel was top of a survey of schoolboys (Salmon, 1888). Girls, as well as boys, encountered it: as Woolf puts it in her essay on Defoe in *The Common Reader*, 'we have all had *Robinson Crusoe* read aloud to us as children' (1925/1984, p. 86). Publishers embraced multiple readerships and so many chapbook versions, abridgements, adaptations, and sequels have been spawned since the eighteenth century that Michael Preston finds it useful to refer to the extensive 'shadow canon' surrounding Defoe's original work (1995, p. 23).

Reading beyond this discourse of popularity and transformation, other autotopographical patterns emerge among memories of this text, situating it as part of a more complex network of connections within readers' life spaces. The fictional landscape of the novel itself plays a part, with the deserted island looming large in accounts of remembering. Dickens reflects that he 'never was in Robinson Crusoe's Island, yet [he] frequently returns there' (1860/1958, p. 148), writing about how he is transported through memory to a specific place where the 'tropical sky shines bright and cloudless' (p. 149), while contemporary British writer J. G. Ballard explains that 'simply thinking about [. . .] the waves on Crusoe's island stirs me far more than reading the original text' (1992/2015, p. 88). Both adult rememberers also highlight the 'worldness' or 'topothesia' of Defoe's text – the heightened description of imaginary place that creates the text's rich invented world and makes Crusoe's island seductive to readers. Both describe how *Robinson Crusoe* is transformed from the words on a page into a vibrant and dynamic virtual world through immersion into that landscape as boy readers, a sense of immersion into landscape that can be revisited well into adulthood through memory.

Ballard suggests that books such as *Robinson Crusoe* departed from the page and have taken on a 'second life' inside his head, not only in the sense of the virtual entity that reader response theory posits as being set in motion when reader and text meet, but also as an ongoing narrative space that plays out again and again over time and via memory. It is a telling phrase, since the term 'second life' has more recently been appropriated for an online virtual platform that replicates and augments 'real life' and actual space.[10] This second life world includes landscapes that can never be visited in bodily person, but which are nonetheless part of experiential reality for its users. The online platform mirrors one of the most enigmatic qualities of the reading act, whereby printed text is decoded and transposed into mental images. Those images then perform as memory traces do and can sometimes be embodied in the sense that a fictional place really seems to have been visited in the reader's past. This process can be plotted according to the different 'registers' of memory and imagination (Fernyhough, 2012, p. 42), which in some cases can cross over or become merged. The point where they meet is particularly resonant in the context of constructing and consuming fictional worlds.

To continue a process of thick mapping, further links can be made between these textual spaces of remembered books and geospatial elements of the actual world shared by different readers. For example, Kipling also recalls reading *Robinson Crusoe* as a boy and his autobiographical account focuses on real-world spaces and the locations of his childhood in which he acted out aspects of Defoe's plot. He describes the 'mildewy basement room' in which he pretended to trade with savages and the imaginative apparatus of a 'coconut shell strung on a red cord, a tin trunk, and a piece of packing-case' with which he created the fantasy world: 'everything [. . .] was quite real', he writes, although it did smell of 'damp cupboards' (Kipling, 1937/1991, p. 8).[11] This location might be termed a 'representational space' – the lived environment in which textual events are reinvented through imaginative play. An important part of childhood reading histories is this doubling or overlaying of fictional landscapes onto real places, whether in the process of play-acting or in the act of relating a text to familiar geospatial locations in the physical environment. Uttley remembers undertaking similar playful re-enactment after her mother read *Robinson Crusoe* aloud to her and it became the book 'above all books [that] brought dreams and visions':

> We listened, carried far away to that island, dwelling in cave and tree-top, watching for the ship, plunged in despair. Night after night the story continued, but for me it was unending. I lay in bed, making up more adventures, reliving Crusoe's life in a brilliantly-coloured dream of my own, where parrots and goats shared my existence. In the daytime I went on with the tale, acting it in my games, with the lawn as the island, and the summer-house as the cave, and the house the wreck to which we sailed our raft. (1937, p. 175)

Later robinsonades provide similar material for building representational space, as I discovered in researching memories of reading Ransome's *Swallows and Amazons*.[12] Two of my interviewees, Tom and Nicki, recalled more about their re-enactment of the novel than about the contents of the story itself. For Nicki, the game transformed her real and very rural home environment into an adventurous camp, while Tom explains that he used Ransome's sketched topography of the setting for his protagonists' heroes to create 'a map of "our" part of the Gower (where we used to holiday each year)'. Of course, the fictional Walker children engage in precisely this kind of imaginative mapping themselves, by naming elements of their Lake District environment after literary spaces (such as 'a Peak in Darien') and play-acting fictional adventures (with Titty taking on the role of Robinson Crusoe on his island).

John Buchan records a variation of this imaginative register in his autobiography, *Memory, Hold the Door* (1940), whereby the geographies of a significant book of his childhood are overlaid onto a real landscape in the reading process rather than in play. Woodlands outside Fife acted as a symbolic setting for textual events so that, as the young Buchan read, he imagined episodes from John Bunyan's *The Pilgrim's Progress* (1678) taking place in the colliery, gravel pit, and bogs of his local surroundings. Biblical stories were also part of his literary experience as a boy, and his environment also helped to bring these narratives to life as he 'built up a Bible world of [his] own and placed it in the woods' (1940/1984, p. 16).

Remembering readers might orient themselves across each of these spatial planes, although, in practice, individual memoirs and interviews rarely cover them all. In the final part of this chapter, I turn cartographer and draw out the overlapping 'thick maps' of two readers I interviewed about childhood reading, relating them where viable to broader histories of response to island narratives.

Mapping reading

Mary was born in 1928 and grew up in Paris until 1940, when her family moved back to England. Simon was born fourteen years later in 1942 and spent his childhood in rural Somerset. Both now live in the south of England. They both took part in my survey and agreed to talk to me about their early reading as well as to undertake my rereading experiment. The books they recalled from childhood and chose to reread as adults are robinsonades: in Mary's case, L. T. Meade's *Four on an Island* (1892) and in Simon's, Johann David Wyss's *The Swiss Family Robinson* (1812). Their reading narratives provide interesting case studies for mapping the different topographical layers I have outlined so far: the common waymarks of reading narratives, actual geospace, fictional or textual space, and representational space. In addition, these accounts reveal evidence of subterranean matter as the act of remembering digs down into the past as well as aiding traversing across various landscapes.

In our re-memorying interview, Mary explains the early years of her literate life:

> I spent my childhood in France, in Paris, and that means, of course, that it affected the books that I read quite a lot, because the choice was rather limiting compared to being in England. And also I was an only child, so I didn't have anything else to do but read, because living in Paris, one didn't run out of doors and play with one's little friends, one was stuck in a flat all day long really, except for doing homework, which took up a lot of time, but all the rest of the time I read.

Mary's Parisian flat is the first actual space to be mapped in her account and it is a rather limited and isolated one. It also signifies a division between two reading identities as she grew up as a bilingual English girl in France. She notes that French 'was for school' while the very few English books that were available to her at this time were for pleasure. She describes the Paris branch of W. H. Smiths' bookstore as 'paradise', expressing something of the visceral thrill also suggested by Lively's account of the Express Bookshop in Cairo, where the young Penelope became 'infatuated, addicted' to British children's literature (Lively, 1994/1995, p. 106). For Mary, then, reading children's books in English is a form of transportation to an alternative and better reality as well as a retreat and escape, which mostly takes place in the first space of her bedroom: she recalls receiving a copy of Louisa May Alcott's *Little Women* (1868) for her seventh birthday, which she took to her bedroom and read, then turned 'straight to the beginning and began again'. She describes the novel as a 'refuge' for her child self, blurring the boundaries between the sanctuary of bedroom space and the fictional text. It also acts as a kind of talisman throughout her life course, and she still has her original copy, which she says she would not part with for anything: 'it stayed with me [. . .] put into storage in the war and coming across to England [. . .] all the houses I've lived in since'.

Like Mary, Simon did not have easy access to books as a child, growing up in the 1950s in a village without a library or bookshop. He recalls finding books in hidden spaces. There is a damp cupboard full of musty leather-bound books left by the previous owners of the house, 'coated with a white powder perhaps to keep insects out' and reminiscent of the 'musty cupboard' in which Crago originally discovered 'exotic' hardback copies of Lawrence R. Bourne's *Coppernob Second Mate* (1927) and W. H. G. Kingston's *Old Jack* (1934) that he then decides to source and reread (Crago, 1990, p. 106). Simon also recalls a 'tea-chest' of jigsaws that his father brought home during the war, which may have housed the copy of *The Swiss Family Robinson* that he remembers reading around the age of nine or ten. These repositories of cupboard and chest are atmospheric and slightly mysterious, and the novel itself is also recalled in terms of its intriguing difference – 'this oldness', as Simon puts it – being the first text he had come across as a child that included unfamiliar chapter subheadings and engraved headings. The enigmatic stores of books and the challenging hardback copy of Wyss's novel mirror Simon's taste for 'adventurousness', both in his regular outdoor activities in the local environment and in his preference of reading matter (enjoying Blyton's *Adventure* series more than her *Famous Five* books, for example). At the same time, as with Mary's account, Simon's primary geospatial description of his childhood reading reflects a more homely concern with comfort and seclusion as he reports that he usually read on the floor in front of the coal fire or in bed.

Geographical movement shapes Mary's reading history significantly, expanding her map beyond her Parisian flat and also into new forms of texts. She places great weight upon her return to England in 1940 for instance, describing fondly her 'very good English teacher' at the Croydon elementary school who introduced her to boys' adventure stories and of the 'absolute joy of a public library' where she could choose her own books for the first time. A year earlier, in 1939, her family evacuated from Paris 'absolutely certain it was going to be bombed to pieces' and moved to an aunt and uncle's house in a village beyond Versailles called Louvecienne. They lived there for less than a year, but Mary explains it was one of the best years of her life: the rural lifestyle transformed her childhood from a lonely bookish one to one filled with French friends and outdoor play. Although Louvecienne is described by Mary as a 'real village where there weren't books', in autotopographical terms it is still a rich site of meaningful literary objects and memories of reading them. While not the most literary of landscapes, the singularity of the village as a retreat, as well as its links to a period of uncertainty and heightened anxiety, embed it and the books encountered there particularly firmly in Mary's account. Louvecienne is a space of discovery. The books Mary remembers discovering there expand her range beyond girls' classics. For example, she reads popular adult books by Edgar Wallace and P. G. Wodehouse that she finds in her aunt's collection, and she recalls coming across a copy of Ian Hay's *Pip: A Romance of Youth* (1907), a sporting tale, that encouraged her later taste for boys' school stories and laid the groundwork for her to expand her reading into the merchant adventure tales of Percy Westerman in adolescence (further, it developed an enthusiasm for cricket she could share with her father).

Mary also discovered Meade's *Four on an Island* at her aunt's house. While part of her paracanon, it has not 'come with her' through age in the same way as *Little Women*, and she is not quite sure why she read it: she identifies it as 'an oddity' and quite 'absurd' but does remember finding it very thrilling and rereading it several times as a girl. Meade's novel is a tale of adventure set in Brazil and its high seas, featuring four English children who are stranded on an island and have to find ways to survive until they are rescued. Mary states that she remembers the story being similar to *The Swiss Family Robinson*: Meade was also clearly influenced by Defoe's work, and was part of a body of female authors rewriting *Robinson Crusoe* narratives for an audience of girl readers (Fair, 2014; Norcia, 2004). Like Crusoe, the heroes and heroines of *Four on an Island* are plagued by numerous challenges – sharks, land crabs, storms, and injury – and yet remain cheerful and resolute throughout. They find an old shipwreck and make a home on it, then use its stores to build a proper shelter on land. Meade offers her readers some of the same 'spirit of adventure' that Defoe does his, but allows them to see this spirit through the actions and endeavours of the main female character rather than through an individualist male hero. The oldest boy, Ferdinand, plays the part of the strong leader as much as he can. However, as several critics have pointed out, it is his sister Isabel who is the true and brave heroine for much of the story: she hunts, climbs trees, and directs the other children. This exchange between Ferdinand and Isabel, when the former explains that he cannot climb a tree to make a flagpole because he has sprained ankle, reveals something of Meade's attitudes towards gender. Isabel responds with very English courage or 'grit':

> What a good thing that I was always as much boy as girl . . . Oh dear, oh dear! my mistress at the old school in England used to prophesy all kinds of bad things of me because I *would* climb trees; and now – if poor Miss Hodges could only see! Well, here goes! Give me the hatchet, please, Tony. I'm going to swarm up the old king. (Meade, 1892/n.d., p. 172)

As Megan Norcia observes, 'Meade recuperates Crusoe's domestic heroism, positioning her hero Isabel Fraser as his most fitting successor' (2004, p. 348). What Norcia does not notice so much is the central role the island setting plays in creating effect in this novel, making it 'exciting and thrilling' as Mary remembers. Certainly, the deserted island allows the children to temporarily escape the norms of social life and the trappings of patriarchy. But it also plays a part in softening the exotic and potentially fearsome elements of the plot: often, the South American landscape is described in positive and familiar terms, as in the example of the cave the children explore, which is described as a 'comfortable little room cut out of the solid rock' and a 'little bower' into which 'the sunlight streamed' (Meade, 1892/n.d., p. 111). Indeed, the episode Mary recalls most vividly features the setting, specifically a makeshift shelter the children call the White Castle, which they ingeniously construct inside the handy shipwreck. She describes a key narrative event that has remained vivid in her memory and is related to this shelter. It is the moment when the White Castle is threatened:

> One of them opened a door or whatever they had by way of a door in this shelter, and could see a great [. . .] bulk of some kind by the fire, sort of monster, [. . .] one of the little ones was terrified and rushed off to get the older ones, and the older ones came along and bravely looked inside. And it turned out to be a Guernsey cow. I don't know how it had got there (laughs). But they were delighted when they found it was a perfectly tame, Guernsey cow. It was completely and absolutely unbelievable, all of it.

The Guernsey cow episode from *Four on an Island* is presented in comic terms by Mary, yet she remembers thinking as a child reading that there really was a 'horrible monster', which is no doubt why the episode has remained in her memory (although she misremembers the breed, since it is actually an Alderney cow). *Four on an Island* may not obviously mark a turning point in Mary's life, but the scene with the shelter and the menacing cow may nevertheless provide one significant dimension to her autotopography by allowing us both to dig down further into her past. The cow reflects the novel's repeated references to the bucolic beauty and familiarity of England even in the midst of exotic descriptions of the South American island – the Alderney even provides welcome milk for the children's sustenance. From the first space of her bedroom to the conceptual space of *Little Women* as refuge, and the threatened White Castle, safety and security feature throughout her account of remembered reading. Perhaps this is a key that unlocks the urges of many children who seek protection from potential threats in familiar and homely places: the element of domestic sanctuary protecting against the wilderness identified by Jane Suzanne Carroll (2012) as a key topos of children's literature. 'Refuge' is also the term used by American writer Verlyn Klinkenborg to describe the selection of books he has chosen to reread over the course of his life, reflecting, as he puts it, the safety of childhood practice which is 'an oasis of repetitive acts' (2009, n.p.). For Mackey, 'yearning for home' factored as a significant theme for her response to the books she read during an unsettling holiday stay with her uncle and aunt when everything around her felt strange (2016, pp. 252–8). The idea of refuge may also have a particular resonance for a generation facing tangible dangers living through a war and for an individual aware of the potential of being bombed in her Parisian home.

The dual pleasures of hazard and security also form an important part of Simon's reflections on *The Swiss Family Robinson*. He recalls the aspect of survival key to the Swiss family's fictional endeavours:

> I engaged with this as I did imaginary things like this myself in my roaming around the local countryside pretending I was this family and had to fend for myself against any odds. Being alone much of the time made it harder for me (in my games) to survive so it stimulated my own mind and ideas about natural conditions around me. I re-lived some of their adventures and loved every minute of it. I made camps or dens in the woods.

Simon admits that he was inspired by Wyss's story as a boy, although he did not enjoy what he calls Defoe's 'contrived' story at the same age; his account combines the sense of individualist epiphany that Rose observed in his readers of *Robinson Crusoe* with something of the urge for refuge I have argued exists in Mary's autotopography and which emerges in an analysis of her response to *Four on an Island*. In demonstrating his immersion into the actual space of the countryside through re-enactment of fictional tropes from the novel, Simon reveals an investment in Wyss's imaginary geography that helped him create his own possible worlds as a child. There are some details about plot and character in his account that I shall return to in Chapter 5; however, once more it is the setting and world-building in *The Swiss Family Robinson* that provides the main scaffold for memories of initial reading. He recalls that the island is very 'lush and productive' and notes that his interest lay in the extensive descriptions of wild animals, birds, and plants that do, of course, make up the bulk of the narrative. As critic J. Hillis Miller reminds us, Wyss's central purpose was 'to teach natural history' (2004, p. 84) and, in his own recollections of reading the novel as a boy, Miller stresses what he calls the 'abundance' of the tropical island 'teeming with every sort of bird, beast, fish, tree and plant' (p. 78). As with Simon, who remembers finding the idea of self-sufficiency on an island very appealing and uses textual concepts of ingenuity and survival to shape his role-playing games in the wood, moors, marshes, and beaches of West Somerset, Miller recalls finding the idea of abundance both exciting and reassuring as a child, giving him the early sense that he could be an independent being. Both stress the importance of camps and dens, Miller glossing the effect of *The Swiss Family Robinson* as the 'deep satisfaction of the nest-making instinct' (p. 78). This response towards a realistic assessment of survival based on textual evidence and the connection of textual actual world to real actual world differs slightly from a common conception of the desert island as a site for childhood autonomy, which may nevertheless be more apposite in relation to alternative types of narratives. For instance, another participant, Virginia, states while reflecting on her early reading of William Golding's *Lord of the Flies* (1954) that she liked the idea of being deserted on an island and 'able to do as I liked', but recognizes the limitations of her own abilities in this kind of situation. She wryly notes: 'as the story unfolded I realized that [my] "Guiding" knowledge would not have been much use'.

The notion of refuge and bounty shapes reading maps for both Mary and Simon. Englishness also plays a part in Mary's autotopography. Having not read *Four on an Island* since she was eleven, Mary enjoyed revisiting it on my request some seventy-five years later in her modest home in Hertford, surrounded by cosy bookshelves lining her living room with books from across her lifespan. In her notes from this rereading of *Four on an Island*, she reflects that 'there is a great deal about the importance of England and Englishness, sentiments which I would have shared'. Later she muses on her enjoyment of school stories by Antonia Forest and Angela Brazil, explaining that they were so completely different from her experience of education in France that they might as well have been fantasy worlds like the desert islands of *Robinson Crusoe* or *Four on an Island*. Tellingly, she also assumed, at first, that *Little Women* was set in England, so pervasive was this national influence as a place of imagination in her early life. It is not clear whether Mary's move back to her homeland in 1940 shifted this perspective, but since she and her family were 'bombed night after night' in Croydon, it is possible that the pleasures of fantasizing about England reduced significantly from this point onwards. Mary's map provides alternative ways of understanding the reception of a Robinsonade such as Meade's *Four on an Island*, as concerned with refuge as well as feminine agency, with fantasies of England as well as fantasies of exoticism. Mary's and Simon's narratives also point to other possible reading histories of *Robinson Crusoe*, ones that focus on multiple dimensions of autotopography rather than a linear journey structured around a turning point.

Conclusion

Childhood books, and encounters with them, can productively be mapped within the life course. Journeying through this terrain leads remembering adults through the contact zone, starting points of literacy, hidden places of personal taste, and shared spaces of schooled reading. Chapters 3, 4 and 5 will continue this voyage to explore further waymarks of the lifelong reading act, including first loves, revisiting through rereading, and the wrong turnings of misremembering and forgetting. Transformative moments also appear on these maps, representing conventional autobiographical turning points that seem to lead readers into new and more mature territory. Reports of transformation are not always to be taken at face value, however, as exemplified by Townsend's wry account of learning to read. For her, Richmal Crompton's *William* books (1921–70) acted as the gateway to an enthusiastic childhood reading habit and she indicates the significance of first encountering them by stating 'there should have been a hundred-gun salute. The Red Arrows should have flown overhead. The night sky should have blazed with fireworks' (Townsend, 1992/2015, p. 219). The bathos of this epiphanic description shows that the notion of a single turning point in a clear trajectory is open to gentle ridicule. Rather, such moments act as one of a series of coordinates that allow for a new form of directional movement across the terrain. Similarly, the very acts of remembering or reimagining childhood favourites regularly return adult readers to earlier stages of the reading journey. Departing from a linear conception of reading helps us recognize that reading childhood books can be an ongoing endeavour and that many points on the map can be revisited through different forms of imaginative engagement.

Memories of paracanonical books represent a significant part of the reading act, as memoirs and narrative accounts attest. These memories are also embedded within the life space, forming connections between childhood books and their geographical and social contexts. I have attempted to describe some common ground in the life space of those growing up in late nineteenth- and twentieth-century Britain. Individual accounts often tell even richer stories about the interrelation between reading and being in time and space. Actual space, representational space, and fictional space form the territory across which a reader moves back and forth over the course of their lives, and this landscape itself is worth scrutiny, as much as the human movement across it. Being equipped to analyse these layers of space through methods of autotopography and thick mapping allows for a 'probing [. . .] in the dark loam' of the past, as Benjamin puts it (1932/1999, p. 611) and means that scholars of reading can understand more about the continuing influence of childhood books in real lives. In the next chapter, I turn from this territory inwards once more and explore how childhood books leave residue in the form of affective traces among the strata of the life space.

3

Affective traces

Any act of excavation reveals strata below and above, in a place of deep origin and in the surface crust 'that must first be broken through' (Benjamin, 1932/1999, p. 611). If an element of the lifelong reading act can be framed as a kind of excavation, then it is worth acknowledging alongside archaeologist Sarah Tarlow that 'emotion, in short, is everywhere' (2000, p. 720). Affective discourse can be traced in mnemonic accounts of remembered reading and rereading as a way of connecting the reading scene and life space throughout the life course. Reading histories are therefore also histories of affect, telling narratives about the intimate relationships that exist between ageing readers, their earlier selves, and the texts that bind them together.

This chapter attempts some of the labour of uncovering accounts of significant childhood texts that have provoked passions as well as ambivalent feelings and that have refused to be eradicated from the adult's remembering mind due to emotional resonance. The production of personal paracanons depends on what is left as residue through traces of remembered emotional response. From Rosemary Sutcliff's reunion with what she calls her 'old love', L. M. Montgomery's *Emily of New Moon* (1923) (1983, p. 97), to Vladimir Nabokov's 'ecstatic moan' (1966/1969, p. 61) on rediscovering as an adult the French children's books that he had been introduced to by his uncle as a child, romantic and erotic ties offer a common theme in the discourse of lifelong reading. As well as love, adults remember and re-experience fear, grief, desire and boredom as they respond to books from their earliest years, the characters that populate them, and the worlds created within them, alongside sometimes uncomfortable memories of their previous reading selves.

I call these points of connection *affective traces*. These act like threads that resonate as they are first spun or as they are touched again in remembering or rereading. They create clear links between reader and book as well as connect the reading scene to elements of the life space in ways that can be broken and rewoven over time. They are sticky, attracting affective language and meanings, binding these to both remembered text and remembering adult. I begin this chapter by laying out some of the theoretical approaches to emotion and affect that have been most useful to me in examining the lifelong reading act. These are drawn from literary and critical cultural studies and also from cultural psychology and archaeology. C. S. Lewis's writings interrogating his personal returns to childhood books further illuminate reading, memory, and rereading according to emotional strata and traces. Each of these starting points helps me to unpick a range of autobiographical and remembering accounts and track histories of response: first, of passionate entanglement with childhood books that can be located within a wider discourse of children's literature as morally affecting; and, additionally, of more ambivalent emotional memories that offer alternative stories about the peculiar influence that books hold over their readers.

Affective traces and resonance

Childhood books exert an influence over individuals throughout the life course, being incorporated by young readers and contributing to 'their growth and their power', in the words of Walter Benjamin (1929/2014, p. 259). Critics have long debated what this influence might be, and how child readers and readers more generally are seduced and shaped by the books they ingest. Maria Tatar argues that 'the emotional landscape of the child' is dominated by 'boredom, wonder, and curiosity' (2009, p. 30), perceiving children's literature as a means for creating interest and awe and encouraging intellectual inquisitiveness. Philip Fisher, in contrast, proposes that literature most effectively models what can be called the 'vehement passions', those eruptive and momentary impassioned states of desire, wonder, fear, anger, grief, and shame that move characters – and subsequently readers – to action. Both perspectives echo long philosophical traditions of yoking affective reactions and aesthetic pleasure to intellectual or moral development, ranging from Aristotle to John Locke. Maria Edgeworth's preface to *The Parent's Assistant* (1796) offers a pithy defence of material that will equally stimulate the passions and the conscience in her young readers: 'to prevent the precepts of morality from tiring the ear and the mind, it was necessary to make the stories in which they are introduced in some measure dramatic; to keep alive hope and fear and curiosity, by some degree of intricacy' (1796, p. ix). The idea that encounters with texts offer the potential for lessons to be learned through emotional response persists, particularly in recent discourses of the development of empathy (see Nikolajeva, 2013; Coats, 2017). However, although accounts of remembered reading and rereading sometimes foreground vehement passions and reflect part of Tatar's emotional landscape in describing boredom as a means to personal enrichment, they do not always stress ethical or imaginative transformations in a younger self. Affective response emerges in autobiographical narratives in more ambivalent ways. Sianne Ngai's cultural analysis of what she calls 'ugly feelings', is helpful in recognizing the way that emotional states 'no longer link up as surely as they once did with [. . .] models of social action and transformation' (2005, p. 5). Even if childhood books have retained some of their purpose to teach empathy towards others or anger at injustice, other emotional narratives play a part in lifelong reading acts.

In uncovering some of these patterns, it is useful to recognize that although 'core' or 'basic' emotions are identified by psychologists and anthropologists as universally experienced throughout history and culture, 'higher' or 'cognitive' emotions develop later in the life course and involve a degree of learning and social conditioning. Both play a part in remembered reading. Cultural psychology is the study of 'the way cultural traditions and social practices regulate, express, transform and permute the human psyche' and it identifies its main premise as the human search for meaning (Shweder, 1990, p. 1): a framework that neatly addresses the rich performance of remembering and rereading childhood books. In such a schema theory, an affective script allows for the process of interpretation rather than focusing on the 'reality' of an emotional event. It is useful in this respect partly because it helps me move beyond universal neurological explanations for emotional states and identify the slipperiness of affective lexicography. Cultural psychologist Richard A. Shweder thus describes emotion as a 'complex synthetic notion' (2004, p. 82) and emotions as 'interpretative schemes' that give 'meaning and shape to [. . .] somatic and affecting "feelings"' (1994, p. 32). In other words, emotions and affective states can be thought of as packages or clusters of feelings that help frame experience. In this respect, emotions help us tell stories about ourselves and can be used to encompass ideas about sensations of the body (such as tears, a blush, or a racing pulse), feelings about the inner self (such as the sense of loss, wrongdoing, or transformation), and more general moods (such as anxiety or ennui). They can also help to connect and explain these different phenomena. For instance, a theory of mood-dependent recall helps to explain how recollections are organized and reconstructed via emotional 'tags'. Intense emotions in a moment help to 'fix' memories more securely for future recall, meaning that moments of strongly felt emotion from the past are most likely to be most powerfully recalled when we feel a similar emotion in the present (Eich et al., 1994).

Shweder describes emotions as 'script-like' (2004, p. 82), stressing the cognitive processes of recognition and pattern making that humans employ to organize the world and their interactions with it. Each emotion represents a complex of interrelated stimuli and affective response, but any single expression of an emotional script is liable to conflate more than one of these elements. 'Love' in this context can refer to a simple indication of interest or enjoyment; stronger romantic implications of affection towards character, text, or material book; a mood of wellbeing, or a series of somatic responses connected to such feelings. Love can also express or explain something of an action towards a book, such as the tender placing of it underneath a pillow. It becomes clear that the words adults use to describe their emotional responses to remembered reading are not always transparent or straightforward and, while 'love' is especially prone to linguistic fuzziness, as I shall show later in this chapter, all emotions are prey to the confusions of human language. Emotional discourse thus exists within systems of interpretation that help reading and remembering individuals, as well as institutional or moral gatekeepers, make sense of their responses and think of them as interpretative scripts, which, therefore, helps to unpick some of the discursive confusion.

Like Shweder, feminist cultural critic Sara Ahmed argues that emotions are not fixed and, moreover, that they cannot be reduced to passive definitions. Instead, they represent embodied actions. For Ahmed, emotions circulate between bodies while ideas or meanings 'stick' to them (and vice versa) (2004, p. 11). Her methodology provides a valuable way of understanding the language that expresses feelings: for instance, her parsing of the term 'impression' demonstrates the way that emotions function in multiple ways to create feelings, suggest responses, and make marks on the surface of individual and cultural 'skin', allowing her to 'avoid making analytical distinctions between bodily sensation, emotion and thought as if they could be "experienced" as distinct realms of human "experience" ' (p. 6). This formulation is particularly useful for thinking about emotions in the reading scene and the life space. Not only is reading itself an embodied act as well as an imaginative one – and childhood books are material artefacts located in space as well as texts – memories of that act also reconstruct a blend of mental and physical phenomena. Where affect is in play, it is both body and mind that are affected. Many of the accounts of remembered reading I have gathered are saturated with affect in ways that Ahmed would recognize. In most cases, reading scenes would not hold together without the affective terms used to describe childhood books and childhood reading selves: rememberers refer to shivers and tears, sleeplessness and laughter; they love and loathe, are thrilled and terrified, and are confused and unsettled. I have, therefore, remained alert to the bodily effects of reading and incorporate moments of physical interaction with childhood books throughout this book as a key part of the narratives of remembering and rereading I study.

In her theory of implicated reading, Lynne Pearce argues that even those critics writing explicitly from within the field of affective studies often fail to 'conceive of text and reader in terms of what it most obviously is: a *relationship*' (1997, p. 19). She posits that human interaction, specifically the development of romance, works as a viable alternative 'model of text-reader relations' (p. 20) that can help us properly move beyond a purely cognitive understanding of reading. Drawing on Roland Barthes's emotional 'dictionary', *A Lover's Discourse* (1977), she explores the way that readers fall in and out of love with texts, interrogating all of the affective stages along this journey. She lists these as 'enchantment', 'devotion' and 'fulfilment' (all aspects of Barthes's first phase of '*ravissement*') and 'anxiety', 'frustration', 'jealousy' and 'disappointment' (characteristics of 'the sequel', in Barthes's terms). Although she does not use the term, Pearce acknowledges the idea of the paracanon, pointing out that many readers recognize 'a feeling of devotion towards those 'special texts' (perhaps very few in number) that have made it onto [their] 'life list' (1997,

p. 107). Pearce argues that there is the potential for all readers to double back on her affective sequence, finding a way back from disappointment to earlier phases of *ravissement*. In tune with the majority of critics of reading, however, she fixes her model on an adult reader and glosses over what happens when reading is transferred from a child's encounter to an adult's long-term memory.

Theoretical notions of the archaeological trace offer a useful way of addressing this gap. In behavioural archaeology, a trace is 'material evidence that a particular interaction [. . .] has occurred' (LaMotta, 2012, p. 67), allowing transmissions of information about the past into the present. Traces can be ephemeral, 'disappearing soon after a particular interaction has occurred' (p. 67), but in some cases they can endure and provide clues to past behaviours and experiences. Traces represent resonance across time, allowing an emotional response from long ago to reverberate and be shared by the modern archaeologist (see Rizvi, 2015; also the concept has been employed in more philosophical terms in Ricoeur, 1988). In corresponding ways, adults encountering texts from the deep strata of their childhoods may feel vibrations from their original encounters and, in some cases, may be able to use these traces to interpret something of their early readerly culture.

Pleasures

As both children's author and literary critic, Lewis wrote cogently and without nostalgia about these affective strata and their relationship to reading histories. Much of his critical writing circulates around reading for pleasure, which has its origins in response to childhood books. His essay 'On Stories' (1947) is often quoted for its pronouncement that 'no book is really worth reading at the age of ten which is not equally (and often far more) worth reading at the age of fifty' (1966/1982, p. 14). Alongside this pithy statement, the rest of the essay is worth looking at in full, not least because by foregrounding elements of story and excitement commonly found in traditional children's literature, rather than theme, character, and style more prominent in the adult novels generally examined by critics, it made 'a unique and important contribution to literary theory' (Schakel, 2002, p. 53). While its aim is partly to set out what makes a good book (or a good reader), it is also salient because it represents a mnemonic scene in which the emotional traces of childhood reading and adult rereading are presented and theorized.

For Lewis, pleasure refers not only to base gratification, but also to a kind of transcendental readerly experience. He argues that a certain 'state or quality' (1966/1982, p. 17) to be found in some narratives awakens a corresponding and primarily affective response in the reader, which is the key to literary reading of story at any age. In an informal newspaper essay published in 1945, Lewis contrasts this idea of enjoyment in reading with the more scholarly activity of contemplation, arguing that the latter can be likened to looking directly *at* a sunbeam's illumination of a scene, while the former is akin to being within that beam and looking *along* it (1945/1970). His discussion ranges into the realm of, what Shweder calls, 'feelings of the soul' (1994, p. 37). Shweder is quick to point out that the term 'soul' is not religiously conceived: it is simply his shorthand for the self that is experienced internally, in terms of dimensions of emptiness and fullness, expansiveness and contractedness, agitation and stillness, and pleasure and displeasure. The word is nonetheless loaded, linking emotional narratives to an understanding of human subjectivity that is relevant to Lewis's critical position.

Lewis's descriptions of the affective qualities he remembers about childhood reading sit within this transcendental framework. He explains the 'sense of the deathly' produced when reading or remembering the scene of danger that occurs in H. Rider Haggard's *King Solomon's Mines* (1885), which includes atmosphere and setting ('the cold, the silence, and the surrounding faces of the ancient, the crowned and sceptred, dead'; 1966/1982, p. 6) in addition to the 'hushing spell' (p. 6) laid on the imagination. He also considers childly reading of fairy and folk tales in which the mythic figures that populate stories are repositories for the elusive feelings. Giants, for instance, may create excitement in the damage they threaten toward characters such as Jack in 'Jack and the Beanstalk', but they also generate sensations of 'heaviness [. . .] monstrosity [. . .] uncouthness' (p. 8) that resonate in the reader as feelings of the soul.

Lewis describes these evocative sensations in terms of elements in a musical theme that underscores the very idea of 'giant' and creates an almost unconscious effect on the listener. Taking a cognitive stylistics approach, Peter Stockwell has recently employed similar musical concepts to help explain literary effect and affect. For him, resonance is 'tone, an atmosphere in the mind that seems to persist long after the pages have been put down', which can 'strike the reader on a first reading, or may emerge only later on, and then several times in ongoing life' (2009, p. 17). It also has dual properties, of 'a *prolonged response* and an *aura of significance*' (p. 18) and can be measured, as sonorous music, in terms of its intensity over time. This is the 'state or quality' that most interested Lewis, too. As well as referring to musical aesthetics to explain its effects, he stresses its elusiveness, likening it to a bird in a net. Where the net represents the simple sequence of events of the story, the living thing it is designed to catch is itself more individual, peculiar, and precious. It is, therefore, not the plot itself, nor the simple thrills of excitement or suspense.

The elusive thing evoked by Lewis might be named, as it is by Schakel among others, as 'atmosphere' (2002, p. 57), a term he uses in his essay and later ones. However, while atmosphere describes something of the detailed description and world-building that he recognizes to be crucial in the creation of great stories, it does not quite encompass the notions of 'giantness, otherness, the desolation of space' (Lewis, 1966/1982, p. 17) that he uses as examples in reference to fairy tales, adventures, and short stories, nor does it capture the affective nature of the readerly responses he deploys to illustrate such giantness in action.[1] Lewis suggests that the young reader can be profoundly influenced by stories, which themselves are saturated with affect and, in turn, left in a different state to that in which he opened the book. Moreover, mood in this form can be connected to early emotional states and can also be conjured and intensified in the process of rereading a childhood book as an adult, a process of trace recovery and analysis that Lewis dwells on in his autobiographical writings, to which I shall return shortly.

In the manner of Marcel Proust before him, Lewis recognizes the importance of early encounters with books as a way of understanding something of the act of reading throughout the life course. However, he stresses, above all, continuity between child and adult in engaging with story. Indeed, he hardly distinguishes between these states in his commentary on the pleasures that books can give up to keen readers, ranging over a variety of 'romances' to provide examples for his discussion, 'from American "scientifiction"' and Homer, from Sophocles and *Märchen*, from children's stories and the intensely sophisticated art of Mr de la Mare' (1966/1982, p. 15). For Lewis, the distinction between the literary and non-literary reader is much sharper than differences of age or experience (he had earlier noted in his memoir that his own childhood was 'at unity with the rest of [his] life'; 1955/2012, p. 82).

However, sensations provoked by the initial act of reading a childhood book as recalled by lifelong readers need to be distinguished from those emotional contexts that inflect memories of the books and reading selves of the past and separated from the further layer of response that takes place in acts of rereading. Such a cyclical structure can be especially useful in challenging assumptions that children's reading is necessarily more 'enchanted' than adult's reading because of its freshness and transformational nature. This is a stance that Tatar sometimes adopts in ascribing children the role of 'enchanted hunters' (a phrase she aims – not altogether successfully – to 'reclaim' for children from its more dubious usage in Vladimir Nabakov's *Lolita* [1995]) to express the way that they are exposed to new worlds and ideas through stories (2009, p. 27), and that Călinescu also risks taking in investing too much in the 'romantic literary invention or myth' of childhood as a way of explaining adult memories of the 'enchantments' of childhood reading (1993, p. 96). Tatar's sense that child readers seek out stories that glitter and sparkle covers up some of the lived experiences that have been recorded or can be retrieved through re-memory work (although admittedly she does pay attention to other affective modes). Ahmed also falls somewhat into the trap of essentializing 'the child' as site of pure emotional response arguing that 'the figure of the child does important work' because '"the child" occupies the place of the "not-yet subject", as the one whose emotions might allow us to differentiate between what is learnt and what is innate' (2004, p. 17). In the rest of this chapter, I counter this view by recognizing that child readers are by their actions of reading immersed in discourse so that they have already learned certain appropriate emotional responses. Moreover, in the lifelong reading act, what Ahmed refers to as the child's 'innocence' may well function as part of the adult's nostalgic memories of reading, but is even more likely to be mixed with other, less idealized ideas about past reading selves. Turning now to accounts of remembered reading, I examine discourses of desire, fear, and grief – first, to explore how they function as immersive passions and how childly reading selves are positioned in autobiographical accounts to adopt the role of a reader 'moved' by text, and then to consider ambivalent feelings that run alongside the passions and provide a richer understanding of childhood reading remembered.

Passions

Desire and a yearning for close physical or emotional interaction between child and book play a significant part in the repertoire of memories that appear in many memoirs and in discussion with adult readers. In some accounts, the relationship is that of companionship with the material book itself and all it represents. The concept of books personified is well acknowledged by commentators and critics. The argument of John Ruskin's *Sesame and Lilies* (1865) is that the common reader should take notice of 'kings and statesmen lingering patiently' in their bookshelves, waiting to offer wisdom (1865/2002, p. 52), while Proust's commentary suggests that the relationship between reader and book is, rather, a friendship purer than others since it involves no politeness or convention on the part of the reader. My participant Karen, born in 1960, notes that when her dog recently chewed her childhood copy of Robert Louis Stevenson's *A Child's Garden of Verses* (1885) she felt 'as if he had mauled a friend'. Patricia Spacks muses on how repetition of favourite books in early childhood relies on the idea that the content is stable: if a book becomes unpredictable, then a 'friend's personality has changed' (2011, p. 1), while Anne Fadiman explores the idea of the relationship, rather than the individual, changing (2005, p. xviii). For Fadiman, a book read while young is a lover who is transformed into a friend when returned to in later life, a process that somewhat complicates Pearce's relational model by introducing a sense of reduced passions and comfortable easiness into the latter stages of the lifelong act. Nevertheless, in accounts of remembered reading, passion is often brought to the fore.

Sutcliff's childhood memoir is saturated with affective language that implicates her in a romantic bond with her remembered childhood book. Sutcliff's reading as a child in the 1920s and 1930s was limited, due to the periods she spent in hospitals and special schools (although, as I noted in the last chapter, her mother read aloud to her and introduced to a rich diet of literature early in life). She recalls one promising book that she managed to pluck from the hospital bookshelf at the age of eight from a selection of otherwise unappealing 'Victorian stories about little girls of great virtue who died young' (1983, p. 95). This was Montgomery's *Emily of New Moon* and Sutcliff writes that she immediately fell under the spell of its 'magic', carrying it off to keep under her pillow 'or clutched to my bosom at bed-making time' (p. 95). She thinks she read it once 'voraciously and then with slow and lingering delight, at least three times on the trot' (p. 95). As a portrayal of early infatuation, this description is both convincing and powerful, portraying the material book as a fetish or love object and a source of sensual pleasure, first accomplished with the pace of initial passion and then savoured over a longer period. Sutcliff uses the language of romance and the setting of intimacy and the literary clinch, adding a flush of adolescent excitement to her description. The episode is also related with a certain degree of nostalgia, as the memoirist elaborates: 'The Evening Star, and the bugles sounding across the misty fields in the summer dusk, and the book hidden under the bedclothes somehow entered into each other and became part of the same enchantment, while I followed spellbound Emily's adventures and misadventures' (p. 96). A sultry season and evocative incidental backdrop (the bugles sounding Last Post came from nearby barracks) add to the intensity of the encounter with *Emily of New Moon*, but also employ the language of generic autobiography, locating it in an almost-timeless past of idyllic summers. In contrast, Sue Townsend's love affair with Charlotte Brontë's *Jane Eyre* (1847) – the first book she lost 'a night's sleep over' – plays out in chillier and altogether more prosaic surroundings, as she reads all night under the covers in her unheated bedroom until her 'fingers and arms froze' and has to finish the last page the next day in the school cloakroom, 'surrounded by wet gabardine mackintoshes' (Townsend, 1992/2015, p. 321). In each case, desire is embodied and the accounts are saturated with scripts of love and romance. It is also noteworthy that Sutcliff and Townsend adopt, no doubt knowingly to a degree, some of the resonant tone of the works of Montgomery and Brontë in evoking emotional traces in their own response.

Although passionate in their own ways, these discourses of love subscribe to certain conventions of the romance that demonstrate their affiliation with higher cognitive affect rather than visceral or base emotion. In contrast, Alison Uttley writes several sharply observed accounts of her childhood reading experiences in *Ambush of Young Days* (1937) that offer small phenomenological narratives about her responses to a variety of texts that, nonetheless, often present vehement affective perspectives. The young Alison is beset by fear. For instance, as adult memoirist, Uttley recalls a link between bedtime stories and night terrors, remembering that 'to be sent into darkness with only a flickering candle which might be blown out by an unseen robber at any moment was fearful' (1937, p. 207). Fear represents a significant part of her repertoire of interpretative schemes, providing the sticky thread that ties her to books that have retained their force over her from childhood into adulthood. One of these is an intriguing volume she found underneath several 'dull-looking books' and 'dry volumes' at the bottom of a drawer in the family bureau, which was a 'dark green volume with gold lettering' of Maria Sherwood's 1818 publication *The Little Woodman and His Dog Caesar* (1937, pp. 202–3). In this highly didactic tale, the boy hero, William, is abandoned by his wicked and godless brothers in a forest, in a scene that is evoked with great atmosphere by Sherwood. The text is designed through its evocative prose to arouse vehement emotions. Scripts of fear, and its counterpart of relief, help to position the young Alison on the hero's side and consequently encourage her to reflect on the structures of danger and safety. Uttley probably had a copy to hand as she wrote her memoir, since she paraphrases the text very closely in her account:

> I shivered with fright as I approached the climax, where the little woodman, lost in the dark wolf-haunted forest, heard footsteps padding behind him. He ran, and the feet came nearer. He stumbled and thought his last minute had come, as the warm breath of the animal touched his face, and the creature leapt upon him.
>
> As I read I was quite as terrified as the little woodman, so that I was trembling and shivering with fear as I sat alone in the sunny parlour. I spelled out the words, with mounting horror, sick with apprehension. Then came the unexpected relief, an ending which amazed me. It was the tongue of Caesar, his faithful dog! The hound had broken loose from the hut and tracked his master to save him from wolves and to bring him safely home. (p. 203)

Sherwood's passage presents a direct if unidentified threat to the character, described in focalized prose with plenty of emotive language ('the wind arose and whistled dismally'; 1818/1827, p. 19). In response, Uttley reports being as terrified 'as the little woodman', and experiencing a sense of threat to herself through identification as well as somatic symptoms of a real belief of danger, such as 'catching [her] breath when the terrible race came' (1937, p. 203). Uttley's reading scene is constructed using the same terms of suspense and embodied excitement that Sherwood deploys in her description of the fictional scene and, as such, it provides an illustration of the paradox of real feelings directed towards fictional characters or experienced via fictional events that has taxed philosophers of reading.

Susan Feagin describes these 'make-belief' truths as 'affective imaginings' (1996, p. 83) and Bijoy Boruah calls them 'children's make-believe attitudes' (1988, p. 55). Cognitive psychologist Keith Oatley's formulation that reading for pleasure is a 'simulation' allowing the reader to mimic and take on a character's emotions as they rise (1994, p. 66) also recognizes the phenomenon, as does Kate Flint in her recent observation that 'we make a very slender, if any, distinction between the mental state of real people and that of fictional characters' (2012, p. 19; see also Walton, 1978; Lamarque, 1981; Carroll, 1990). This phenomenon has often been the basis for an assumption that young readers will imbibe moral edification from their engaged reading. As an ideal reader, the young Alison certainly seems to have felt encouraged by the imposing narrator to identify with William through his goodness and his vulnerability as the youngest and smallest of the brothers. Uttley describes her remembered reading in these terms, explaining that she did indeed internalize the message that goodness leads to salvation. She states that 'this story was my own, my very own! I felt as if I too had escaped from imminent death' (1937, p. 203). The conventional notion of the reader 'trembling and shivering' through the effects of fear as she experiences the frightening conditions along with the hero, even in the safety of the 'sunny parlour', is, however, tempered by Uttley's gentle indication that as a just-literate child she was decoding at a basic level as well as responding affectively to the text's events. In fact, she draws together the effect of the text and this context of early literacy, allowing the slowness of her reading pace to add to the atmosphere of 'mounting horror' as if it is part of the intended form of the story. As a remembering adult, she carefully constructs a distinct emotional script about her early reading self, not just one that reproduces the text's ideological intentions.

In my corpus of remembered accounts and parallel texts, sadness or grief, and its partner empathy, emerge as one of the clearest affective scripts that adults use to discuss favourite books or reading experiences that have been retained in memory most vividly. Such accounts often refer to nineteenth-century popular fiction or classics of children's literature, which, despite much diversity, might be characterized as broadly didactic in purpose. In our conversation about Louisa May Alcott's *Little Women* (1868), for example, Rachel recalled identifying with Jo March but weeping for 'Amy and her limes' and 'especially for Beth – and the reunion with her father', noting that she reread Alcott's novel several times and wept even more on each rereading because she knew Beth was going to die.[2] Claire has vivid recollections of the end of Hans Christian Andersen's 'The Little Match Girl' (1845). It took her some time as a child to realize that the female protagonist has died by the end of the story when she is to be found sat at the corner of two houses 'at the cold hour of dawn'. Claire comments, 'when it dawned on me I was devastated'. She explains that the grief was so overwhelming that she has since 'shelved that story along with other unpleasant memories'. Joan Aiken writes about the influence Elizabeth Wetherell's 1850 bestseller *The Wide, Wide World* had on her because of the sad details of this 'harrowing prototype orphan book' (1974, p. 162), and Richard Adams recalls feeling upset by the 'heroic, self-sacrificing death of Elzevir Block' in J. Meade Falkner's 1898 *Moonfleet* (Adams, 1990, p. 101). When my participant Geraldine reread Falkner's novel as part of my project, however, she had misremembered or forgotten so much detail that she wonders if she had 'wiped much of this' from her memory because she had found it so traumatizing as a child. It is not just human suffering that evokes pain and grief. Adams also recalls being rendered distraught by the fate of a number of animal characters in his childhood reading, including Raggylug's mother from Ernest Thompson Seton's story of the cottontail rabbit in *Wild Animals I Have Known* (1898), who was 'pursued onto the ice, fell through it and drowned' and the sparrow who 'hanged itself in a loop of horsehair' (1990, p. 101). Several of my participants refused to consider rereading Anna Sewell's *Black Beauty* (1877), remembering that it made them feel sad in unmanageable ways as children and explaining that, like Claire's response to the match girl, they did not want to revisit that set of emotions.

Reflecting and extending critical discourses that link childhood with romantic ideals of sympathy and sentiment, these mournful and empathetic responses in accounts of remembering reveal an affective script that allows adults to speak of emotion in detail and with great potency. In examining adult memories of affective encounters such as these the extent and range of emotional responses might be traced across the lifespan. Adams elaborates on his remembered reading of Harriet Beecher Stowe's *Uncle Tom's Cabin* (1852) in these terms, recognizing that the death of little Eva has become 'a symbol for the worst kind of Victorian sentimental mush' (p. 101), nevertheless consciously owning the range of soulful and somatic feelings he recalls experiencing on reading the novel as an eight-year-old schoolboy. Despite embarking on it for the sake of pleasure and to learn more about its anti-slavery narrative, he was instead exposed to what he describes as 'levels of grief which I had never imagined', resulting in devastation and copious weeping (p. 101). Rather touchingly, he admits that he must have been 'a bit of a trial to the family for a day or two at least' after finishing reading (p. 102). In stark contrast to those adult readers of sentimental novels who wept, according to Q. D. Leavis in her *Fiction and the Reading Public* (1932), because of an intellectual sense of pity and because they felt they should, Adams makes it very clear that the 'shock' of Eva's death could not be contemplated disinterestedly by his childly self, and could only be felt vehemently and authentically.

The emotional investment felt by young readers, as remembered by their adult selves, is not always so closely linked to feelings of empathy, shame, or other moral reactions. Alternative types of affective response also fall under the emotional scripts of fear and grief and these often reveal connections between childly and adult reading selves more than they suggest any clear ideological influence of the remembered books themselves.

Grief

Melissa is in her fifties when she rereads Patricia M. St. John's *Treasures of the Snow* (1950) for my project, having first encountered the novel as a young girl. Feelings saturate her account and the term itself is overdetermined in her description of rereading a key scene from the text: 'But I did feel [. . .] I felt for Lucien, I really felt for Lucien and his ostracization after he'd done it [threatened to kill a kitten]. And he didn't mean to do the bad thing, so I really felt for him. And I think I felt for him [. . .] it feels like a feeling that I felt at the time of when I read it myself'. 'Feeling' is used here, as it is by a number of participants, as shorthand, a way of digging up a remembered response to a childhood book, including the moods that accompanied the experience of revisiting it, as well as encompassing emotions towards the character, episode, and the previous reading self. The term often overlaps with other affective scripts that are harder to express.

Melissa's life space is of interest because in her rereading account she sets her encounter with the novel against a tense period in her home life. Her family had recently moved and her mother had started a teaching job that took her away from her children, but also encouraged more directed reading with them. Melissa speaks of the strict Calvinist Christian philosophy that formed her upbringing as well as the tensions between her parents at this time, all of which put pressure on her own relationship with her mother, who she considers to have been overly strict and restrictive. St. John's novel is a sentimental story about loss, anger, redemption, and rebirth in the tradition of nineteenth-century children's literature such as Johanna Spyri's *Heidi* (1884), with which Melissa confuses it at one point. She points out that reading aloud was a 'very new thing' and a 'Christian thing' for her mother to do with her children and she suggests that tackling *Treasures of the Snow* in this manner was employed partly as a way of teaching moral lessons and partly as a way of practising newly acquired teaching methods. Melissa received *Treasures of the Snow* as a Sunday School prize and her mother attempted to read it aloud to her and her younger sister. However, in Melissa's account of remembering, she explains that the event did not end well:

> Early on in the story the Grandmother dies and it made my sister and I cry and cry. My mum had to stop reading because we were so upset [. . .] a few days later she tried to read some more of the story. However in the next bit a kitten went missing and this started us off crying again [. . .] My mum got very exasperated [. . . and] said she wasn't going to read to us anymore and didn't finish the story.

On rereading, Melissa realizes that it is the mother, not the grandmother, who dies in the first chapter, going to 'spend Christmas with the angels' (St. John, 1950, p. 12): a curious misremembering considering the fraught maternal relationship she has related in providing context for this account of remembering. Rather than directly reflect on this slip, Melissa theorizes that her sister must have felt separation anxiety on hearing about this traumatic event (a condition she herself admits to suffering later in life). The sister's tears set off her own weeping and they both 'cried and cried buckets'.

The episode featuring the kitten is no less traumatic for the siblings than the loss of the mother character, according to Melissa's memories. In fact, it is somewhat the more dramatic scene in St. John's telling. Whereas the death of the mother is gently implied by her absence one Christmas, the kitten's peril is directly reported. The creature is initially described in the text in emotive and sentimental terms, weak and thin with a 'smudge on her nose' found 'curled up in the furry lining' of a slipper (St. John, 1950, p. 27) and fed warmed milk until 'it put out a wee pink tongue and its dim blue eyes grew bright and interested' (p. 28). When the novel's child villain, Lucien, drops it into a 'dark ravine' (p. 41) in a highly suspenseful scene, the reader is potentially as passionately attached to the kitten as its owner the young hero Dani is, and as likely to feel terror on its behalf. The moment is certainly designed to be affecting, and it is surely for this reason that the visual image Melissa recalls most clearly in her imagination when she remembers *Treasures of the Snow* is precisely that of Lucian and the threatened pet rather than of the illustration of Dani that appears in the modern edition she rereads for me.

In contrast to most accounts of reading aloud I explored in the last chapter, Melissa's analysis of her remembered reading scene casts her mother as an obstructive and emotionally distant figure in this contact zone, adding an additional affective resonance to her own tearful response to the death of the good mother in St. John's story. She is keen as an adult to reread the book in order to understand more about her childhood, and, thus, is self-aware of the effects that reading and narrative can have on an individual's imaginative life and sense of self over time. In this example, it is also difficult to pinpoint from affective traces the exact object of the expressed feelings of sadness and anxiety or its location in the strata of encounters with the text: is it simply a matter of empathy with the child characters who lose their mother and kitten, or perhaps concern for the seductive kitten itself? Is there a specific sense of identification between remembered child reader and motherless characters, or is the adult rememberer feeling sadness towards or about her earlier self or experience? Is the sadness remembered, or re-experienced in recalling these dramatic narrative moments and the specific context within the life scene in which they were first encountered? The adult Melissa's connection between grief in the text and sadness about her own relationship with her mother as a child is implied rather than explicit, yet displays a vivid set of affective threads tying the present to the past.

A comparable example of a reading memory saturated with grief and implicated in early home life can be found in the parallel text that academic Veronica produced for me, in which she claims that she still cries when she rereads the moment in Ethel Turner's *Seven Little Australians* (1894) when Meg tries to comfort her sister on the occasion of their mother's death. It is unclear if this response is because of the emotion the adult Veronica feels about the sentimental scene at the time of reading (in the early 1950s), because of her memories of the sadness her seven-year-old self felt, or due to the way that this sadness was compounded by the almost simultaneous announcement by her mother of the death of her pet rabbit (her account is certainly poignant).

Not all reading events in childhood are so saturated with affect, but beyond these most personal of accounts is a more general point to be made about the potential for overwhelming emotions to obstruct childhood reading and curtail a reading act. In Melissa's case, her mother's exasperation and incapacity to deal with two crying listeners meant that the story was left off at a moment of heightened drama and emotional draw: while it appears to a reader abandoning the text at this point that the kitten must have fallen to its certain death in the 'rushing torrent of melted ice', in fact it has 'stuck fast on a ledge of overhanging rock and clung there mewing piteously' (p. 22), a consoling fact that Melissa and her sister would have been unaware of (although stopping reading at this point saved them from the labour of dealing with five-year-old Dani seemingly meeting the same fate as his kitten). Clive, who remembered being read Charles Kingsley's *The Water Babies* (1863) by his mother around the age of five or six, reported similar feelings of profound sadness and pain as a child as Melissa does, with similar results:

> Well my mother read it to me and I, I, it upset me greatly and I, I made her stop reading it. I said I can't stand this, you know. And I think, I mean the incident of the drowning I think is what I found. Well firstly, of course, I mean, Tom is very badly treated, you know. Um, and that was all very painful. Um [. . .] and then of course when he, when he jumps in the river and, and drowns, no I found that very distressing.

Again, a refusal to continue reading means that the remembered account cannot incorporate the 'consoling' fact that, even if Tom does drown, he is reborn as a water baby in order to have underwater adventures. One of the potential dangers of strong affective traces is therefore the loss of a full reading experience or a skewed memory based on partial knowledge. On rereading Kingsley's novel at my request, Clive notes that he no longer has the same affective response to Tom's fate: 'Well I just skated past it [. . .] obviously at this age it didn't distress me at all'. I have explored this response in detail elsewhere[3] and it seems that, in some cases of acute affective experience, the interpretative scheme constructed reclassifies emotional response to allow for a connection between initial reading self and remembering self, even when rereading self reacts in a new and different manner. It may be that, as Clive points out, rereading adults are not directly affected by the same sadnesses, anxieties, or terrors as their childhood selves and are less likely then to notice the textual features that upset them earlier in the lifelong reading act. On the other hand, Melissa and Veronica's experiences demonstrate a much tighter bond between early childhood encounters and later memories or rereadings. The fact that this moment of trauma when Tom appears to die has remained in Clive's memories of the book and of the initial reading act with his mother also suggests an altogether more implicated connection between the text and self throughout time.

Such dynamic examples of emotional resonance suggest that grief plays a part in reading histories that goes beyond the provocation of vehement passions as development of moral response. Indeed, rather than reflecting on the lessons they might have gleaned from reading and remembering sentimental childhood books, the recollections offered by Melissa, Veronica, and Clive appear to function as a way of re-activating early experiences of loss and dissolving the division between textual other and reading self, as that self is assembled in the temporal life space.

Fear

When the ideological mechanisms of a remembered book are themselves uncertain, or where a reader engages with evocative fragments rather than character or narrative, other interpretative schemes can emerge in adult narratives. When young readers approach texts that are designed to provoke emotion but are not aimed at a child audience, for example, the experiences can reverberate over time in troubling ways. A number of remembered encounters with adult ghost stories or tales of the unexpected occur across my corpus, indicating the genre's popularity as a way of sampling 'grown-up' literature or testing boundaries. Adams writes about his schoolboy enjoyment of Edgar Allan Poe, at the same time describing how his short stories gave him 'the screaming hab-dabs' and were 'unsuitably advanced' for his age (Adams, 1990, p. 105). Some of the remembering adult rereaders I spoke to depict similar experiences of literary precociousness. Like Adams, my participant Geoffrey, who was born in the late 1940s, recalls picking up a copy of some ghost stories (this time by M. R. James) without his parents' knowledge and frightening himself 'witless' reading 'Canon Alberic's Scrap-Book', 'Lost Hearts' and 'The Mezzotint'. He makes the repercussions of reading such scary and adult tales clear: 'oh, I didn't want to go to bed for a week and, er, that book was quietly hidden [laughs]'. Similarly, Rachel, also a child of the forties, enjoyed the short stories of H. G. Wells but reports that her parents found her 'sitting scared on the landing one night' and subsequently took control by marking up 'those it was safe to read'.

Looking more closely at Geoffrey's remembered account of reading 'Lost Hearts' (1904), it is clear that while fear is the common affective cluster characterizing his memories of this reading event, the statement 'M. R. James's ghost stories scared him' would not quite do justice to the range of emotional responses he experienced:

> One of the episodes in 'Lost Hearts' I could see it. The fact that where we were living in Portishead at the time [. . .] There's a particular incident where [. . .] the child, who was a hero, the child the hero at the centre, the main figure of this story, was not very much older than I was and he was walking along a corridor which was very much like our corridor, and the

> bathroom which he found, the horrible things which he found, was pretty much located where our bathroom was [. . .] so that made a huge impact. And the fact that it was written so beautifully as the James stories are, I mean, they were written to be read out loud and my goodness they just sing off the page at you.

Geoffrey's fear of the corridor incident itself is multifaceted. His repeated reference to the boy in the story as hero suggests that in some way he put himself into the character's place when he was a child reading, and like Uttley and the hero in Sherwood's tale, empathized with the terror that the fictional boy Stephen experiences in the story, prompted by seeing haunting figures in the bath. Although in our interview we did not discuss the age at which Geoffrey read 'Lost Hearts' it is quite possible he was at the 'child as hero or heroine' stage identified by Appleyard as that when young readers are inclined to engage with characters who can represent both what they 'want to be and what they once were' (1991, p. 77). Since Fisher observes that the ghost story, gothic novel, or fright film unsettle the reader by creating 'the duplication in the reader of the aroused state of the central character' (2002, p. 10), it is possible that a childhood reading experience such as Geoffrey's would be an especially potent one (the kind to lead some commentators to worry about the influence of such fictions on young readers, in fact[4]).

Geoffrey's memories of the content of these tales are tied up with his admiration of James's writing that 'sing[s] off the page at you' so that his fear at the terrifying incident of the child looking in at the bathroom window is blended with a quite different aesthetic response to the style of that content that chimes more with Lewis's sense of affective response. Adams, too, reflects on Poe's style in similarly aesthetic terms, noting its 'force and credibility' and the way it 'reft you out of your world into his and held you gripped there' (1990, p. 105). Geoffrey's own separate childly fear also emerges in autotopographical memories of the context of his reading 'Lost Hearts', where the conflation of fictional setting and real place encouraged him to be scared by James's description of Stephen in the corridor because it reminded him of his own surroundings. Perhaps more significant is the fact that Geoffrey remembers being scared when he visited the bathroom at Portishead because it reminded him of the story. In this latter case, it is not the content of the reading event itself, but rather the representational space that is the object of fear. Such bleeding of the fictional threat into real-world contexts results in an especially richly felt account of remembering.

Marina Warner argues that the main function of horror stories told to children at bedtime is not to provide invigorating moral provocations. Instead it is to produce talismans against fear by evoking frightening figures, listing 'giants, ogres, child-guzzlers, ghouls, vampires, cannibals, and all their kind' (1998, p. 6) as culturally inscribed symbols that 'materialize fear in some kind of living shape' (p. 4). There is some evidence for this direct and visceral emotional response in autobiographical accounts I have gathered: Lucy Boston admits to being terrified by Giant Despair in *Pilgrim's Progress* (1973/1978/1992, p. 24); while Roger McGough claims that fairy-tale fiction was as dark as his nightmares (1992/2015, p. 152); and Enid Blyton states in her autobiography for children that she did not like 'frightening things' in the Grimm's fairy tales, 'any more than you do', making it clear that she assumed the same response to conventional monstrous figures from her readers (1952/1986, p. 49).[5] However, only a few of the accounts of remembered reading or rereading I have worked with in my research deal in such obvious and culturally ingrained signifiers of fear: monsters, witches, and vampires rarely emerged among the discourses of fear that circulate around remembered childhood reading, and even the ghost stories discussed evoked fear more from the atmosphere of suspense and a general feeling of uncanniness than because of ghostly figures themselves. If fear is intentional (that is, if it must be felt *towards* something), then the objects of terror recalled by adults can be highly personal and obscure.

In his autobiography *Surprised by Joy* (1955), Lewis connects one of his remembered childhood books to the bad dreams he used to suffer as a child, wondering if his night visions of insects developed due to the scariness of this nursery book, or if the memory of the nursery book itself is in fact 'a product of nightmare' (1955/2012, p. 8). It is a mnemonic scene of unsettling ambiguity. He blames his nightmares on the influence of this 'abomination' of a moveable book his mother allowed into the nursery, in which a 'midget child [. . .] stood on a toadstool and was threatened from below by a stag-beetle very much larger than himself' (p. 8). He recalls that the beetle's horns were designed to be moved by a 'devilish contraption' operated by the active reader, so that they 'opened and shut like pincers: snip-snap-snip-snap', marking the scene with an especially dynamic image of menace for a child such as him who was already phobic of insects with their 'angular limbs, their jerky movements, their dry metallic noises' (p. 7). There is nothing nostalgic in this recollection. In linking this vivid memory of a childhood movable book to the machinations of his night-time terrors, Lewis draws affective threads from the image of a tiny figure being attacked by an otherworldly creature to the fears of a small child both drawn to and repulsed by the action of exerting control over the very movements of otherness. The boy Jack not only seems to have returned again and again to this book, since it is described in habitual and familiar terms, with the note that adult Lewis can still visualize it as he writes; but he also appears to have been compelled to work its mechanisms, to make the pincers move and shock himself into the feelings of fear that, as he puts it, were like a 'window opening on what is hardly less than Hell' (p. 7). Lewis does not report on any rereading of the disturbing book that included the stag-beetle illustration. However, he does reflect on his changing affective relationships with insects, noting that later in his teens he developed 'a genuinely scientific interest' in them from reading John Lubbock's *Ants, Bees and Wasps* (1882), and that during this 'entomological period' his fear 'almost vanished' (p. 8).

Lewis's pop-up insect is not quite of the same order as Uttley's woodcutter nor the bedtime tales Tatar describes nor the ghost stories endured by Adams and Geoffrey. It is tied to a subtly different package of feelings in which his remembered child reader struggles with fear that is both imposed upon him in dreams and self-administered through his playing with the book and its sinister stag-beetle image. It is also a highly focused recollection of a solitary page, specifically an illustration. The interiority of Lewis's engagement with the moving illustration is brought to the surface through repeated references to the way it might be contained and controlled. Karen Odden has noted the correspondence between rereading and the infant game of 'fort/da' related by Sigmund Freud to explain separation anxiety (1998, p. 140), and the same action of disappearance and return may also help to throw light on psychoanalytical mechanisms for managing fear.

This mixture of revulsion and intrigue appears in other memoirs and remembered accounts of childhood reading and is often remembered within a similarly constrained reading scene and in the context of vivid imagery. Uttley's sense that she would have enjoyed the works of Dickens as a child if she had 'never seen Cruikshank's pictures' because the 'odd queer-looking people' frightened her (1937, p. 207) indicates something of this power of imagery to unsettle, particularly imagery that deconstructs normalized ideas of what it is to be a human. Picture book creator Shirley Hughes reports a similarly terrifying, if inspiring, encounter with Heath Robinson's illustration of Andersen's 'The Marsh King's Daughter' (1858),[6] which depicts the king as part-botanical, 'an elder stump in the quagmire' (Hughes, 2002, p. 46). This retention of an image that has been seemingly purged by the child self is reiterated in Mary's remembered account of reading, in which she describes her first glimpse of a copy of Carroll's *Through the Looking Glass, and What Alice Found There* (1871), illustrated by John Tenniel:

> I nearly had a fit. I can remember vividly – now this really does remain with me – turning over the pages and coming across [. . .] there's a picture of her holding the Red King between her finger and thumbs, and his mouth is wide open, he's screaming really. And this horrified me, I was really, really frightened. I suppose I was about seven, an old six perhaps. And I just sort of put the book down and I didn't pick it up and open it again for I should think years. And nobody could persuade me to, you know.

Warner argues that Tenniel's visualizations of *Through the Looking Glass* are frightening in ways that the text is not because they do not 'hollow out' moments of terror as Carroll's use of humour manages to do (1998, p. 325); Mary's response to the Red King's fear as it is signified through the open mouth and suggestion of a scream of terror supports such a reading of these illustrations. Moreover, for Mary it is not simply the image itself but the moment of shock and fear she experienced herself in turning over the page and which remains with her in visceral form. A similar account is provided by Naomi Mitchison, who notes that she found the image of 'Alice with the long neck' in *Alice's Adventures in Wonderland* (1865) so shocking that she developed a practice of turning the page it appeared on very quickly 'so that she couldn't get out' (1973, p. 51). I am struck by what Mackey would describe as kinaesthetic and embodied forms of reading that are evident in these accounts (2016, pp. 484–92). The bundle of feelings categorized as fear are organized by the body, which not only turns the pages and then puts the book down or skips ahead, but also threatens to fit and lose control (albeit metaphorically). The Red King's physical distress is itself signalled through the manipulation and dramatic responses of his body, and Mary's remembering places her as child reader alongside the suffering character. While control might be at the centre of these accounts of remembered childhood reading, in each mnemonic scene the terrifying image is retained throughout the lifelong reading act despite initial encounters being nothing more than a 'fearful glimpse'.

The physical mutability at the centre of many fairy tales, and of Carroll's classic novel to some degree, invites certain reactions in a child reader, traces of which can still be identified and felt by a returning adult. Whatever might be said about the images discussed here, however, they do not offer a coherent visual theme or ideological message and cannot be said to represent a consistent idea of imagined threat to the child encountering them. They evoke, not cathartic vehement passions, but rather ambivalent feelings that work to create sticky associations rather than moral improvements in the childly and remembering reader. In the final part of this chapter, I want to consider the traces that are most elusive in narratives of remembered childhood books: those affective scripts that speak of desire, hidden emotion, and – most abhorrently – boredom.

Desire and boredom

Although not a children's author, Edward Said's candid mnemonic scene of early reading is worth citing because he articulates what is usually unsayable in the context of childhood and children's books. In his memoir, *Out of Place* (1999), he writes about the gratification he gained as a boy from browsing a copy of the *Collins Junior Book of Knowledge* (probably an edition of Arthur Mee's *The Book of Knowledge: The Children's Encyclopedia*, published by Grolier from 1910 to 1964), given to him by a well-meaning relative. Specifically, he found a kind of intriguing thrill from looking at an entry on circuses that featured tiny, grainy, and blurred photographs of Kalita, a girl performer who performed 'miracles of strength and self-punishment' that showed her doing 'amazing, unimaginable things with her body' in appealing bathing suits:

> I read and reread the three grittily printed pages on Kalita and I examined and reexamined the two photographs that drew me in every time I opened the book. But it was their very insufficiencies – their minuscule size, the impossibility of actually being able to see the woman's body, the alienating distance between them and me – that paradoxically compelled, indeed enthralled, me for weeks and weeks. (1999, p. 32)

Barthes's 'erotics of reading' (as it is described by Richard Howard in the American edition of *The Pleasure of the Text* [1975a, p. vii]) offers one way into analysis of the sensual rhythms or disjunctions that attend pleasurable reading experiences and that can help bridge the uncomfortable distance between conventional ideas of childhood innocence and accounts of remembered reading that foreground sexual details. This is the territory explored in Jacqueline Rose's exposition of the fictional child as a creature of erotic desire (1984). However, Barthes's concern is with the pleasure of the text more generally and in theoretical terms. He points out that readers rarely read any text word for word, instead reading descriptions, conversations, or plot development with different levels of intensity depending on what they expect to get out of it. He develops his notion of this rhythmic quality of reading for pleasure through the metaphor of the children's game of 'topping hands', where 'excitement comes not from a processive haste but from a kind of vertical din' (1973/1975, p. 12) and where the object is to create a kind of 'hole' or 'gap' (an imaginative vacuum, almost). This image suggests that reading, like playing, can work through a frantic movement where meaning is destabilized in the effort to get to the 'win', which is itself an absence. For adults remembering early reading acts, absence can easily be coded as sexual content: not because there is so little in the literature of childhood, since readers can find such material wherever they look for it, but because it most often (if not always) signals the gap between imaginative experience and real knowledge and experience.

The gap in Said's account between Kalita's potential as object of desire and the 'insufficiencies' of the images offered up to the young Edward does not impede any excitement to be had in engaging with this text. Said points instead to the liberating distance between his boyhood self and the prospect of real interaction with such a womanly body and, although it might be uncomfortable to think about the child reader resembling, in Barthes's terms, 'a spectator in a nightclub who climbs onto the stage and speeds up the dancer's striptease' (1975a, p. 11), the metaphor is astute in describing the rhythms of reading for pleasure, where the reader skims and skips in order to get to the 'warmer parts' (p. 11) of the text in the same way as the paying customer tears off the stripper's clothing.

On a very basic level, McGough's embarrassed admission that he borrowed his sister's copy of *School Friend* each week to 'marvel at the drawings of girls wearing tutus or hockey shorts' speaks to warmth as it is sought by child readers of a certain age and in certain dispositions (1992/2015, p. 153). Few of my participants made any reference to such moments, however; it is, in any case, improbable that in the face-to-face conversations I conducted such material would arise in discussions about childhood. There are some hints of awareness of the 'gap', however. Jillie points out that she did not originally spot that the character in the childhood novel she rereads gains a girlfriend during the course of the plot, for instance ('probably because of how naïve I was and the age I was'), while Chloe remembers fancying the hero of one of her favourite books as a child of the 1970s and thinks she would probably still find him attractive on rereading. Adams recognizes that among his own polite society, 'sexual things simply "didn't exist"', so that his adolescent reading was more likely to be saturated with sadistic cruelty than sexual fantasy (1990, p. 104). Hints and glimpses are all that are provided in accounts I have explored, but it would interesting to pursue this topic among readers such as Chloe, who grew up later in the twentieth century and who will have had access to teenage fiction that addresses sexual desire directly.[7]

There are ways in which the hidden and unsayable can be exposed and celebrated in the lifelong reading act: ways in which the warmth of desire is played out as an ambivalent feeling or sticky affective thread in remembered accounts. In an early chapter of *Surprised by Joy* in which he establishes the main theme of the memoir, Lewis describes how after a succession of encounters with books that gave him certain basic pleasures and gratification as a boy, he found 'at last beauty' in Beatrix Potter's picture books (1955/2012, p. 14), specifically *The Tale of Squirrel Nutkin* (1903). The moment is described in the manner of what Barthes might call a *ravissement*:

> I loved all the Beatrix Potter books. But the rest of them were merely entertaining; [*Squirrel Nutkin*] administered the shock, it was a trouble. It

> troubled me with what I can only describe as the Idea of Autumn. It sounds fantastic to say that one can be enamoured of a season, but that is something like what happened [. . .] the experience was one of intense desire. (p. 17)

Squirrel Nutkin transcends the more ordinary pleasures of Potter's other creations, tapping into something of 'another dimension', for Lewis as adult remembering as well as himself as a young boy emerging into the world of sensation. His 'intense desire' is not for a glimpsed woman's body. Instead it attaches itself to Potter's lush illustrations of autumnal vegetation and the vivid portrayal of the red squirrel character Nutkin. In this respect, desire has much in common with fear. Shock is central, as is some kind of embodied quality that through memory in the reading scene binds the child self and his or her personal circumstances to text or character.

Lewis's aesthetic appreciation of Potter's animal stories elsewhere is, in fact, mixed. In *An Experiment in Criticism*, he describes some of her work as 'ugly, ill-composed, and even perfunctory' (1961/1969, p. 14), but since this later publication is an attempt to define 'good' and 'bad' books through an examination of the way they are read, literary judgement is more prominent in it than in his more personal autobiographical writings. For Lewis the critic, illustrations such as Potter's have only an anthropological function rather than an aesthetic value for the child reader and are to be made use of rather than appreciated. For Lewis the memoirist (and, not insignificantly, the Christian convert[8]), there is, however, an emotional thread between Potter's *Squirrel Nutkin* and his boyhood self that is more crucial and is what makes this particular text powerful. It would be possible to gloss over *Squirrel Nutkin*'s affective influence on Lewis as Brian Attebery does, describing it only as a 'keen response to Beatrix Potter's evocation of autumn' (2014, p. 73) in order to move on to discussion of Henry Wadsworth Longfellow's 1849 translation of Esaias Tegnér's *Balder the Beautiful* (or 'Tegnér's Death'), which Attebery sees as Lewis's crucial 'touchstone' (p. 74). Yet the mnemonic scene places emphasis equally on both texts to articulate central elements of what he ultimately describes as 'joy' (Lewis, 1955/2012, p. 16), a form of transcendental experience that encompasses reading, autobiographical moments (such as a memory of his brother's construction of a toy garden), romantic love, and spiritual fulfilment. This balanced account shows quite clearly that, for Lewis at least, children's literature seeps into the affective life space with as much tenacity as other forms and that a seemingly slight textual encounter can continue to exert emotional impressions through a lifelong reading act.

Lewis's remembered response includes affective markers that can be plotted against Pearce's model of implicated reading: of enchantment ('the shock') and fulfilment (becoming 'enamoured' of the portrayal of Autumn) as well as indicating how such feelings can be shaded by anxiety ('it was a trouble'). There is an affinity in his terms between remembered reading and the ambivalent pleasures of erotic play that Barthes describes. For Pearce and Barthes, these affective stages are followed by difficulty: by frustration, jealousy, and disappointment. Lewis, on the other hand, reports that when he goes back to *Squirrel Nutkin* he does so 'not to gratify the desire (that was impossible – how can one *possess* Autumn?) but to re-awake it' (p. 17), and so he rereads in a manner that speaks instead of devotion to a text, part of the early relational phase. He goes on to note that 'in this experience also there was the same surprise and the same sense of incalculable importance' (p. 17). Several points are worth making about these statements. First, Lewis's ambition to reawaken this overwhelming feeling of desire shows a willingness to value his childhood emotions, a willingness I have already argued is no doubt fostered through his own practice as children's author and an innate recognition of the nature of childness as a shared spectrum between experiencing child and remembering adult. In addition, the account demonstrates an openness to the idea that these sensations can be accessed once more, after the first encounter is over; in other words, resonance can be felt over time and across years and experience (this is a topic I shall return to in the next chapter). Finally, it is an illustration of how atmosphere in this case the 'Idea of Autumn' rather than 'world-building' – is closely related to desire, and how both should be distinguished from ordinary pleasure or even the more straightforward passions of wonder, anger, fear, and grief. The shock of joy for Lewis is the entry point into the 'imaginative air we breathe or element we swim in', as Michael Ward puts it (2012, p. 15). Enjoyment can encompass fear, in fact, since it does not refer to straightforward gratification but to the immersion in a book that allows both textual atmosphere and readerly feelings to be fully experienced: what is illuminated in the beam of enjoyment is not the crucial thing, and it might be pleasurable or frightening, sad, or hilarious.

The peculiar influence of books or textual encounters that trouble, open gaps, and offer glimpses is an inherent feature of the reading scene in the lifelong reading act. When Ward objects to the term 'atmosphere' in his discussion of Lewis's 'On Stories', he points to the original title of the essay, which was first delivered as a lecture to a Merton College undergraduate literary society in 1940 about the 'Kappa Element' of romance. The 'kappa', or hidden and cryptic element in this instance, ties the boy Jack to Potter's tale through surface detail in the text (the description and illustration of Autumn) and the shock of recognition of a profound quality of seasons and the passing of time to deeper feelings that are evoked through these details. These feelings may be commonly held ones, reflecting Potter's artistry and the intensity of her representation of the natural world. But they may also be quite specific to Lewis as individual and help to show how he makes himself as a reading subject. It is worth comment that the encounter with *Squirrel Nutkin*, the memory of the toy garden, and the introduction to Norse mythology through Longfellow, are related to the most momentous episode of his youth, his mother's death. Crago goes further in relating the kappa element to Lewis's specific life space, arguing that as well as representing the 'Idea of Autumn' as a common threat of the coming Winter against which squirrels and children are powerless, *Squirrel Nutkin* may have provided the young Jack with images of a father figure (in the character of Old Brown) and brother companions (Nutkin and Twinkleberry). Further, he points out the absence of female characters as significant ('It is as if the very idea of a 'mother' has never existed'; Crago, 2014, p. 87) because it spoke to Lewis's own childly context. I am not convinced it is necessary to psychoanalyse Lewis to quite this extent to find useful material about how an adult rememberer might recover the remembered text and recast it in terms of personal meanings as well as childly aesthetic appreciation, although the impact of the life space certainly throws light upon the persistence of Potter's text in his reading history. *Squirrel Nutkin* 'sticks' and bears the impression of emotions that have in turn resonated with the memory of reading and subsequent rereadings.

These traces endure, yet not all childhood books are so resilient. If, according to Barthes's view, desire is a contract between reader and text that circulates around gaps and hidden pleasures, that contract is broken when the surface of a childhood book offers only obstruction. As noted earlier,

Tatar argues that 'boredom, curiosity, and wonder form a dense tissue of connectivity central to the experience of growing up' (2009, p. 194), suggesting that boredom is the initiating factor in this trio that represents the natural and necessary mechanism leading to more productive affective schema. Boredom is rarely expressed in such terms in autobiographical narratives about reading, however, apart from in the kind of autodidactic accounts that rely on moments of epiphany that I dealt with in the last chapter. Spacks stresses the importance of boredom as a cultural concept originating in the eighteenth century and signifying various ideological meanings as an indicator of class-bound listlessness and decadence, youthful rebellion, or postmodern malaise. She demonstrates how it appears in discourse, not always as a spur for curiosity and wonder, but sometimes as an 'interpretative category' that implies 'an embracing sense of irritation and unease' in which the individual becomes more and more important but less and less powerful (1996, p. 13). In my accounts, too, boredom is represented as a common affective response that does not necessarily result in the positive corollary of curious action.

My participant Helen recalls being sent Cynthia Harnett's *The Great House* (1949) by a relative as a Christmas present while she was living in America with her English mother and American father in the 1950s. Despite treasuring the material book itself for its sentimental attachment to her grandfather, as a story, *The Great House* is a signifier of negative affect:

> I was an avid reader and was pleased to receive this book, but when I started to read it, I was BORED!! It was so ENGLISH! I was 'into' Nancy Drew, the Hardy boys, and Trixie Belden not some wimpy English stuff! My mother was disappointed that I didn't like the book, and she encouraged me to read on, assuring me it would get better. It didn't! It was still BORING! It lacked excitement, and I found the language so old fashioned. Nevertheless, I finally finished it, vowing I would NEVER read it again! I tended to read it in bed at night for 10–15 [minutes] each evening [. . .] it was guaranteed to put me straight off to sleep!

Helen's boredom reflects the lack of power referred to by Spacks. She explains the pressure she experienced from her mother to keep reading, most likely based in a desire for the young Helen to appreciate 'quality' literature and also to maintain some national ties with her homeland. In addition, the regularity of reading for ten to fifteen minutes every night suggests stolid doggedness rather than passion, and contrasts with other accounts of beloved texts that are consumed voraciously, all at once, through the night. Such determined and decidedly non-vehement reading mimics reading as school work or as moral duty, where boredom might be expected as a primary emotional script. Boredom in this context is also intentional rather than indicating a particular mood. There is no doubt left in her account that Harnett's novel about two seventeenth-century children is the affective object and the reasons given for her response are convincing. Cultural difference is often described by remembering readers as exciting because of its exoticism or desirable otherness: however, in the context of 1950s American series fiction, Harnett's relatively conservative historical fiction (her later work, *The Wool Pack* won the Carnegie Prize in 1951) is coded as 'ENGLISH' and 'old fashioned'.

As with other affective bundles, boredom is very often centred on the stories that remembering adults want to tell about themselves, and covers a number of interlinked phenomena in the lifelong reading act. A book or situation can seem tedious either to the remembered child self or the rereading adult, or an adult can remember feeling bored in a certain reading context. Helen agreed to reread *The Great House* for me, despite her childhood vow never to return to it, and notes that she expected to like it much more as an adult. Somewhat unfortunately for her, she still found the process a 'chore' and the novel unexciting and 'turgid'. Although she overlays memories of childhood reading with more adult terminology and insight, otherwise she discovers more overlaps than difference in the reading scene. Her honest response represents a clear trace of the past and demonstrates something of the continuity of this most childly seeming emotion, allowing for boredom to enter the repertoire of adult response to classic children's literature in ways that affirm early childhood reactions.

Conclusion

Reading events feed into the dynamic life space but are initially crystallized, as Rosenblatt puts it, from 'the stuff of memory, thought and feeling' (1978/1994, p. 12). This chapter has demonstrated how affective traces can connect childhood books to the autotopographies of remembering adults in terms of both vehement emotions and ambivalent feelings. This emotional residue saturates the layers of memory and past experience of each individual readerly self, revealing how the surface is often in tension with deeper strata.

In the practice of rereading affective threads can also be broken, traces erased. Pearce's final stage in the relational model of reading is disappointment, which she describes as the most difficult because it 'compounds the loss of the textual other as a presence in one's life with the loss of one's desire for them' (1997, p. 170). In other words, revisiting a beloved childhood text and finding lack, confusion, or problematic content can provoke difficult feelings about both the book and previous self. Boredom is at the mundane end of this spectrum of feelings, yet it can still inflect the reading scene as a site of potential tension. Both Grace (a retired teacher born in the 1930s) and Lauren (born about a decade later) told me that, as adults, they were bored by the books they had chosen to reread for my project, despite having only positive memories about them from childhood. Grace's remembered delight in Richmal Crompton's 'William' books – books that made her 'laugh and laugh' when she was a girl – is replaced by serious boredom at the 'repetition of themes, language and William himself'; and, while Lauren recalls enjoying the language of *Children of the Dark People* (1936) and thinking its subject matter interesting as a five-year-old, as discussed in Chapter 2, she reports that she found it 'fairly boring' on rereading as an adult. She explains this response to herself and me by noting that more successful books have been written about aboriginal children since 1936, but perhaps more importantly she has simply encountered more of these over the course of her life and can tease out nuance and historical detail from her greater fictional and historical knowledge. Grace's displeasure in the repetition that Crompton employs also implies a wider knowledge and appreciation of variation and invention in her later reading so that what has become tedious and familiar for an adult is still fresh and interesting earlier in the life span. Yet this interpretation rather essentializes both childhood and adulthood and downplays the validity of different emotional responses in different sites of the life course.[9] These accounts of early pleasure taken in language and humour do not necessarily have to lead to conclusions about children's pure emotionality, and might acknowledge the sometimes shifting nature of the relationship between object and response.

Pearce's category of 'disappointment' looms large in much general discourse about rereading childhood books, as I shall discuss in the next chapter, although, for some adults, it ultimately masks other affective schema, such as fear and embarrassment. Discussing one of the books she remembers most vividly and with the most affective resonance from childhood, Jillie told me that she was looking forward to rereading it, to see how this effect was achieved. In the end, the experience is saturated with disappointment: 'And I have to say the final thing was a bit of a disappointment really, that actually it doesn't live up to what I had expected it to live up to. And it just [. . .] although it's the same story and the same book, it just didn't have any impact at all [. . .] Yeah, disappointment was what I felt most.' Although it is 'the same story and the same book', Jillie's significant childhood book lacks the life it had in her remembered narrative: it neither 'lives up' to her expectations nor has any impact or impression to make. It makes no mark on her, as Ahmed might put it, and thus has nothing more to add to her affective script about her reading self. In other accounts, disappointment does mark the remembering readers with much more troubling inscriptions, often prescribing readerly identity rather than shaping and self-narrating it. I will return to Jillie's experience in my final chapter on misremembering, but her language and perspective act as a handy preface to Chapter 4, in which I will identify and interrogate different types of rereader stance – what I call rereading attitudes – and explore different ways that adults approach and interpret their acts of rereading childhood books.

4

Rereading attitudes

So far in this study of adults and their experiences of childhood reading, I have worked to build a model of remembering and rereading as part of the lifelong reading act. I have dwelt on the reading scene as a virtual zone in dialogue with an individual's life space through the workings of memory and the force of affective traces. This scene encompasses spots of time related to books through reminiscence as well as textual details that are revived through recall, recognition, and imaginative reconstruction. Remembering and rereading also function as emotional processes, bound to feelings inside and outside of texts. In the next two chapters, I draw out some of the specific practices and consequences of rereading that emerge out of that model. I explore individual motives for rereading childhood books in adulthood and consider what happens when rereaders misremember or forget.

In this chapter, I am mostly concerned with questions of how books from the past are recovered and used. Matthew Grenby calls for a theoretical model of reading that does not rely on the idea of a book as 'a conveyor of exclusively textual gratifications', instead taking into account 'its material and status-forming appeal' as well as focusing on 'specifically juvenile practices', such as repeated readings, memorization, extraction and misuse (2011, p. 287). Much excellent work has been produced in this area (e.g. Bernstein, 2011; Immel, 2013; Rodgers, 2016), but as yet, little has been written about the practice of adults rereading childhood books and the uses to which older readers might put the memories of their paracanons. Reasons for rereading – for returning to remembered childhood books throughout the life course – are multiple. Parents, teachers, and librarians often retrieve old favourites to pass on to the next generation of child readers, for instance, while writers, publishers, and producers might use memories of early reading to develop ideas for creative projects, as we have already seen. For many adults, simple curiosity to find out whether they remember books accurately over time is enough of a reason to return and reread. An individual might spontaneously remember a book from childhood in the course of everyday life and be compelled to dig it out to satisfy nostalgic urges. Some individuals are also prompted to recollection through the trigger of re-encountering the material object itself; some are reminded by stage, film, radio or TV adaptations, or documentaries to seek out an old childhood book; while others have developed an interest in a geographical area or theme that they recall is featured in a book they read when they were young. Involuntary memories of books can provide imaginative starting points for philosophical musing about readerly identity over time; thus rereading can become a form of personal research. Research of a more professional sort drives many academics to study and teach books they remember from their own youth within the field of children's literature, producing insights about the literary works themselves, and often also revealing much about scholarly attitudes towards personal autobiography.

Accounts by parents and grandparents of revisiting remembered childhood books with or for the children they care for offer alternative perspectives to those memories of being read to by parents discussed in Chapter 2, and provide different ideas about the mechanics of what Tatar calls the 'contact zone' (2009, p. 3). Further insights about how a sense of self past and present can be shored up through the practice of rereading are presented by looking at why adults reread childhood books *without* children, particularly considering how scholarly identity is constructed through processes of reassessment of texts and how far the influence of interpretative communities can inflect an adult's stance towards a younger reading self. Throughout this chapter, I interrogate rereading as a purposeful act, but one that comes with risks as well as opportunities: for example, the potential for rereading to disenchant represents a rich affective seam of discourse in accounts about childhood reading. I am particularly concerned with what I call *rereading attitudes*: the way that layers of identity are exposed by the pseudo-archaeological practice of rereading and what position might be taken to deal with such exposure. Childhood books function within an ongoing reading act encompassing other purposes than nostalgia, such as vivid readerly pleasure, the passing on of paracanons, professional practice, or identity formation. I explore some of these further uses of rereading in the following sections, paying particular attention to interview responses and then to bibliomemoirs and autobibliographic accounts. To establish a theoretical basis for this framework, I begin by re-examining the metaphor of rereading as a process of excavation that can reveal sites, artefacts, or time capsules with links to the past.

The uses of childhood books and *rereading attitudes*

I have been arguing that rereading can be understood as a process of 'digging up' and processing the paracanonical text, an archaeological practice that implies an interest in gaining authentic insights into the past. What Nick Campbell calls the 'archaeological imagination' (2017) infuses the adult's recovery of childhood paracanons with the possibility of a thrill of discovery, as remembered stories and images, meaningful material books, and ideas of the earlier self are revealed through memory work and in the process of rereading. Alongside the thrill comes risk. As I mentioned in the last chapter, one potential hazard is the prospect of uncovering uncomfortable passions such as fear and grief that then must be relived and dealt with anew. Perhaps more crushingly, the ambivalent feeling of boredom may be invoked in the practice of rereading, overlaying images of early desire and jeopardizing any firm sense of the continuity of taste or even identity between child and adult. In his work on collective memory, sociologist Maurice Halbwachs makes a case for the dangers of nostalgia based on unreliable memory in terms that touch upon this sense of a loss of continuity. He observes that memories of childhood are mutable and not like 'intact vertebra of fossil animals' to be easily reconstructed into a direct version of past reality (1952/1992, p. 47); rather they are continually reproduced or repeated at different stages of life. As an alternative metaphor for memory, he proposes the archaeological remains of a human settlement, since these give a hint of an original event's real meaning but are always fragmentary and subject to interpretation. Both tropes help him explain the workings of nostalgia in the context of childhood books: for example, why coming across a well-loved book from the past provokes unrealistic anticipation in the nostalgic adult reader because we erroneously 'believe that we can recall the mental state in which we found ourselves at that time' (p. 46), thinking we can see again the extinct creature or live again in that ancient home.

In Halbwachs's critique, nostalgia is a problematic attitude because it rests on a realist philosophy of memory that takes as its starting point the idea of a relatively stable archive of memory images stored away that might provide, if not direct access to childhood experience, at least some truths about the past. For others, the problem rests in the cultural practices that accompany memories of childhood artefacts and the self-deception that can affect whole populations when they lack proper awareness of the difference between *then* and *now*. Valerie Krips incorporates Pierre Nora's work on *lieu de mémoire* alongside Halbwachs's ideas to suggest that childhood books as remembered by adults are 'sites of memory' that perform on a cultural axis to protect the story of the past. To illustrate this practice, she offers the example of the rebranding of Beatrix Potter's *The Tale of Peter Rabbit* (1902) by Ladybird in the 1980s, which resulted in communal horror from adult readers who compared this simplified version of the picture book classic with its photographed images of stuffed toy animals to their recollections of Potter's original delicate watercolours. Drawing on Walter Benjamin's phrasing, Krips argues that in the vitriolic responses to Ladybird's adaptation in popular press articles 'we can recognize signs of alarm, of "memory flashing up"' (2000, p. 44). The cultural response she uncovers was to try and reconstruct a version of Potter's work that represented a coherent version of childhoods past for the majority of adults. Krips's implication is that if the same readers were to revisit the primary text of *The Tale of Peter Rabbit* itself, they may find their nostalgic vision just as shaken, since the story of childhood that has been produced through the *idea* of Potter's classic tale is constructed through forces of nostalgia, heritage, and cultural currency, narratives that are perhaps particularly strong in the world of British children's literature of the Golden Age.[1] She does not go so far as to investigate rereading along these lines, however, or to ask what actually happens when adults return to childhood books.

Although Halbwachs and Krips use them to signify nostalgia, archaeological metaphors can represent a range of ideologies, promoting everything from unrealistic sentimental expectations to the most radical of uncoverings. Time capsules might be found at one end of the spectrum: fixed museum pieces, representing lifeless artefacts secured for the record rather than objects with the potential for further lived impact on their readers. As Maurizia Boscagli points out in her work on 'stuff theory', time capsules can be thought of as 'archaeology in reverse', creating the kind of past that a present society thinks its future counterpart will want to see. In this sense, the time capsule 'wants to close the lid of history and turn history itself into a museumized, catalogued, and packaged memory for future generations' (2014, p. 215). The risk of cultural petrification is particularly high for items that have been gathered or curated in a specific historical moment in order to reveal something of the past for future generations. Krips includes children's literature in this category.

Rereading can also be likened to digging up less carefully curated material, since the original reading experience is both created and unearthed by the same individual, meaning that wider social significance is less consciously produced across time (although it may still be important). Significant childhood books continue to exert influence and shape readerly experience and response throughout the life course, at the same time that they evoke elements of that initial encounter and of the child reader who experienced it. They may be conceptualized as sites of meaning or meaningful artefacts, both of which require thoughtful treatment and recovery – or 'meticulous examination' (Benjamin, 1932/1999, p. 611) – as discoveries are made. Each instance of remembering or rereading represents a new encounter that may well primarily participate in nostalgia, but can also move towards new types of response, in the same way that historical sites can shift from one function to another, or old buildings, artefacts, and relics can continue to find uses in new cultural circumstances. Part of my purpose in this chapter is to explore some of the reasons for rereading childhood books, taking into consideration their ongoing *uses* for the adult reader, while looking closely at different attitudes towards the practice of rereading that to a greater or lesser degree subscribe to the 'museumizing' or archaeological discovery and treatment of those remembered texts.

What became clear as I analysed accounts and interviews is that rereaders consciously or unconsciously orient themselves in relation to children's literature and relationships between younger and older selves. As a form of pseudo-archaeological activity, rereading childhood books can disrupt earlier layers of identity and experience in ways that are uncomfortable; it can also contribute further layers to an autotopographical reading narrative, as the very practice of return contributes responses to the text and meanings to a sense of readerly self. The degree to which these processes are acknowledged or cultivated by individuals depends very much on their rereading attitude; that is, the values ascribed to meaningful objects from the past and the sense of an ageing self mapped onto a personal reading history. As with any process of uncovering the past, rereading exists as a practice in constant tension with the present and future. Questions of what should and can be recovered, to what extent, and for what ends, underlie the personal recovery of childhood books, whether such queries are expressed explicitly or not. These questions can fruitfully be couched in terminology from archaeology and museum studies: restoration, renovation, and conservation. These terms help to draw attention to methodological assumptions at the heart of any encounter with an artefact from the past, as well as offering creative ways of thinking about the instinctive responses adults might have when faced with emotive texts from their childhood.

A restorationist finds a way of returning to experiences of the past by allowing a relic of that past to reflect its former status in as natural a way as possible: this can be achieved through an active engagement with the artefact, along with a recognition of the layers of change that might have occurred over time. The *restorationist stance* must be distinguished from Svetlana Boym's (2001) 'restorative nostalgia', which vainly struggles to return to a lost past and which has more in common with, what I have called, the preservationist attitude. My terms differ from Boym's, working within archaeological paradigms. John Ruskin's notable repudiation of the nineteenth-century movement to restore by 'false substitute' (1849/1903, p. 245) is softened in modern conservation theory, which more often complies with his sense of the importance of the 'golden stain of time' upon historical sites or artefacts and the ability of these monuments to display a patina of change over time (p. 234). In her study of rereading, Patricia Spacks offers a slightly different starting point for thinking about repeated engagement with a single book over time that nonetheless speaks back to Ruskin:

> The layers of experience accruing from early readings, partly erased, remain partially discernible. Each new layer both adds to and subtracts from what has gone before. It subtracts in obscuring old reactions by new ones; it adds

> new response to those still remembered. The final product – if one can ever speak of finality in connection with rereading – includes more than is readily visible. Although one never altogether recovers previous layers, they add texture and meaning to the ultimate version. (2011, p. 274)

Spacks suggests that the original response can never be perfectly recovered, but that, like an ancient monument or relic sensitively restored, the addition of new reactions contributes to the overall meaning of the whole and provides a valuable history of the reading act over time.

A *preservationist attitude*, in contrast, prefers to prevent any disruption of relics, aiming to maintain artefacts or archaeological sites as static souvenirs of the past. In terms of rereading, this stance can manifest itself as a 'forlorn nostalgia' for the 'innocent credulity' of a child's first encounter with a book, as J. Hillis Miller confesses he feels in his essay on rereading *The Swiss Family Robinson* (1812). He mourns that child's conviction that the Robinson family's island 'still exists somewhere' and that the family are 'always having new adventures and always encountering new animals, plans, birds and fish' (2004, p. 91). The adult Miller aims to preserve his child self and his early version of the text as if in amber, despite his adult knowledge of the complexities of the text and its literary history.[2] Related to this approach is an extreme *conservationist stance*, which refuses to dig relics up in the first place. The hero of Marcel Proust's *À la Recherche du Temps Perdu* (1922–31) articulates this attitude when in the final volume, *Finding Time Again*, he stumbles across a copy of George Sand's *François le Champi* (1848) on the bookshelves of a friend's library, and realizes it is the novel given to him by his grandmother and read to him by his mother when he was a boy. The stimulus of the childhood book, which 'in its red binding' is enough to evoke a 'peculiar essence' in the adult protagonist, initially brings the child he once was 'back to life' (Proust, 1927/2002, p. 192) in the way that digging up a time capsule is designed to bring to the surface material realities of living in the past. However, the hero rejects the idea of actually rereading his original childhood copy of Sands's novel, stating as his reason a fear of inserting his current, adult impressions into the book 'until they had completely covered up old ones' (p. 196). In a slightly sinister extension of this analogy, he suggests that the child brought back to life by the idea of the remembered book would be 'for ever buried in oblivion' (p. 196) by the act of rereading. Proust's hero's comments construct the paracanonical book as time capsule or archaeological find, pregnant with meaning and information about his childhood. However, it is also portrayed as a form of crypt for the previous child self. The dead and therefore perfectly untouchable child is not a particularly unusual figure for Modernist writers in an age fascinated by the past and its relationship to the present; Boscagli also argues that time capsules 'fetishistically deny death by embodying its very stillness' (2014, p. 215), mirroring a fascination with the paraphernalia of death and life beyond death that was very current in the late nineteenth and early twentieth centuries and manifested itself in spiritualist movements, such as Christian Science and Theosophy, cultural mourning of the world wars, and archaeological finds, such as Tutankhamun's tomb in 1922. This idea of burial by influx of memory idealizes the child self, then, whose innocence and unsullied response cannot withstand the clumsy interpretative force of the adult self and his interference.

A *renovationist stance* tends towards the present, rather than the past, leading individuals to make use of unearthed artefacts or sites in new ways, or to attempt to make them 'as if new again'. For the rereader returning to a childhood book, this can manifest itself in new ways of interpreting or responding the original text that prioritize adult sensibilities. Remaking a favourite fairy tale into a site for identity politics or assessing a previously beloved children's story book according to the altered tastes of later life gives a new lease of life to these objects, but can override earlier childly responses. For many scholars of children's literature, this is the default position for rereading: indeed, 'rereading' is often a synonym for reinterpretation or new reading according to the principles of deep critical understanding and research rather than a return to earlier layers of response.[3] In these approaches, there is also a dislocation between the moment of rereading and earlier interactions, what Roger Sale calls the cutting of 'some real or imaginary umbilical cord' that allows him to 'read and write about children's literature without confusing it with myself as a child, or with the study of children's habits, tastes, or ways of thinking' (1978, p. 20).

I employ these terms – restorationist, preservationist/conservationist, and renovationist – as a shorthand for the various ways that adults resist or embrace earlier versions of their reading selves and the ways that they accept or deny the possibilities and value of re-experiencing childhood books throughout the life course. They are a way of stepping somewhat outside of debates within aetocritical discourse that are concerned with power relationships between generations and which also tend to critique theoretical positions for being more or less naïve, or more or less child-centred.[4] It is useful to locate rereading narratives within a discourse of difference and kinship instead, by considering how far the earlier child self is positioned as experiencing an authentic response of a childhood book, or to what degree childly reading experience is bound to be impenetrable and incomplete. Using these terms, I hope, avoids overt judgement value. Although there are fierce and ongoing discussions around the philosophical and ethical implications of conservation within practicing fields of museology, archaeology, and architecture (see Richmond and Bracker, 2010), there is no obvious set pattern of intellectual or aesthetic superiority attached to modes of archaeological practice from a literary or reader response perspective (although it might be obvious from my interest and approach that I am most aligned with the restorationist attitude myself). Certainly, they help to frame the motives behind rereading childhood texts, motives that go beyond critical traditions of interpretation towards what Lynne Pearce calls 'implicated reading'. What rereaders *do* with childhood books is as important as how they understand them.

Recent investigations into 'the book' acknowledge that it is not just a literary entity or an affective text, but also a material object and a basis for social interaction. Leah Price's focus on the 'operations' that surround printed matter in the Victorian era, for instance, helps her recognize that readers in the past and nowadays handle and circulate books as much as they actually read them (2012, p. 5), while Danielle Fuller and DeNel Rehberg Sedo use the terms 'processes' and 'actions' to stress the importance of readers as active agents who *experience* books as much as they *respond to* them (2013, pp. 37–8). The uses of paracanonical books change throughout the life span as rereading functions as a form of nostalgia, an act of sharing and inculcating, a way of reassessing literary texts, or an entry into autotopographical reflection and identity building. In the next sections, I will explore these uses, remaining alert throughout to the rereading attitudes on display and the implications these have for the process of excavation.

Nostalgia

Adults sometimes use remembered childhood books as a kind of magic talisman to obtain *nostos*, or homecoming. For instance, as I noted in the Introduction, Susan Hill, in her *Year of Reading from Home*, refers to Lewis Carroll's *Alice's Adventures in Wonderland* and *Enid Blyton's Treasury* as the two special books on her shelf that act as Proustian madeleines, with 'the power to catapult' her back sixty years (2009, p. 25), while Rachel Falconer uses J. K. Rowling's fantastical teleportation device '*Portkeys*' as a metaphor to indicate how books can transport readers to an earlier time in their lives (2008, p. 157). Despite the obvious energy and dynamism of these images, they might also be accused of nostalgic undertones. Nostalgia is suspect, not only because of its potential to obscure truths about the past, as discussed in Chapter 1, but also because of its solipsistic nature and the gratification it promises. In Kantian terms, gratification represents interested, rather than disinterested feelings, and when such individualist pleasures are aligned with reminiscence about childhood books, the adult can be figured as self-indulgent or in danger of misunderstanding the proper purpose of children's literature. When Fred Inglis claims that childhood books can act as natural gateways to a past self on some levels, suggesting that 'the joy they bring revives in us the childlike qualities of freshness and innocence and delight' (1981, p. 7), he commits Halbwach's nostalgic fallacy in precisely these terms. Doris Lessing does much the same in her assessment of the importance of one of her childhood favourites, Walter de la Mare's *Three Royal Monkeys* (1924), which she summarizes thus: 'Some books read in childhood put such a spell on you that for ever after you remember something like those sunset clouds illuminated pink and gold' (1999, p. 150). Her 'sunset clouds' evoke William Wordsworth's 'clouds of glory' and are likewise sentimental, drawing on the idiom of innocent and magical connection between a reminiscing adult and a cherished childhood text.

Rosemary Sutcliff goes beyond theorizing to enact this fond sense of connection when she manages to retrieve a copy of her childhood favourite *Emily of New Moon*. Many years after her initial encounter with the novel, and long after she had forgotten its title, a Canadian friend reminds Sutcliff of

Montgomery's work and sends her a copy. In her childhood memoir Sutcliff writes that she was 'almost afraid to open it' because it was 'a little like going back to a place where one was happy, years ago, even meeting an old love' (1983, p. 97). Her experience of rereading, which I have previously noted for its affective discourse of love in Chapter 3, is related by merging a specific memory with the generic backdrop of nostalgic reminiscence:

> I took the book to bed with me that night, opened it, and started reading. And the magic was still there! Even without the evening star and the distant bugle, it was still there! But in a strange way it was not without them, for they had entered into *Emily of New Moon* and were still there, waiting for me; a small fragment of my own childhood given back to me again. (p. 97)

In this mnemonic scene, Sutcliff falls into the nostalgia trap that Halbwachs identified, of believing that she can recall as an adult the mental state she found herself in on first reading Montgomery's work as a child, and of reconstructing the initial conditions of childhood reading. Not only this, the original book also offers an authentic 'fragment' of the past, precisely the fossilized piece of reality that critics of nostalgic thinking suggest cannot exist.

Freudian psychoanalysis might be invoked to censor such statements, since it suggests that for individuals to proceed safely into the measured and mature phases of adulthood and its appreciation of deferred pleasures, they need to move beyond early psychosexual stages, including the oral stage of instant gratification. In childhood reading practices, the oral stage can implicitly refer to the urge to 'consume' books with haste and compulsion, a trope commonly discussed by many critics and commentators (see Tatar, 2009, pp. 24–5; Spufford, 2002, pp. 4–12; Nell, 1988, pp. 98–113), or, more explicitly, it might refer to the visceral pleasure that one of my participants, Paulina, remembers enjoying as a child when she read A. A. Milne poem 'At Home' (1924), which is 'all about cream and cream cakes'. Moreover, within this model, childhood books themselves can act as 'love objects', or 'object(s) of attachment', as Keith Oatley describes them (2010, n.p.). The compulsion to retrieve such cast-off objects of desire is the proper work of infancy, not adulthood, presenting a process of control and management of desires that should be completed in a healthy childhood. By returning again to meaningful texts through reminiscence or rereading an adult undermines such psychological work and is thus performing neurotically. This theory can be detected in plain terms in academic Mary Warnock's 1971 article titled 'Escape into Childhood'. In this piece, she despairs of her undergraduates, who return to childhood books rather than engaging with current affairs in their spare time, who she claims are 'metaphorically thumb-sucking' (p. 823).[5]

For Warnock, nostalgia is distasteful, childish, and irresponsible. In addition, there is an emotional risk in the very idea of returning to a book that was once a pleasurable source of gratification. The risk is pain or anxiety in a disconnect between present and past experiences, and a yearning for a direct line to 'the time of our childhood, the slower rhythms of our dreams', as Boym puts it (2001, p. xv). Elizabeth Goudge articulates this stance when she writes fondly about her paracanonical text: 'Perhaps I could find a copy of *The Cocky Olly Bird* in the world if I looked a bit harder, but I think I am rather afraid, if I found it, of finding him perhaps not so wonderful after all' (1974, p. 29). Several of the adult readers I have corresponded with, and interviewed, also express this preservationist 'rereading anxiety'. In a pleasing parallel, Madeleine remembers reading Goudge's *The Little White Horse* (1946) as a ten-year-old in the late 1960s, and is also reluctant to reread it, worrying that she would lose the 'special feeling inside' that the book engendered in her childhood reading self since it is, according to her perspective, 'impossible for an adult to return to that space – it is too innocent and hopeful'. For other adults, that magical space or special feeling is still accessible, but only within the right conditions. For Philippa, born in 1941, the strong affective responses she recalls from reading Erik Linklater's *The Wind on the Moon* (1944) are dependent on the specific edition she owned as a child: 'I bought my daughter a copy in a jumble sale years later and all the memories flowed back – the paperback I've ordered from Amazon has no such effect. I wish I had the old hardback to read again'.

Similarly, Karen's desire to reread *Robinson Crusoe* or *Little Women* is tempered by her need to find the exact same editions she read as a child, with the same illustrations, to 'recreate the emotions of childhood' as she puts it. The restorative urge to recreate the *nostos*, or lost homeland of childhood, differs from the more pessimistic nostalgic stance taken by rereaders who express doubt about the authenticity of the outcome of their actions and anxieties that a book they enjoyed as a child 'would probably be rather disappointing' to them in adulthood (Rachel) or that the experience of rereading would be 'not too satisfying' and the book would seem 'shallow and irrelevant' (Brenda). Both positions assume that there is a real and stable event in the past that might be tested against their current, adult situation, however, and thus both display elements of the nostalgic fallacy.

While nostalgia and its counterpart of therapeutic reminiscence, discussed in Chapter 1, have a major part to play in a poetics of rereading childhood books, there are other ways in which rereading represents an active and ongoing part of the lifelong reading act rather than a point of division between present and past. Other reasons for rereading can bring out these alternative modes of remembering and revisiting, although the full range of rereading attitudes can still be found. Most obviously, rereading paracanonical texts with children, who might be seen to have a 'pure' and unsullied relationship with them, could be proposed as a way to avoid nostalgia completely. At the same time, real children offer tangible opportunities to return to childhood books that might otherwise have been left alone through embarrassment or anxiety.

Rereading with children

Ursula Le Guin has observed that a child or grandchild provides a 'good excuse' to return to old favourites (2006) in order to access these nostalgic pleasures. There are other reasons for rereading alongside younger relatives, of course, and co-reading with real children can give a public purpose to the cultural practice of revisiting childhood books. In an educational context, personal paracanons have the potential to become rich literary sources of teaching material. Several of my participants were or had been involved in teaching in some way, and several indicated that the main reason they had reread paracanonical texts before taking part in my study was because they offered up suitable material for working with schoolchildren. For instance, retired teacher Virginia lists a number of titles from her own youth that she went on to use in the classroom along with explanations for why they were productive choices: a collection of poetry by Robert Graves she read aged ten subsequently worked well as 'a trigger for those pupils who claimed a dislike of poetry, especially the boys'; her beloved *Black Beauty* by Anna Sewell (1877) became a valuable class library book to help those with poor reading skills;

and the 'Just William' stories provided a 'hilarious close of our week' for the whole class, nicely restoring Virginia's original reading experience of Richmal Crompton's work in a completely new context through her rereading activities.

These books work as 'generational texts' in the sense of objects passed from teacher to pupil, parent to child, and sometimes from grandparent to grandchild, through what might be called the practice of *re/reading*; that is, the form of textual encounter in which the adult is rereading and the child is encountering the text for the first time. This activity can often be a positive experience. For instance, educators can feel invested in using such texts in the classroom and pupils can benefit from the deeper knowledge and emotional connections towards these texts that their teachers may well reveal through co-reading. On the other hand, some argue that there is a risk of museumizing the world of literature for young pupils if those introducing them to texts in the classroom only reproduce the canons of their own childhoods and do not maintain a liberal and current perspective on children's literature available (see Cremin et al., 2008).

The classroom represents one contact zone in which re/reading takes place and generational books can be experienced, both as historical objects and as sites for pleasurable encounters and cultural exchange between teacher and pupil. The contact zone of parent or grandparent reading to child or grandchild offers another scenario for such re/reading. Although a common aim among teachers and caregivers is often to help encourage a love of reading for pleasure among younger generations, accounts from parents and grandparents suggest that the familial bond can shape this contact zone in terms of conflict as well as exchange. I have already explored some of its inherent tensions from the child's perspective through memories of early reading in Chapter 2. The generational contact zone can also be viewed from the adult's point of view as a scene of rereading occurring later in the life space, in which memories of early reading are then overlaid onto the activity of passing on a paracanonical book to a son, daughter, or grandchild.

The adults who remembered and reread for my project ranged from age eighteen to eighty; however, a high proportion of the participants were in their sixties or older when they responded to my survey or spoke to me interview, and most were parents and/or grandparents.[6] This locates the majority of rereaders I worked with in a particular sociocultural grouping similar to that covered by the University of the Third Age's 'You Must Remember This' project. The editor of the findings from this project notes that books formed 'a vital part' of identity for this generation, especially since there were few other indoor entertainments available for wartime and post-war children: 'Reading books was for most of us an absolute necessity' (de Bóo, 2008, p. 27). For many of my participants, books were a central medium for entertainment, then, not just during their own childhoods but also as they organized their offspring's upbringings. It is not surprising that the importance of introducing 'good' books to the next generation is rarely in question and that early twentieth-century classic children's books feature in many narratives of re/reading with children or grandchildren in these terms.

Unlike overtly pedagogical and didactic discourse, in which 'good' usually means 'good for' in the form of literature that might be morally improving or that might grow the mind of the reader through its aesthetic qualities or intellectual content, 'good' books re/read in the familial contact zone usually mean pleasurable or emotionally appealing ones. For instance, like Virginia, Jack mentions Crompton's work in terms of shared fun, claiming that it delighted both him and his son without feeling dated at all (so that he only felt compelled to substitute words such as 'emulsion paint' for 'whitewash' to bring the reading experience fully into the contact zone for them both). The 'Just William' books are regularly cited as boyhood favourites among my cohort of rememberers because of their humour.

However, by far the most frequently mentioned author in my data in this context is A. A. Milne, whose *Winnie-the-Pooh* (1926) and *The House at Pooh Corner* (1928), along with *When We Were Very Young* (1924) and *Now We Are Six* (1927) represent consistently successful shared childhood books for parents, grandparents, children and grandchildren of both sexes. Richard Adams points out that when they were first published 'everyone read [them . . .]: everyone quoted them' (1990, p. 21), and it seems viable that the very performability of Milne's work and its potential for shared pleasures among different aged readers has prompted their regular use as family texts to be reread through the generations. Owl's advice to Pooh about how to help Eeyore find his missing tail presents an excellent example of how adult and child co-readers might interact in reading the following extract aloud:

> ‘The thing to do is just as follows. First, Issue a Reward. Then –’
>
> ‘Just a moment’, said Pooh, holding up his paw. ‘*What* do we do to this – what were you saying? You sneezed just as you were going to tell me.’
>
> ‘I *didn’t* sneeze.’
>
> ‘Yes, you did, Owl.’
>
> ‘Excuse me, Pooh, I didn’t. You can’t sneeze without knowing it.’
>
> ‘Well, you can’t know it without something having been sneezed.’
>
> ‘What I *said* was, “First *Issue* a Reward”.’
>
> ‘You’re doing it again’, said Pooh sadly. (Milne, 1926/2000, p. 45)

The playful invitation for adult reader to exaggerate Owl’s officious language to replicate the sound of a sneeze is made more tempting by the repetition of the expression, which allows the child listener to come in on the joke. Certainly, parents and grandparents I spoke to described the satisfaction they remember feeling on first encountering Milne’s linguistic humour, characterization and the illustrations (particularly of 100 Acre Wood), and often imply that they can now share – or attempt to share – such pleasures with younger readers to whom they introduce his work. Little mention is made in these accounts of the often overwhelming sentimentality of the portrayal of childhood in the Pooh stories or in Milne’s poetry. Re/reading adults instead express forms of renovationist attitudes towards Milne’s work, accepting fresh responses to the texts brought to them through co-reading as well as seeking out nostalgic enjoyment. These responses are shaped by the mechanisms of a successful contact zone, where pleasure is shared equitably by rereaders and new readers alike. For Shelley, born in 1944, for instance, *Winnie-the-Pooh* is comforting, ‘like a friend’ who she is delighted to re/read to her grandchildren. Mary and Sue both note that they recognize new jokes aimed at parents when they revisit the book to introduce it to their own children, and even Rachel, who mentions that she would not have read Milne’s writing again for her own sake, finds entertainment there when she re/reads it alongside her daughter. These elements of what Barbara Wall (1991) would call Milne’s ‘double address’ aimed separately towards adult and child readers (but what might in fact be understood as ‘treble address’ to encompass the remembered child self) explain something of the popularity of his work as generational texts.

Clive recalls his father reading *Winnie-the-Pooh* to him in bed many times from the age of four onwards, and he continued this practice of reading Milne with his own sons and daughters, although he admits he may have been somewhat less 'assiduous' in this practice of reading to his children than his own father had been with him. He is prompted by taking part in the project to think about reading it to his great-grandchildren now that his grandchildren are 'too old for it'. Nicki reports that her father was also the reason the whole grown-up family re-experienced *Winnie-the-Pooh* on a recent camping trip, as he sat down by the river and reread chapters to them all, 'which was quite emotional actually, after all that time'; while Mary too feels that the Pooh books are truly generational texts, since they are passed on like heirlooms to her children and she also feels that she has been 'rereading them all [her] life!'.

Philippa also finds re/reading useful for building dialogue with family and for excavating the past. She chooses to reread Linklater's *The Wind on the Moon* for my project, having been given it by her father when she was a girl and remembering identifying fiercely with its mischievous heroines, Dinah and Davina. The novel marked a departure in her father's usual recommendations, which were more prone to be swashbuckling yarns featuring boys, such as Robert Louis Stevenson's *Treasure Island* (1883) or Linklater's other work, such as *Pirates of the Deep Green Sea* (1949), and Philippa recalls particularly observing and enjoying a sense of female adventurousness portrayed by the naughty protagonists in *The Wind on the Moon*. She did not read the book to her own children when they were growing up (thus she is able to participate in my rereading experiment with a fresh eye), but she did get hold of a copy in a jumble sale for her young daughter to read independently. In preparation for revisiting Linklater's novel, Philippa discussed her memories with this now grown daughter and she reports how they negotiated an account of remembering between them, both recalling individual details and also forgetting much of the same content. Her daughter feels she enjoyed *The Wind on the Moon* partly because her mother loved it so much, and Philippa tells me that the book is now going to be passed on to her grandchildren, 'who lead very different lives, to see how it goes down with them'. Although the contact zone in this case is rather more complex than for most parent re/readers, dispersed as it is over time and family branches, it still represents a valuable point of connection between generations and can be seen working productively when both co-readers are in fact rereaders.

Winnie-the-Pooh and *The Wind on the Moon* function here more as heirlooms might, rather than time capsules or archaeological sites or relics: never completely buried out of sight, but rather in constant use as a way of stitching a family together in shared reading. Heirlooms imply precious or valuable objects, so while part of the purpose of re/reading with children can be to build shared cultural memories that can sustain future discussions and relationships within a family, it can also intend to influence and develop their taste towards worthwhile literature (as I suggest in Chapter 2). The act of re/reading appears here as a purposeful act of parenting, albeit sometimes one with mixed intentions. Critic and writer Anne Fadiman explains, 'reading a favourite book to your child is one of the most pleasurable forms of rereading, provided the child's enthusiasm is equal to yours and thus gratifyingly validates your literary taste, your parental competence, and your own former self' (2005, p. x). As her wry comment suggests, when that formula breaks down, other objectives and functions might be revealed.

Intended influence can flow in different directions, for example. Some accounts portray a complex picture of generational reading that illustrates the potential for influence to shift and contact zones to metamorphose over time, as the distance between parent and child ebbs and flows. Robert Louis Stevenson's *A Child's Garden of Verses* (1885) represents happy memories for Adrian, both from his own childhood in the 1940s and 1950s, and in sharing poems with his children and grandchildren, but when he explains that he tried to introduce these offspring to his all-time favourite childhood books, Arthur Ransome's *Swallows and Amazons* series (1930–47), 'sadly they weren't interested'. In this instance, what is significant terrain worth re-exposing for the parent turns out to be wasteland to be left unexplored by the younger generation. In this instance, Adrian finds a new way to engage in re/reading with his daughter, however, whose school studies of Richard Doddridge Blackmore's *Lorna Doone* (1869) encourage him to return to the novel (which was also part of his own childhood reading history) so that they can discuss it together.

The desire to warn susceptible young readers of the dangers of certain texts is another common aim. Such ambivalence about the suitability of certain texts in the context of re/reading parents and children is rarely directly addressed by the remembering parent in accounts and interviews I have examined. A parent, after all, stands to gain little by admitting having read unsuitable books themselves as a child or by discussing questionable parenting practice, and he or she may also prefer not to reproduce any of the ambivalent feelings they experienced themselves in childhood reading during the supposedly safe and secure contact zone of co-reading with their own offspring. However, hints about adult restorationist attitudes on this matter can be found in writers' memoirs directed at a child audience, as the memoirists take on a kind of pseudo-parental roles to advise their young readers about appropriate books. Writerly parental figures sometimes seem to seek to protect and secure their younger co-readers, while at the same time indulging in the illicit or merely intriguing pleasures of a book remembered as somewhat unsuitable for children. Enid Blyton advises her audience not to read 'unsuitable' classics until they are older, for example, otherwise these books (which she leaves unspecified) will be spoiled for their more mature selves (1952/1986, p. 48), while Jacqueline Wilson sagely recommends that her child readers avoid Vladimir Nabokov's *Lolita*.

As I argued in Chapter 2, Wilson's original adolescent encounter with this novel acted as a challenge for the young Jacky, morally, aesthetically and intellectually, and it is notable that her warning to contemporary children is in tension with the very enticing description she gives of the pleasures it provided for her early teenage self:

> It was a revelation. I hadn't known language could be used in such a rich and elegant way. I whispered each sentence, tasting the words on my tongue.
>
> [. . .]
>
> I wasn't particularly shocked, just enormously interested. It's strange, nowadays I find the whole story so troubling, so distressingly offensive, that I can't bear to read it. I strongly recommend that you don't read it either. It's truly not a book for children. (2009/2010, pp. 98–9)

Wilson's epiphanic moment of 'revelation' marks a deviant episode in her youth that is first held up with passion and then soundly rejected. This formulation acts to close down generational re/reading, as Wilson takes on the voice of an advisory adult who refuses to share this particular paracanonical text. At the same time, the thrilling idea of the novel's words being tasted 'on the tongue' is a hint of the unsettling sensual pleasures to be found in *Lolita*, marked by an emotional script of desire, and more likely to entice in the same way it enticed the teenage Wilson, than to warn off young readers. The convention of an epiphany borne of deviance also leads Wilson to refuse to reread the novel herself, although it is unclear whether she writes with a censorious tone towards her younger, unenlightened self, or simply a growing queasiness about the discourses of childhood and adulthood inherent in Nabokov's work. Exploring a grown man's desire for an underage 'nymphet', *Lolita* can certainly be considered questionable literary matter for a child. Note too that Proust's hero's love of his childhood book *François le Champi* is shaded by ambivalence, since it was not written with children in mind and has a disturbing storyline of a growing romantic love between an orphan child and his adoptive mother.[7] No wonder Wilson and this character share a conservationist urge to leave the initial encounter buried.

Fadiman's narrative of her experience of re/reading C. S. Lewis's *The Horse and His Boy* (1954) with her son, Henry, reveals a different preservationist attitude and one that speaks further to the contact zone as an encounter of possible conflict and coercion, in which the adult reassesses the value and meaning of a paracanonical childhood book and attempts to co-opt a child co-reader into sharing these new views. In the foreword to her collection of rereading gathered from contributors to *The American Scholar* magazine, she remembers her response to this paracanonical book as she first read it as a child. Her memories are concocted in romantic terms, as at the age of eight she recalls the novel 'had seemed as swift and pure as the [. . .] river that divides Calormen from Archenland' (2005, p. xii). She goes on to compare this recollection with her later response, which is shaped by the 'complicating lens' of adult perspective, forcing her to reinterpret the novel's treatment of female and non-white characters that she did not notice when younger and to conclude (with her tongue slightly in cheek) that Lewis is, in fact, a 'racist and sexist pig' (p. xi). As well as challenging Henry's enjoyment of the text by asking him to see it through her critical eyes (an act that provokes his outrage and a look 'he might have used had I dumped a pint of vinegar into a bowl of chocolate ice cream'; p. xi), Fadiman struggles to accept the viewpoint that her own excavated childhood memory of *The Horse and His Boy* offers her, and her account initially seeks to renovate the text, layering her feminist and postcolonial adult analysis over her childly experience of narrative immersion, burying the latter and aiming to extinguish Henry's similar childly response through her act of re/reading.

The question of how far adults should make use of rereading to assess children's literature of the past in these terms has wider implications for individual parents, teachers, and guardians, and for the larger community of children's literature specialists who may work in publishing, educational, or academic contexts. It is underpinned by what Fadiman describes as the distinction between 'velocity and depth' (2005, p. xii) and what Miller has referred to as 'allegro' and 'lento' reading (2004, p. 79): the difference between succumbing to 'innocent', immersive, narrative pleasure couched as the practice of first-time and childly reading, and submitting the text to critical, contextual demystification as an adult returning to the book. When adult rereaders such as Fadiman fail to remember or refuse to admit their own childhood practice of reading for narrative pleasure – or prefer to suppress it – then within these terms they risk imposing forms of lento reading that may be uncomfortable or unnatural to their young co-reader. What the discourse does not immediately allow is that childly reading may also be lento, and that adult rereading can be immersive and quick-paced in certain contexts. Pleasure in beauty in its purest Kantian sense should be a free delight experienced independently by any individual through subjective response. However, there is a strong temptation for adults to mould an individual child's experience of a text, either to bend towards their own personal and recalled childly tales – 'I loved this so you should too' – or to learn from their misreadings – 'I loved this but you should not'. On the scale of children's literature scholarship, in which adult rereading may influence children's access to books but where there is no real child co-reader involved, the same patterns and urges to renovate are often in evidence, although as I shall go on to show in the next section, such personal attitudes are often masked by critical discourse and an appeal to the interpretative community.

Towards the end of her short essay Fadiman revises her account, admitting that her rereading practice could in fact make room for the pleasures of storytelling she recalls from her original encounter with the novel. She explains that she needed help from Henry and evidence of his first-time enjoyment of

Lewis's fast-paced narrative to help her reach a more restorationist stance, in which the palimpsestic layers of past and present can co-exist. Determined and independent response from the child reader can help add nuance and prompt an adult to adjust his or her autotopographical attitude. But what happens when there is no live child, only an adult's excavated child self, and what attitudes are formulated when childhood books are reread to be reassessed? In the next section, I move onto examine the self-indulgences of scholars and memoirists who turn to paracanons for mixed reasons and with mixed attitudes.

As scholars

Fadiman's metaphor for her autotopographical attitude is perceptual rather than archaeological. She describes the experience of rereading *The Horse and His Boy* as like wearing a set of bifocals (2005, p. xii), an image that Hugh Crago argues 'splendidly captures the re-reading experience' (2014, p. 179; see also Tatar, 2009, p. 4). The visual metaphor she uses to grapple with her layered response to Lewis's fiction might be compared to his own critical distinction between observing a beam of light (contemplation) and viewing the world *through* that beam (enjoyment) discussed in the last chapter, of course. Unlike rereading Milne's Pooh books or poetry, where pleasure in first childhood reading is usually matched by pleasure in adult rereading through the same sorts of delight in linguist play, setting, and character, Lewis's *Narnia* chronicles provoke complex negotiations between past and present that seem to require such dual vision more often than not. Once unearthed as paracanonical texts, these novels pose particular problems for adult rereaders because of their potential to both betray and disenchant, in the manner of Pearce's 'sequel' in the reading romance (1997, pp. 169–80), which proceeds through anxiety, frustration, and jealousy to disappointment. As such, *Narnia* presents a useful case study for thinking more generally about the function of critical rereading in the field of children's literature.

As Falconer has argued, Lewis's novels are prime stimuli for nostalgia because of their inherently familiar forms and themes. They also establish fertile ground for rereading, as they model 'coming back' as a natural and fulfilling process for characters and reward their readers for revisiting the stories to notice connections between times and places. The character of Lucy embodies this flexible movement, being the first to travel into Narnia through the wardrobe. When she tumbles back through the wardrobe from the magical secondary world after her first encounter with Mr Tumnus, she thinks she has been away for 'hours and hours' and yet in the chronology of her primary-world England only seconds have passed. Nevertheless, she persists in asserting the reality of Narnia, presenting a childly and open-minded perspective that privileges remembrance. By the end of *The Lion, the Witch, and the Wardrobe* (1950), the seeds of a new kind of reality have been sown, rendering Narnia the primary world and the Pevensie children's England the 'other place'. Even *The Horse and His Boy*, which is in most respects a self-contained adventure story set 'when Peter was High King' (1954/1980, p. 11) rather than a fantasy in which children from England are transported to Narnia, establishes itself as familiar through various tropes first introduced in earlier volumes: perhaps most vividly the narrator's direct address and the sumptuous delight characters take in eating ('There were lobsters, and salad, and snipe stuffed with almonds and truffles, and a complicated dish made of chicken-livers and rice and raisins and nuts, and there were cool melons and gooseberry foods and mulberry fools'; p. 64). In this way, the books subvert the conventional quest or heroic structure of home-away-return home, making the 'away' more satisfying and homely than 'home', what Colin Manlove has described as representing a 'growing love-affair with Narnia' as a homeland (2003, p. 85).

The comforts of return can be misleading, however. Madeleine reports in her survey response that she reread the *Chronicles* several times throughout adulthood from her early twenties to her current fifties for various reasons: because she was inspired by the film *Shadowlands* (1993); as part of her professional practice as a teacher of reading to a class of children; and to 'verify the knowledge that there was a religious connection that as a child I knew nothing about'. However, she also muses that she felt 'cheated somehow' when she comes up against the religious symbolism of Lewis's character of Aslan in her rereading. This is the feeling underlying Fadiman's account, and one that is mirrored in many other oral and published accounts of rereading the *Chronicles of Narnia*, including journalist Laura Miller's popular study *The Magician's Book* (2008). In this account, Miller attempts to deal with her horrified realization that she has been 'tricked' by her beloved Narnia books and their 'thinly concealed theological messages' (2008, p. 9). As Francis Spufford observes: 'Some people feel got at by the Narnia books' (2002, p. 102).[8]

Despite issues of betrayal and estrangement, Miller finds that she is unwilling to resign herself to accepting 'a fathomless gap' between 'the reader I was as a child and the reader I am now' (2008, p. 9), leaving herself open – as Fadiman does – to accessing memories of Narnia through 'bifocal lenses' and accepting the layers of response she has identified in herself. Naomi Wood also offers a brief personal account of rereading the *Chronicles of Narnia* to frame her critical interpretation, similarly highlighting changes in worldview and attitude that have drawn her back to Lewis's work in different situations throughout the life space. As a child, the *Narnia* series offered Wood 'a larger world' than the one she inhabited and the novels taught her to dream of becoming 'an English professor and a female C. S. Lewis' (2005, p. 56). However, 'along the way to adulthood' she became 'disenchanted' with the books for their values and ethical treatment of minority characters. 'Even now', she notes, the narrator's pronouncements 'slight my politics' (p. 56). Nevertheless, she recognizes the way that her own parallel text of the *Chronicles* has been constructed incrementally, its meanings formed by concerns and ambitions that emerged at different stages of life that can be unearthed and examined through the process of rereading. Rules and pleasures surrounding food and drink appear to be crucial to Wood's most childly reading self (following the example of the texts, she remembers developing a yearning for 'fried mushrooms and tea' and learning that 'alcohol was not sinful'; p. 56). Politics, on the other hand, emerge as important in her response once she has developed her own liberal philosophy. As with Fadiman, bifocal vision presents itself as a shorthand expression of the split between the intimate connection Wood continues to feel with the voice of Lewis's narrator and the weft and weave of storytelling, and the disenchantment she experiences encountering many of the plot points and ideological subtexts of the *Chronicles*.

It is valuable for literary critics to recognize that a range of motives might shape their treatment of books first encountered in childhood, including a need to reassess early response as well as to understand texts in their historical or literary contexts. As rereaders, they often inhabit a borderland of sorts between expert and lay commentary when discussing books they recall from their own reading histories. U. C. Knoepflmacher suggests in his discussion of the role of the critic 'in purporting to talk about literary texts we are covertly talking about ourselves' and any concealment of that fact is harder than usual to 'carry off' for critics and teachers of children's literature (2002, p. 5). While talking about themselves, critics are also talking to others, so that any personal response to a paracanonical text published for scholarly consumption is undeniably also a response aimed at the interpretative community, or what Pearce calls 'extratextual others' or interlocutors. She explains, 'a reader might realize the *possibility* of becoming very intimately and emotionally bound up with a certain text, for example, but, knowing that a prospective interlocutor to the reading will feel very differently about it, may be pushed towards a more defensive engagement' (1997, p. 235). In other words, children's literature critics who remember paracanonical books in a professional context – particularly those texts that enchanted them on first encounter – might be expected to work to elaborate on what could be seen as early and naïve responses in order to demonstrate their analytical prowess or ideological sophistication, or to reflect on their childly reading self as an object of scholarly contemplation.

This kind of split response between personal and professional, with its attendant need to overlay or reconstruct, can be seen at play most clearly in feminist criticism of children's literature. Here, as with *Narnia* criticism, expressions of disenchantment are often the result. This affective script is also shaped by an apparent need to defend a position against extratextual others, including one's older reading self. Spacks explains that feelings on returning to a text from the past can assume two forms: 'disappointment in a book and disappointment with the self' (2011, p. 278), and the latter appears with some regularity in accounts by feminist children's literature scholars. For instance, Judith Armstrong is scathing of her younger self in her account of her adult rereading of *The Children Who Lived in a Barn* (1938) by Eleanor Grahame. Grahame's novel tells the story of five siblings left to fend for themselves, which was first published in 1938, then reissued by Puffin in 1955 (when Grahame was acting as editor for the imprint), and most recently by nostalgia publishers Persephone in 2001 in an edition aimed more at adults than at children. Despite its respectable pedigree, as an adult critic Armstrong regards it as ideologically suspect because of the gendered representation of domestic duty it presents in the guise of a realistic adventure story. Her rereading forces her to ask why she had to have loved this book in particular: 'Why, with [my] passion for freedom and adventure, did [I] not suspect that there was something undermining going on here?' (2003, p. 253). Her recollection of an early reading experience encourages her to undertake an 'energetic reassessment' (p. 251), meaning a complete renovation or reinterpretation based on greater knowledge, critical ability, or readerly perspective gleaned through experience over time. In moments such as this, scholars use rereading to expose themselves and to demonstrate the object lesson they have learned about their younger identities, offering up a narrative of developing critical reading skills that overlays naïve early engagement with adept adult response.

I have detailed similar autotopographical attitudes displayed by feminist critics of *The Secret Garden* (1911) elsewhere.[9] As with *Narnia* criticism and with Armstrong's response, many individual scholars rereading Frances Hodgson Burnett's classic text assume a position of readerly disappointment: overtly towards the novel, but covertly also towards their younger reading selves (see Knoepflmacher, 1983; Foster and Simons, 1995; Dolan, 2013). For example, when Faye Cheatley revisits what she calls some of the 'icons of the Golden Age', including *The Secret Garden*, she insists that the 'magic' of Burnett's novel still existed for her when she returned to the book as an adult, indicating that some elements of the pleasures of childhood reading have been accepted and incorporated into a later rereading in a palimpsestic manner; however, her framing discussion is telling in representing underlying concerns about the project that are preservationist in tone. She explains, 'to approach and reread childhood literature is *fraught* with *problems*. The recollection is often replaced by a new adult version of reality, much of which *threatens* to *shatter* the illusion of the child reading. Therefore it was with *trepidation* that I approached the task, *armed* with [. . .] adult critical tools [. . .] An *arsenal*' (1994, p. 104, my emphasis). The idea of warfare is strongly coded in Cheatley's use of the language of threat and armament, and this rhetoric sets up the ideological difference between a vulnerable, innocent child reading that needs to be protected and an aggressive adult rereading the same text in order to destroy. These terms are also saturated with affective language of fear and threat. Since Cheatley's chosen texts for rereading are all ones she remembers with pleasure, there is a marked contrast between joyful recollection and the experience of horror and feelings that this joy has been 'swamped' in adult rereading, which is her reported experience revisiting the two other Golden

Age favourites (*Little Women* and *The Coral Island* [1858]). Coded language also positions Cheatley as rereader in a position of defence against potential extratextual others, and it is no surprise that in her final analysis she feels the need to report that she is disappointed by the ending and not surprised that in her 'inner child version' she remembered 'only Mary's adventure' (p. 104).

Feminist criticism is a field perhaps more open than most to drawing on personal lived experience to illuminate the practice of rereading. Some critics working in this area make use of rereading as a pure form of autoethnography, making even clearer the connection between encounters with a text and intimate development of the critic himself or (more often) herself through the life system. Here, interpretative community plays a lesser role; indeed, such accounts can be unsettling, in their focus on adult uses of childhood literature and in their inward-looking dynamic that appears not to engage in the game of speaking to or towards others. Roberta Seelinger Trites's essay about reading Alcott's juvenile fiction, 'Academic Grief: Journeys with *Little Women*' (2009) is a pertinent example. In this piece, Seelinger Trites uses personal responses to Alcott's female characters over time to reflect on her own professional experience as a female academic in the United States, and employs emotional themes of anger that feature in both text and life to build an argument about new forms of feminist response built on 'gentle dignity' (Amy March's own refrain in the novel). The content deals with difficult topics about the role of gender politics in academia and risks being confrontational towards its intended audience, but, by employing the practice of rereading childhood books, Seelinger Trites manages to ground these issues in a commonly understood discourse that is likely to appeal to her interpretative community. In the same collection, another US-based scholar of children's literature, Karen Coats, writes about her professional engagement with psychoanalytical theory and its usefulness in constructing a personal narrative about rearing her first daughter alongside the flow of narratives stemming from fairy tales and their Disney retellings. In her essay, titled 'Wet Work and Dry Work: Notes from a Lacanian Mother', she calls her child 'the little shit' (2009, p. 77), and argues that the troubles of potty training they both endured infuse her dry – that is academic – work with something living and fluid' (p. 79), deliberately winding together theory, fiction, and material bodies in a 'braid' that ignores boundaries of private feelings and public meaning.

Few scholarly writers go this far in entwining the practice of rereading childhood books with the process of understanding or constructing identity: indeed, when I asked a number of academics to participate in an early version of my rereading project, a number returned responses that were basically critical analyses of their chosen texts, rather than reflections on the process of returning to paracanons. Despite being given the opportunity to dig up personal time capsules and respond freely – in an implicated rather than hermeneutic manner, to use Pearce's terms – the urge to apply adult interpretation seemed too compelling for some. One also noted that the process could expose 'childhood feelings which maybe don't need to be unleashed', a sentiment that has to be respected in undertaking this kind of work.

One instance of a critic restoring a paracanonical text through layers of response over time can be found in Falconer's work. As with other critics of Lewis's Narnia chronicles, she uses the term 'disenchanted' as she first returns to reread Lewis's *The Silver Chair* (1953), but in her case she means she was in a state of 'mental paralysis' in her own personal and intellectual development during this period of adulthood and that Lewis's work offered her a way out of this stasis (Falconer, 2008, p. 183). She explains that rereading *The Silver Chair* transported her back in time to a point prior to her academic training, in which she felt somewhat freer to respond to texts in an implicated rather than purely hermeneutic manner. In rereading without a specific scholarly purpose, she responds emotionally to the scene in which Prince Rilian slays the witch in serpent form, which appears to her almost as a vision, 'forcibly and unannounced' (p. 183) and frees her from her previous state of stagnation in terms of this paracanonical text. As such, she recognizes that remembered verbal images from favourite books such as this one can return to the adult critic in 'unexpected ways' and open up new avenues of investigation.

The explosion of autobibliographic writing and bibliomemoirs, which I described in my introduction, points to uses of rereading that are similarly unexpected and that go beyond the practical purpose of introducing literary works to young readers or the importance of reassessing old favourites. The value of early childhood literary encounters and later re-encounters for forging an understanding of identity and selfhood over time is key, and it is to this practice that I turn for the final part of this chapter.

Understanding literary life

Spacks signals the impossibility of detangling life from the practice of rereading when she states that her main aim in writing about revisiting the books of her past is to create autobiography 'mediated by literary works' (2011, p. 18). She has other intentions, too, notably to assuage the guilt she feels in the lazy pleasure of returning to the same books again and again rather than tackling new ones, but also to build a defence of reading more generally. Childhood reading in particular represents a compelling and fundamental part of the life space for many reflective individuals; rereading allows for a certain systematic method of tracing and giving shape to this aspect of past life that can otherwise be relatively vague in memory, of articulating links between 'the rise of fledging identities' to books found in an 'early environment', as Tully Barnett puts it (2013, p. 87). Spufford's *The Child That Books Built* and Margaret Mackey's *One Child Reading* are the most comprehensive rereading projects to focus on remembered childhood books. Mackey's bibliomemoir – which aims to include 'all kinds of texts that normally slide under the radar' (2016, p. 499) – represents an especially impressive and full attempt to show the interaction between individual and paracanon: there are a number of ways in which she demonstrates the ways in which books that have come with her through life throw light on aspects of her personality and development, and vice versa. Although she does not use the term, she performs autotopographical research, attempting to understand the literary life through examination of remembered books and reading experiences.

One way that this activity manifests itself is as a way of testing identity over time. Rereading allows adults to state 'this is me now' and ask 'was this me then?': another kind of archaeology in reverse. In her autobibliography, *Nothing Remains the Same* (2002), bibliomemoirist Wendy Lesser expresses her feeling that Dodie Smith's *I Capture the Castle* (1948) reflects something of her own changing selfhood in its narrative: 'Peering back down the years through the telescope of *I Capture the Castle*, I see not only the girl who first read the book but also the woman she developed into, as if the book itself were in some way responsible for that development' (2002, p. 35). Penelope Lively's rereading of Arabella Buckley's *Eyes and No Eyes* also falls into this category. As discussed in Chapter 2, Buckley's natural history primer formed a significant part of Lively's home schooling and shaped her keen interest in the flora and fauna of her childhood home in Egypt, as well as her growing pleasure in participating herself as a girl in naive methods of botany and science writing. Ordering up a copy of Buckley's *Eyes and No Eyes* at the British Library in later life, Lively is less than impressed with the text. First of all, she did not remember that it came in individual little booklets rather than in a single volume. And through her adult perspective, she notices and bristles at the didactic and 'cosy' quality of writing in the work, expressing distress at the fact that 'the text no longer had the command and authority I recalled' (1994/1995, p. 101). She wonders whether this could really be the same book that had originally fired her 'with scientific enthusiasm' (p. 102).

Lively's overt attitude is preservationist: she acknowledges a distance between child and adult reading responses and would prefer to leave the memory of childly encounters with books in tact if possible, noting that purest and most pleasurable form of childhood reading is inaccessible to adults, 'extinguished by the subsequent experience of reading with detachment, with objectivity, with critical judgement' (p. 108). Nevertheless, this stance, it seems, is partially ironic. Lively goes on to describe retrieving her own creative writings from this period of childhood, and reports that these reflect the actual weighty language of *Eyes and No Eyes* quite accurately, suggesting that as a girl she consciously recognized the literary style of Buckley and aimed to emulate it. The exercise in memory and rereading is itself a literary one, of course, as Lively is shaping a life through words in her memoir and claims to want to turn her 'the anarchic vision of childhood' and her 'headful of brilliant frozen moments' into something meaningful through the power of language (p. vii). Other writers are much more explicit in acknowledging the direct influence of childhood reading and later career: Joan Aiken, for instance, enjoyed hearing the French fairy-tale collection *L'Auberge de l'Ange-Gardien* (1863) translated by her mother as a child and when she found a copy later in adulthood she 'read it again with just as much pleasure, and thought what fun it would be to translate. And so it was' (cited in Lathey, 2010, p. 176).[10] For Lively, the self of the past is not exactly the same as the self of the present as it seems to be for Aiken. Rereading acts as a tool to show the links between the two, as well as helping reveal some of the indirect influences on her later writing career that might otherwise have been forgotten.

While many paracanonical childhood books are idiosyncratic and very personal, some texts transcend the individual and become part of a broader cultural autotopography, shaping multiple individual narratives and providing common ground for identity formation into adulthood. No childhood books are more publicly entwined in British culture than Carroll's *Alice* novels and there is no doubt that Alice and her travels through Wonderland have had an impact on many reading histories of British readers throughout the nineteenth and twentieth centuries, and into the twenty-first century. Much of this influence can be traced via rich cultural evidence in the contemporary epoch: events such as the annual 'Alice Day' held in Oxford and an exhibition celebrating Alice's influence in the world of style and fashion held at the V&A Museum in 2015; tourist attractions and accommodation such as Disneyland's 'Alice in Wonderland' ride or Brighton's 'Wonderland House'; and the clear webs of intertextuality that can be found in works such as Neil Gaiman's *Coraline* (2002) and the ongoing online narrative *Inanimate Alice* (Pullinger, et al., 2005–2018); as well as adaptations and retellings into film, game, ballet and other media. In *Alice to the Lighthouse*, Juliette Dusinberre looks further back in time and makes a convincing case for the influence of Carroll as the literary figure 'against whom almost every new writer in the early twentieth century formed her or his artistic identity' (1987, p. 159), and for the particular resonance of the character of Alice as an emblem of childly individualism and intelligence. Virginia Woolf, for instance, recognized Carroll's power to make adult readers childlike again through the creation of Alice's appealing and enquiring mind (1947). However, Dusinberre's study makes no claims about precisely how Woolf and other Modernist writers might have actually consumed Carroll as child readers.[11]

Although by no means mentioned in all the writers' memoirs I have examined, the *Alice* books do emerge in a number of accounts, most often as a key text against which readers remember their own burgeoning identity. Lucy Boston was read *Alice's Adventures in Wonderland* during an infant illness, as I noted in Chapter 2, and she was grateful for it being what she considered her 'first non-pi[ous] book' (1979, p. 43). Boston's comment, albeit brief, hints at the excitement Carroll's novel could still provoke among child readers at the turn of the century as a corrective to overly didactic or sentimental classics. Adults who were children growing up later in the twentieth century make more personal claims for what might be called the 'Alice effect'. Lively writes about her expatriate childhood in Cairo during the 1930s, and reflects on these early years and the relationships 'rich with ambiguities' forged during that time with the servants in her parents' house. In the strange atmosphere of class boundaries and the independence of her own early experiences she recognizes 'the world [. . .] of Lewis Carroll' (1994/1995, p. 36). Aligning her child self with the character of Alice, she notes that she warms to interpretations that see 'Alice's anarchic vision as an attempt to penetrate the confusing codes of an adult world' (p. 36) because these reflect her own sense of subjectivity. Having read the *Alice* books as a child, Lively's adult knowledge of them allows her to reassess her own childly selfhood through the lens of the subversive fictional heroine. Rereading the novel itself also refashions her own autotopography, demonstrating the power of representational space to merge inner and outer worlds through memory. 'Reading today of the White Rabbit or the Red Queen', writes Lively, 'I see myself sitting in the bushes outside the kitchen door at Bulaq Dakhrur, observing [the servants] Abdul and Hassan and Mansour' (p. 36). The dreamlike moment of time-travel back to her Egyptian childhood reveals the influence of Carroll's work over her own labour of autobiography, and also something of the social realities that she lived as a girl and now recognizes as an adult as partly shaping who she was and continues to be.

In his semi-autobiographical collection of essays, *A Reader on Reading* (2010), Alberto Manguel describes journeying with Alice (as a boy, an adolescent, a student, a parent, and a scholar), employing autobibliographic methods to show how his own changing identity can be comprehended alongside different aspects of Alice's character evident in the two novels. Manguel's account stresses the distinctiveness of his relationship with Carroll's works and with the heroine, and he calls himself 'a jealous reader' who is in special 'kinship' with the *Alice* novels. Spacks also casts herself in the light of Alice, stating in her bibliomemoir that *Alice in Wonderland*, as she calls it, 'enchanted' her as a girl, not because it imitated her own life in the way it did for Lively, but because she wanted to *be* Alice: for her, Alice was 'my contemporary, my friend, almost my double' (2011, p. 25). In the same way as Manguel, she remembers being protective of this connection, thinking that the character and the book 'belonged to me alone' (p. 25). Rereading the novel as an adult allows Spacks to reflect further on this identification with Alice and the feelings of possession that attended reading her adventures. She concludes that it is the heroine's 'rebellious potential' that appealed to her (p. 31) as well as the way that the narrative foregrounds Alice's life of the mind. As a child and as academic adult, the 'equation between thinking and being' (p. 32) that is personified in Alice's strangely literal transformations speaks directly to Spacks across time. Other adults remember finding Alice's intellect and ambiguity less directly illuminating to their own sense of selfhood. My participant Georgina remembers thinking that the novel was 'silly' and wondering why anyone would want to read it, and Paulina similarly 'couldn't understand what everybody saw in it'. Judith Kerr 'loathed' *Alice's Adventures in Wonderland* and its complex puns as a girl (1992/2015, p. 53).

Alice functions as a 'textual other' for many remembering adults. According to Pearce, the textual other is 'whoever or whatever causes us to engage with a text in a manner that is *beyond the will-to-interpretation*' (1997, p. 20). Recognition of this other does not have to take place during the first encounter, as it can be activated at any point in the lifelong reading act, 'seep[ing] in' during adulthood, as it does for J. Hillis Miller (2002, p. 156), who claims to have taught himself to read at the age of five in order to read *Alice's Adventures in Wonderland* independently and, like Manguel, Lively, and Spacks, thinks that something of this significant childhood book has 'helped make me what I am' (p. 156). As they develop and look back, readers can identify with characters, not because of shared experiences or personality traits, but for more opaque reasons of recognition and resonance. Identification with a character is just one of the ways that the textual other works. It can also manifest itself in any aspect of that text (language, style, narrative voice, setting) or its material production (e.g. the author-function, or the physical book).

Alongside testing a Lockean notion of identity as sameness over time, then, rereading can be used by adults to nudge them into understanding more about this identity and to provide insights into how elements of childhood books have been evoked or lived through in order to crystallize the reader's 'sense of the work' and how he or she 'may seek to recall it or to relive different parts of it', as Louise Rosenblatt explains (1978/1994, p. 70). New Zealand children's writer Margaret Mahy is self-consciously alert to the way that books and life intertwine, arguing that 'reading and writing are two sides of one coin [. . . that] buys access to many things' and that they are part of the 'imaginative machinery' of children (1987, p. 151). In one of her many essays in which identity and reading are explored, she reflects on rereading one of her beloved childhood books, H. Rider Haggard's *King Solomon's Mines* (1885). She recalls that her initial encounter with this adventurous narrative was through her father reading it to her, and claims – somewhat fantastically – to still be able to remember the 'actual *look* of the page, the cheap yellowish paper, the curious spindly map on page 27', which all seem to her like a 'thrilling but uneasy dream' (1987, p. 154). Her subsequent rereading does not distance her from her childhood self, but adds an additional layer of information about why she found the story itself so exciting. She relates a desert scene, in which Haggard's heroes are waiting for nightfall to be able to continue their journey to reach the Mines, and they are exhausted and dangerously thirsty (these events take place in chapter 5 of the novel). On rereading this moment, Mahy is alerted to the fact that as both child and adult she took pleasure in the fact that there was danger and excitement. She also recognized that she could only enjoy it so much because it was vicariously experienced through fictional characters. The insight subsequently illuminates events in her own life space, when she describes finding herself in the midst of a dramatic crisis in which she and her children have to run away from a burning car. She reports visualizing the key scene from *King Solomon's Mines* and spontaneously using the knowledge of her own lifelong taste for adventure, sourced from rereading, to help her convince herself and her offspring that they are merely having 'an adventure' (2000, p. 83). Like Lively, Mahy is adept at coercing memory and rereading experiences into autotopographical narrative, but her account is valuable reminder that adults rereading may be searching for meaning at deeper levels than simple curiosity about books from the past might suggest. Some of these themes will continue to emerge in the final chapter.

Conclusion

If rereading is an archaeological practice, its purpose can be understood as helping adults understand cultures of the past, where those cultures are childhood experiences that might otherwise be lost or subsumed. Although there are different attitudes towards the activity represented in accounts I have explored – ones that indicate greater or lesser confidence in such a project – I have only unearthed one or two instances where rereading childhood books in adulthood is seen as a wasteful or pointless activity. Lesser's determination to reread only books that 'hold up under the close scrutiny of a second look' discounts for her most children's literature and in the case of J. D. Salinger's *The Catcher in the Rye* (1951), read in adolescence, she refuses to reread it because she 'can't bear to. If you think it's so important, *you* reread it' (2002, p. 28). The implication is that Salinger's novel is only good for one particular moment in life and cannot or should not be revisited. This chimes with a more serious point illustrated by my participant's sense, quoted earlier, that some childhood feelings bound up with books 'maybe don't need to be unleashed'. In one case I was confronted with a rereader who was clearly traumatized by the memories exposed through her experience of rereading, but it is possible sometimes the time capsule's 'will to memory', as Boscagli puts it (2014, p. 215) is too painful or dangerous to submit to. I am also sure I would discover more resistance to the whole practice of rereading if I looked outside the self-selecting group of project participants or the body of writers already explicitly interested in childhood and childhood reading.

In discussing the reasons for, and uses of, rereading paracanons, I have dug up individual and personal motives that suggest purpose and order. In the next chapter, I move into altogether less certain territory and consider the transformations that occur through the various ways that texts are misremembered. I also ask what happens when we forget childhood books.

5

Transforming, misremembering, forgetting

While adult readers often express ambivalence about their remembered encounters with childhood literature and their experiences of revisiting them, a positive discourse that stresses the pleasures and benefit of reading in youth underlies many of the autobiographical accounts and interviews I have gathered. This is perhaps not surprising, since I have selected memoirs by those already committed to children's literature, and have interviewed those who are generally self-selecting as avid lifelong readers. In his personal account of childhood reading, Richard Adams exemplifies something of the general attitude I have noticed:

> Reading was highly reassuring. It was the perfect escape – into other worlds which often seemed more valid and valuable than the real one [. . .] And the thing that happened in books didn't evanesce, like last Christmas or yesterday's picnic. They [*sic*] stayed put, to become familiar, to be re-experienced as often as you wanted; and as they were dwelt on they grew in grace and power [. . .] The permanence of books and the memorability of dialogue are well up among the most supportive things I have ever found. (1990, p. 100)

Adams's words reflect the way he locates childhood books within the pattern of his everyday life and develops a bond with them that has aesthetic and emotional potency. As I have suggested in earlier chapters, childhood books also work as permanent artefacts against which memory can be tested. Unlike many phenomenological experiences, such as eating the consumable items of a picnic, some small part of the original reading act can be compared with response to the same text many years later. As Margaret Mackey puts it, 'however faulty my memory, the books and other materials I encountered in my youth have not materially changed' (2016, p. 12). Nevertheless, Adams's claim that the contents of books 'stay put' cannot always be supported. There is, in the first instance, the basic poststructuralist tenet that every literary work is 'eternally written here and now' and will yield multiple meanings for each reader through individual readings and rereadings (Barthes, 1977, p. 145). Beyond this destabilizing premise, there are also many tangible ways in which specific material objects encountered in childhood might transmute into something strange and new for the returning adult, as well as instances when permanent memories dissolve and books are forgotten completely.

In this final chapter I turn to black holes in the reading scene; those shadows that are cast, not from the ideological and aesthetic disconnect that might occur between child and adult readings as discussed in the last chapter, but from transformations, inaccuracies, gaps, and silences that emerge when adults return to childhood books that are not the same in material terms, or when they misremember or fail to remember significant aspects of those texts. For archaeologists, a black hole is 'a significant absence of specific data in a synchronic landscape' (Groube, 1981, p. 189); for those excavating memories of childhood books, the data around certain texts or reading moments can be frustratingly fragile and surprisingly revealing of the surrounding autotopography. As Walter Benjamin suggests, excavations require a plan, but 'no less indispensable is the cautious probing of the spade in the dark loam' (1932/1999, p. 611).

To tackle these errors and absences, I will make use of my earlier discussions of memory and its limitations as well as existing critical work from translation, adaptation, and transmediation studies, which is useful for understanding ways in which texts themselves transmute and proliferate in tangible ways. A structuralist methodology of examining gaps and attending to the 'strangeness' of ordinary texts, and Freudian alertness to slips and false memories, provide other entry points for thinking about childhood reading experiences and 'transformed texts' as inherently foreign and unfamiliar. There is an additional mass of early reading encounters that seems to be lost from memory, and a final aim in this chapter is to theorize those personal lost paracanons of forgotten childhood books. It is worth thinking about the value of forgetting as a philosophical stance and as a practical attitude towards the shaping of a life narrative that includes books as a major ingredient. I will end by asking whether the practice of *anamnesis* – of the active recovery of knowledge from a previous life – is possible or even ethically sound in this context.

Transformed texts

Childhood books occupy a particularly unstable position in the 'literary polysystem', a model of hierarchies proposed by Itamar Even-Zohar (1979) that has an acknowledged canon at its centre and locates children's literature at the periphery. Accordingly, translators, abridgers, and adapters of classic children's titles are more likely to 'manipulate the integrality of the original text' (Shavit, 1981, p. 174) than they might in the system of adult literature, respecting authorship and literary genealogy rather less, while recognizing the great potential for a popular store of narratives. This situation is also true in the case of adapting adult books into the children's system, because these texts need to be 'adapted to the child's level of comprehension (as the adults understand it), or to the moral norms which are allowed in the children's system' (p. 174). The 'original childhood book' in the lifelong reading act should thus be understood as a book as it was originally experienced by the remembering reader, often – if not always – in abridged, adapted, transmediated, or translated versions, and not necessarily the text in its source language, original shape, or full character as it might be recognized by literary critics. Longstanding conventions of manipulating childhood books – both children's classics and crossover texts from adult publishing – have in some cases resulted in questionable practice, reducing the complex and original work of established authors and illustrators to simplistic plot and character as well as erasing key traditions, locations, or contexts in cultural translation. At the same time, 'there is also great potential for literary creativity in translating or retelling well-known tales for children', as Gillian Lathey has noted (2015, p. 113), and transformation of any kind can be the start of new meaning that means 'interacting with the child, listening and responding' in a kind of ethics of translation (Oittinen, 2014, p. 35).

As I intimated in Chapter 2, *Robinson Crusoe* (1719) by Daniel Defoe is regularly remembered by adult memoirists in terms that suggest familiarity with one of the chapbook versions of Defoe's novel rather than with the original source. Charles Dickens's nostalgic memory of encountering the book in boyhood requires him to journey backwards through the plot of the full text to reach something more reminiscent of a children's adaptation, for instance. He explains, 'the colony [Crusoe] established on [the island] soon faded away, and it is uninhabited by any descendants of the grave and courteous Spaniards, or of Will Atkins and the other mutineers, and has relapsed into its original condition. Not a twig of its wicker houses remains, its goats have long run wild again' (Dickens, 1860/1958, p. 148). This is a form of remembering that is more akin to forgetting, as significant aspects of Defoe's tale are erased one by one and only the truly resonant images remain: the hilltop, the sandy beach, the cave, the hut, and the powerful image of that 'memorable footstep' (p. 148). The aspects of the text that bring a political or social flavour are, as in many children's editions, omitted from this version, but the memory of the original childhood book retains its resonance for the remembering adult.

Such 'shadow canons' of well-known works of fiction have continued to make up a huge part of the children's book trade and maintain their prevalence throughout the twentieth century, along with other forms of textual transformation. There are clear distinctions to be made between abridgements and other types of adaptation or transmediation as well as cultural and linguistic translations, and I do not wish to conflate these different creative endeavours or suggest that they all work in the same way within the economy of children's literature publishing. For the purposes of this chapter, however, they share something in common in terms of their effects on reading response. I use the term *transformed texts* to describe all such childhood books that differ in original childhood encounters from subsequent adult rereadings. In most cases that I report on here, movement is from adapted version in childhood towards original source version in adulthood, although the direction could just as easily be reversed and is not always immediately evident or straightforward. Adaptations and abridgements made with child readers in mind often resonate with power and clarity in the mind of the remembering adult – as a simplified retelling of *Robinson Crusoe* seems to have done for Dickens – and rereading the original or complete version later in life can be a challenging endeavour, involving new affective responses. The same effect can take hold when a translated text is read in its source language: for instance, Judith Kerr lived in Germany for the first ten years of her life and admits that she did not realize that nearly all the books she read in German as a child had originally been written in English (1992/2015, p. 53). In her account of rereading Hugh Lofting's *Dr Doolittle* books (1920–52) in English she explains a certain level of uncomfortable readjustment and some rejection of Lofting's terminologies, since for her the pushmi-pullyu 'was always a *Stossmichziehdich*' (p. 52).[1] Recognition of cultural markers and differences offers one set of clues as to how transformed texts can lodge themselves in particular ways into the lifelong reading act. On the whole, adults rereading texts originally published in a language other than English are likely to encounter the same translations they read when they were children, as retranslations in English are rare. Classics represent the exception, however, and remembering adults may find themselves confronted with recollections of a different translation to the one they have accessed to reread, or an abridged version of that translation. Similar shadowy terrain must be tackled when transmediation is at work, and sometimes whether a childhood book is recalled via its textual form or through its televisual or filmic form is not necessarily clear either to the rereading adult or to me as researcher.

Such encounters, although common in the lifelong reading act, rarely feature explicitly in 'official' reading histories and narratives. Problems are certainly highlighted by a number of autobibliographers, such as Hugh Crago (who I will return to later), but most tend to relate to questions of rereading attitude towards a previous childhood self, in the ways I explained in Chapter 4. In this chapter, I have therefore worked in the most part with parallel texts produced through the interviews I conducted with participants in my rereading project. In contrast to published memoirs, these interviews could be used to actively guide rereaders to examine some of the more unstable elements of remembering and rereading transformed texts.

Structuralist methodology is useful in analysing these accounts and looking beyond 'manifest content' (Culler, 1975/2002, p. 304) in order to isolate the codes at play in remembering and rereading. Jonathan Culler argues that critics are most successful when they turn to conventional and familiar works from another period, which 'make considerable use of traditional codes' and which 'contain large portions of "shadow"' (p. 305). It is in these kinds of texts that critics can best attend to the 'strangeness' that naturally permeates their fabric and by doing so, can capture something of the 'force' of literature itself (p. 304). Adult re-encounters with childhood books can be partly conceptualized as engagement with conventional texts existing within another historical period, that is, an earlier phase of the lifelong reading act. In this sense, they might be considered in the light of feelings of estrangement from initial ideological, literary, and stylistic conceptions of those childhood books. Alternatively, accounts of remembering and rereading might be interpreted as conventional texts themselves, as intimate narratives of a familiar past self, by the adults who have created them and who may feel more or less in touch with that previous readerly identity. Such narratives, especially the gaps and black holes within them, are open to interpretation.

By approaching memories of transformed texts in the context of strangeness, shadows can be revealed and meaning identified. This is quite different from Perry Nodelman's use of the term 'shadow text' to represent a virtual text that an ideal reader might access 'by reading the actual simple text in the context of the repertoire of previously existing knowledge about life and literature it seems to demand and invite readers to engage in' (2008, p. 77). For Nodelman, the shadow represents the shading of an expert eye and life experience that an adult might bring to a children's text, rather than the dark spaces and murky corners of the reading scene. Culler's statements and approach thus offer a framework for thinking about how adults approach texts from the past as 'strange' in different ways, not as repositories of shadow meanings necessarily, but as signifiers of shadows that materialize in the lifelong reading act, as readers are faced with alternative versions of the objects they once read or misremember childhood books. As I will show through a series of extended case studies in the rest of this chapter, there is substantial evidence of the force that such texts continue to exert over time, even if – or sometimes especially if – the processes of remembering and rereading reveal significant disparity and confusion. Probing the black holes that appear in the reading scene offers a way of understanding childhood reading as it works in direct contrast to Adams's autobiographical picture of reassurance and familiarity. I begin with readers' responses to material changes in the books they remember reading as children, exploring the importance of the physical object and embodied reading, before turning to texts transformed by translation and transmediation, including Johann David Wyss's *The Swiss Family Robinson* (1812) and Johanna Spyri's *Heidi* (1884). Finally I will consider a case in which it is the reader's memories – and not the texts – that appear strange and unstable.

Material mismatches

The book as transformed object, as well as other non-textual artefacts, form part of the backdrop of memories in the reading scene. As Danielle Fuller and DeNel Rehberg Sedo explain, reading can be understood 'as involving more processes and actions than a hermeneutic practice or a text-reader transaction' (2013, p. 37) and I have shown in previous chapters that adults sometimes remember illustration or cover art and other paratextual elements, including transmediations, as much as – or more than – they recall textual content. Merchandise, film or TV adaptations, and other such cultural items circulating around children's literature contribute to the accounts of remembering adults, diluting, or enriching their memory scenes, and just as often causing confusion. Indeed, when accounts dwell on the mismatch between remembered materiality and revisited reality, a common theme of disconnection and dislocation emerges: there are regular complaints from participants about different editions with different cover art or illustrations, or even the same edition but not the self-same childhood copy with its personal annotations and colourings.

Most often, disparity in the visual elements of the original and reread texts provoke the strongest feelings of disjuncture in the reader, destabilizing what one of my participants, Victoria, called the 'beckoning power' of a childhood front cover. For example, Martha's rereading of Enid Blyton's *The Magic Faraway Tree* (1943) is influenced by the 2007 Egmont edition that she uses for the project. This has different cover art to the edition she owned as a child, which contained the original illustrations by Dorothy M. Wheeler. The cover of her rereading copy, created by Paul Hess, depicts a brightly coloured scene with the magical tree foregrounded, but Martha admits that this does not beckon her and she prefers the central position of the children in the cover art of her childhood version: the new image 'just doesn't have the same impact on me'. Similarly, she recalls that Wheeler's illustrations appealed to her as a child because of their realistic rendering of character, while Jan McCafferty's modern pictures in the Egmont edition are 'too much like a cartoon'. It is not certain whether Martha's taste has remained consistent over the course of her life or whether the desire for nostalgic pleasure plays a part in her disappointment as a rereading adult.

Since Martha reports that she could not help but be drawn to the new illustrations and that their jarring difference made her stop reading to examine them (this 'did actually distract me from the story a little'), it is apparent that the impact of this transformation goes beyond provocation of nostalgic dismay and affects the phenomenological process of rereading itself.

Another of my participants, Sue, reports on a dramatic sense of dislocation on choosing to reread Louisa May Alcott's *Little Women* (1868). She obtains the 1957 Dean's Classics abridged edition because she knows she owned a number of these titles throughout her childhood in the 1960s and 1970s. However, on receiving the copy she says she is unfamiliar with the cover art. In fact, she recalls *Little Women* fairly scantily, merely as a story of four sisters, and during the reread she becomes '99% sure' that she never actually tackled the novel as a child after all. We discuss the possibility that she had perhaps attempted to read the first chapter as a girl and then discarded the book because she became bored, or that she had read an even more severely abridged version that bore little resemblance to the Dean's text and which gave her some knowledge of the characters and plot but no experience of Alcott's narrative style (highly simplified versions of the story 'retold' by Mary Farrer, Josephine Page and Margorie Rowe were all published when Sue was a girl). There is a chance that Sue heard other children discussing the story and subsequently felt she had experienced it first hand: a case of what Pierre Bayard calls 'non-reading' (2008, p. xiv). Alternatively, she may have encountered a film or TV adaptation, although she cannot verify this fact. Sue's strongest memories of *Little Women* turn out in fact to be organized around the affective traces that connect memories of the book to a merchandizing tie-in: an 'Amy' doll she owned, which was bought from the Maltese factory nearby during her time abroad while her father was in service. It is this object, created to promote to Alcott's novel (it was one of four 'Little Women' dolls on offer) that has remained with Sue, rather than the literary text itself, a reminder that readers 'are not only conceivable as active, meaning-making individuals, but also as embodied, situated subjects' (Fuller and Rehberg Sedo, 2013, p. 37).

Alongside the materiality of books, autotopography plays a part in shaping adult memories according to shadowy points of uncertainty. Paulina experiences a similar sense of distraction to Martha when she comes into contact with the cover art of an edition of L. M. Montgomery's *Anne of Green Gables* (1908) that she obtains to reread for my project. Interested in pretty dresses as a girl, and pursuing this interest in semi-retirement by running a fabric business, Paulina is primed to take notice of Montgomery's descriptions of clothing, and since her original copy of the novel had a plain green binding and no illustrations, her memories of Anne's clothes are vividly constructed in her reading scene through imaginative visualization. In contrast, the 1964 Penguin edition she rereads presents her with a picture of Anne in her Sunday School outfit on the front cover. Paulina's response reflects her autotopographical journey towards enjoyment and expertise in dressmaking, and also a kind of indignation at the fact she is forced to deal with what she considers to be an inaccurate image:

> The dress is supposed to be a stiff black and white checked satin, but the illustrator clearly did not understand what that would have looked like. Because the checks, those checks are huge, I mean they're more like a chess board, I mean that's not the sort of check you would have got on a dress at that time, or a fabric at that time, that was then used to make up a dress.

Paulina find gaps, not just in her thwarted memories of the text but in what she sees as an unacceptable false rendering of a key image in her reading scene. Her comments partly rely on adult knowledge of fabrics and fashion style built from a childhood interest through to professional practice. I would suggest that much of this particular response also reflects a common dismay felt when the physical book does not match the mental images previously conjured through initial reading and concretized through memory.

The disparity between Paulina's vivid interior imagining of Anne's dress and the public, commercial reality of the reprinted book cover, produces what at first glance might seem like an overly fastidious response (after all, few implied readers would know much about the size of check used in early twentieth-century North American dress fabrics). Further scrutiny of her rereading account reveals a common theme, however; not just in her interest in fashionable dresses (which of course, mirrors Anne's own delight in pretty things), but also her rebellion against her mother's taste in clothing and in literature. This theme can help to explain her concern with mismatched detail between original childhood book and adult rereading text. Paulina notes in our initial conversation that until she read *Anne of Green Gables* she had never enjoyed the books that her mother had recommended ('my mother's other great love was Dickens who I loathe, always loathed'), and makes an interesting comparison between her own relationship with her mother and the heroine Anne's relationship with her adoptive mother, Marilla:

> Because my mother never allowed me to wear anything frilly or puffed sleevey or (laughs) the sort of clothes that I would have liked to have wear [*sic*]. I never had a party dress, for instance. I always wanted a party dress (laughs). Whether or not I had a party to go to, I would just like to have a party dress [. . .] My mother always dressed me in very, very plain things. So yes, very similar. Um, no wonder my mother liked the book so much, cos she would have related very much to Marilla. In fact there's quite a lot of Marilla in my mother (laughs).

Although she does not talk in terms of identification, it is clear that Paulina sees her own struggles with her mother in the character development of Anne and Marilla, and uses aesthetic taste and propriety as the codes to explain her own affective ties to this novel. Taking an autotopographical approach to such a reading history, it would be possible to probe Paulina's earlier response to the 'wrong' depiction of the checked satin and interpret it according to her proprietary sense of the text as she first encountered it and the central role that clothing played, both in her concretization of Montgomery's novel, and also in her own sense of selfhood as 'other' to her mother.

Remembered details that initially seem to be irrelevant or too idiosyncratic to take into account can reveal some of the shadow that lies beyond manifest content, pointing – albeit obliquely – to the force of childhood books across the lifespan. In the following discussion of reading histories featuring translated and transmediated texts it is the act of noticing, by the remembered child and the remembering adult, that brings to the surface some of the meaning of the reading act. I start by returning to Simon's account of his childhood book, *The Swiss Family Robinson*, first discussed in Chapter 2.

Translations and transmediations

In his account of remembering, Simon provides evidence that he was an attentive reader as a boy. He noticed that the language used in *The Swiss Family Robinson* was old-fashioned and deduced that it was the account of happenings in the past (around 1800, he thought). Yet his account of rereading this novel is fraught with anxiety and confusion. First, he is forced to overturn his fervent belief that Wyss's novel was 'true and not made-up', a belief which he maintained from childhood into remembering the novel as an adult, one that is shared by other remembering adults: J. Hillis Miller similarly reports thinking as a boy that 'the words on the page were a true report of events at a place that actually existed somewhere' (2004, p. 79). Simon also discovers on rereading that the text he encountered as a boy in the early 1950s is a translation (as is the one he comes to in adulthood), although as he puts it 'at the time this would have meant nothing to me'. These beliefs and responses, maintained through memory over the life course, reflect a consistent fantasy of the transparency of the text to represent no more than what is 'on the page'. This works in terms of narrative events and with regards to language itself. Rereading reveals gaps, additions, and disorienting transformations in what Simon considers to be a paracanonical text he thought he remembered well. The strangeness he experiences is not so much a matter of disparity between child and adult selves, such as is in evidence in the reflections of Laura Miller that I touched upon in the last chapter; rather, it is the shadow cast by completely new material overlaid upon memories of the original. Simon writes, however, with an increasing sense of certainty in his own recollections and awareness of the instability of the text: 'This sounded to be what I wanted but on reading it is clearly not'; 'I didn't know any of this – that the original book was unfinished'; 'I do not remember this at all'; and 'I definitely have no memory of this and really believe it was not in my book'. By the end of the reread, he has realized that he is in possession of a different edition to his childhood one, not just that the print is bigger and the engravings that featured at the start of each chapter are absent, but that the story itself, and the language used to write it, have metamorphosed from the text initially formed within his reading scene.

Written by Wyss as a form of creative response to *Robinson Crusoe* and based on the stories he told to his family – and thus partly collaborative, episodic and makeshift in nature from the start – *The Swiss Family Robinson* has 'proved immensely inviting to adaptation', according to Karen Sánchez-Eppler (2011, p. 437). Indeed, for Lathey, it is one of the 'intriguing instances where a translation becomes far more popular than the source text' (2010, p. 208) and her comment might be extended to cover all forms of popular transformation of Wyss's work. Its publishing history reflects most dramatically the textual instability of a children's classic, as noted by Zohar Shavit: the original manuscripts were edited and published by Johann David's son Johann Rudolph in 1812/13, followed a year after by a fairly free French translation of the two volumes by Mme la Barronne Isabelle de Montolieu, and both German and French versions were used in William and Mary Godwin's first English edition of 1814, titled *The Family Robinson Crusoe*. In the years after this initial foray into the world of children's literature, *The Swiss Family Robinson* was adapted, retranslated, expanded and developed so many times that John Seelye has argued that it 'resembles the adventures of the family themselves, in that it is a communal, even corporate, product' (1990, p. 5). Subsequent retellings of the story – begun by de Montolieu, continued by many others, and incorporated into English translations – extended Wyss's original narrative so that it no longer ended with the family left isolated on the island, philosophizing about the value of their mode of self-sufficiency and reliance on 'providence', instead offering closure in a rescue and return to home, and the additional character and plot devices of a missionary, natives, and a castaway English girl to provide romance as well as a distinctly enhanced Christian subtext.

It is no wonder that Simon's account of rereading is peppered with contradictory details where memory and text do not match up. To take part in my project he obtains a copy of one of the extended transformed adaptations of Wyss's source text, published in 2010 by *readaclassic.com*, probably using the 1910 Everyman Library text by an anonymous translator published by Dent. Simon soon discovers that this is not the same in language or in content as his original childhood book, which was probably a copy of the 1879 shortened English translation of de Montolieu's French version completed by

Agnes Kinloch Kingston under the name of her husband, William Henry Giles Kingston. (Simon's original childhood book is no longer in his possession, but he notes in email correspondence with me that it probably came from the collection of Victorian novels left in the family house his parents bought in the 1940s and verifies with his brother that the version they read included an episode in which a donkey is 'eaten whole by a giant snake'; this is the wonderfully gruesome and memorable account of Grizzle's demise included in Kingston's translation, among others.) Like Martha drawn to the new illustrations of her paracanonical Blyton book, Simon is provoked to focus on what is different, new, and 'wrong' in his rereading. His rereading notes proliferate around the parts of the narrative he 'does not remember at all' and the account becomes a refrain of excess and of absence: 'I do not remember anything about a rescue'; 'no memories of this storm and lightening'; 'map of the island – not in my edition'; and 'the mother's fall – new to me'. He also states that the contemporary edition 'refers to God whereas I remember Providence being used'. The plot elements, illustrative map, and language that he identifies as superfluous to, or inconsistent with, his memories represent some of the most conventional features of the text: codes that might, in fact, be expected to feel familiar in a more general and generic sense. But the sense of disparity is too strong for Simon to reread them without resistance. They are shadows, or rather black holes, pulling the remembering reader into unfamiliar and uncomfortable zones.

Not all rereadings of translated texts in new editions result in such confusion, although memories of 'foreign' books do multiply the strangeness of childhood reading as part of a historically felt experience and an insight into earlier, less-informed reading experiences, as Victoria's accounts reveal. Victoria agrees to remember and reread Spyri's *Heidi* for me, which she first discovered as a girl of eleven in the early 1960s. The novel was initially published in German in two parts: *Heidis Lehr-und Wanderjahre* (1880) and *Heidi kann brauchen, was es gelernt hat* (1881), and then in an anonymous English translation as *Heidi's Early Experiences* and *Heidi's Further Experiences* (1884). Later English-language translations dropped the lengthy subtitles, sometimes cut the second volume, and usually published the text under the simple title, *Heidi*. Victoria buys the 2002 Kingfisher Classics edition to reread for my project, which was based on Eileen Hall's 1956 translation and divided into two parts corresponding to the original German titles: 'Heidi's Years of Learning and Travel' and 'Heidi Makes Use of What She Has Learned'. Although she is seemingly unaware of the original nature of the text as written in German, Victoria acknowledges that as a child she responded to the fact the story was set in a different country: it 'made it exciting to read and a little hard in understanding, having to read and remember unusual names and place names'. Lathey argues that it is the combination of a 'traditional Swiss village story' with a 'strikingly modern portrait of an unstable young girl' that has made the text such an enduring favourite among international audiences (2010, p. 129); Victoria's reflections support the idea that the exotic location and empathetic heroine were attractive to her, and that the translation she encountered balanced these elements in a way that appealed to her tastes.

Victoria does refer to her awareness of the 'foreignness' of this childhood book, then, even if the plurality of forms that translated versions might take is not obvious to her. In her remembering account she picks up in particular on the unusual word 'dirndl', which describes a traditional Alpine skirt, and which she claims to recall appearing in Spyri's text because it was 'strange' to her and helped her to realize that she knew 'very little of the world and its people'.[2] On rereading, however, she discovers that the term does not occur in the edition of *Heidi* she has selected. An aura of uncertainty surrounds this minor detail in the account: did Victoria read a different translation as a child, one that did use the German term to add local flavour to the text?[3] Or did she insert the word 'dirndl' into the remembered story herself, recognizing the cultural markers that connect the description of Heidi's clothing in Hall's translation – 'two frocks, one on top of the other' (Spyri, 1956/2002, p. 15), one of them her 'best dress' (p. 27) – to the information about forms of traditional dress that she may have encountered in her classroom, through other transmediated versions of *Heidi*, or elsewhere in her life space. It is quite possible that the interesting word itself, which invites speaking out loud, ensures that it is lodged in Victoria's memory, as is the case for another participant, Megan, who remembers encountering the word 'diaphanous' while reading Thomas Hardy's *Under the Greenwood Tree* (1872) for her O Levels. Meagan retains a clear sense of this term relating to a piece of ham in that novel, but similarly she discovers on rereading that it does not actually appear in Hardy's text. The dirndl skirt is also related to Victoria's ongoing pleasure in clothing, and, like

Paulina's interest in Anne of Green Gable's outfits, these aesthetic details are as important to her as the story of Heidi's psychological development. Victoria recognizes that much of the aesthetic force of the reading experience is developed within the imaginative workings of the reading scene rather than in the reality of the text. For instance, the Kingfisher cover, illustrated by Angelo Rinaldi, shows the colours of the flowers in the meadows as yellow, but she explains that she had distinctly remembered them as pink, probably 'because it was my most favourite colour as a child'. Similarly, her interest in the dirndl skirt can be interpreted as a reconstructive strategy, focusing remembered reading on such distinctive images of exotic clothing.

Lathey points out that 'memories of childhood readings of [*Heidi*] centre on an idealized, wholesome Swiss landscape suffused with sunlight and pure mountain air, home to a quixotic child at one with nature' (2010, p. 129), although she does not provide specific examples of these adult responses. She goes on to note that 'Spyri's novel is far more complex than this scenario suggests, especially in the Frankfurt scenes that many adults seem to have forgotten' (p. 129). Victoria does recognize this complexity in her adult rereading account; however, she admits that she had remembered 'very little of Heidi's time in Frankfurt' from her childhood reading. In this way, she situates her younger self as more naïve and less able to understand the intricacies of an adult viewpoint than her current reading self. In contrast, academic Laila, who is in her late twenties when she agrees to participate in my project, remembers the Frankfurt sequence from a childhood reading and describes her eleven-year-old self as acutely aware of the change in atmosphere and ideology between the two parts of Spyri's work. She recalls disliking the 'boring lectures on religion in the book's second half' and, although she can now recognize more successfully the complexity of the themes that emerge in the novel, she finds rereading the latter parts of *Heidi* in adulthood as 'boring' as in her younger years. Unlike Simon and Victoria, she is also alert to transformations the text has gone through, which seem to her more stark than any development in her own reading identity.

It is important to note that Laila could not read German as a child and her first reading of the book *Heidi* as an eleven-year-old was an English translation (probably the 1980 Windmill edition), in a sense a rereading of an even earlier encounter with the Japanese anime series, *Heidi, a Girl of the Alps* (1974), and thus she had already gone through a process of reassessing her younger reading self before her participation in my project. She watched this series when she much younger, living in Germany where it was very popular. Since the TV title sequence she recalls depicts key imagery of the 'Arcadian idyll' of Heidi's Alpine days in a classic anime style that emphasizes bright colour and cute characters, it is not surprising that she remembers feeling a 'cold douche' of disappointment when she read the novel in full as a pre-teen and encountered its darker and more didactic second volume. Laila's accounts move from initial familiarity with the adapted cartoon form to exposure to the translated version of Spyri's original German-language text, pointing to ways that texts evolve within the reading scene, and highlighting the fact that remembered childhood books work within a broad culture of artefacts. This sequence reflects what Lathey describes as a process of 'reinterpretation in multiple forms', which is signalled by the shift towards the single-name title *Heidi* that acts as 'icon for multiple abridged, film, television, and animated versions' (2010, p. 129). Laila admits that the 'pop culture image of Heidi on a mountain, amidst a pastoral otherworld', which had been part of her infant consumption of fiction, had begun to reassert itself through a kind of folk communal memory into adulthood, despite her knowledge of the more complex version she had read as an eleven year old. On rereading the novel for my project, it is no longer the second half that comes as a surprise to Laila's reading self, but the beginning, in which 'nothing was so bland' as she had remembered. Reversals of expectation often cross over with experiences of remembered reading that beyond the original childhood book into adaptations and other types of transmediated intertexts.

I will come back to this issue as it is represented in adult memories later in this chapter. Now I would like to move away from transformed texts and towards transformations inherent in the lifelong reading act. These can be caused by misremembering: that is, when rereading exposes material errors or absences in an account of remembering. This mismatch differs from the personal sense of dislocation engendered by changes in rereading attitude, that sense of difference between child and adult reading selves I explored in Chapter 4. Instead, it is the reading scene that is unveiled as changeable and unstable. Nevertheless, the reading self is still crucial to an understanding of misremembering. Where translations and transmediations reveal much about the potential strangeness of childhood books, memory failure dramatizes the strangeness of the reading scene as a reflection of readerly identity. Details lying under the surface remain central to understanding, and Freudian theory can be helpful here, alert as it is to slips, mistakes, and reconstructions. Crago's published rereading experiments also provide a useful model for this approach: as a trained psychotherapist himself, he points out that interpreting types of memory error as evidence of deeper suppression and conflation of the psyche is 'acceptable to psychoanalytic thought' (1990, p. 112).

Memory errors and misremembering

In 'Screen Memories', Sigmund Freud writes 'what is recorded as a mnemic image is not the relevant experience itself – in this respect the resistance gets its way: what is recorded is another psychical element closely associated with the objectionable one' (1899/1959, p. 307). I want to explore this sense of a mnemic image – or memory trace – overlaying an objectionable reality through a single case study. Although the focus is how misremembering functions in the gap between remembering and rereading accounts, some background to the participant in question is helpful to establish possible reasons for resistance.[4]

Jillie grew up in the 1960s and 1970s, during what is often called the Second Golden Age of British children's literature. Despite the wealth of literary material circulating during this period, her memories of early reading experiences are limited. She reports that she found learning to read painful and was not an avid reader for pleasure until her mid-teens. As a child, she enjoyed stories and being read to: she liked the 'safe and familiar world' of the often-read *Downey Duckling* because she knew it so well she could recite it by heart and it therefore provided respite from having to interpret words on the page (see Chapter 2). She explains that she just 'didn't like reading'. Part of the reason for her reticence seems to have been the difficulties she faced in decoding and comprehension. Throughout her account of remembering she provides detailed information about her difficult process of becoming a reader, of the 'anxiety and fear of having to read at home and at school', and the way that memories of being punished for her poor performance in literacy continues to make her feel 'choked up'. Jillie also gives valuable insights into her own sense of lack in terms of the skills of reading for pleasure, explaining that although 'most children must miss things in the text when they read' she thinks she 'probably missed more than most'. She develops this idea through the concept of overlooking 'clues' in Harper Lee's *To Kill a Mockingbird* (1960) that would have aided her in making sense of the story and helped her to sink into it for enjoyment. The process of enchantment with the practice of reading and with individual books only began at the age of thirteen when Jillie found herself having to read thrillers aloud to her ill father and discovered that she 'wanted to actually read the next page, and the next page, and then carry on'. Her love of reading has since become firmly entrenched and she shares her love of books with the primary school children she teaches, although she still considers herself to be a poor decoder.

For my project, Jillie agrees to reread one of the books she encountered herself in primary school, aged about ten, at a point when she was clearly still unsure about her decoding abilities and when pleasure in reading was still hard to achieve for her. Her choice proves challenging for us both in practical ways as, although she recalls some details about the protagonist, storyline, some individual scenes, and the cover art, she cannot remember the title or author of this book. It is included in her paracanon due to the affective traces that connect the book to her reading scene: she remembers it primarily as a 'very emotional book about a boy that went blind' and recalls 'really empathizing' with the guide dog that helps him come to terms with his disability. At first she thinks her remembered childhood book must be one of Blyton's titles, but then realizes that Blyton's writing rarely evoked such strong emotions for her. The other book she remembers in similar terms from the same period in her life and considers rereading is Adams's *Watership Down* (1972), so despite her claims to be a weak reader, Jillie obviously had developed her own taste for affecting animal stories by this point as a young girl.

The first text we unearth as a contender for the 'emotional book about a boy who went blind' is an American novel called *Follow My Leader* published in 1957 by James B. Garfield, which Jillie soon discovers is 'definitely not the book'. One of the offshoots of this kind of research is being introduced to quite random texts you would otherwise have no reason to read, and our search for the mystery book is also a pithy reminder that reading histories are often messy things, partial and tentative, hiding as much as they reveal. It is in some ways surprising that more of the accounts I have worked with do not deal in these kinds of shadow texts, half-remembered yet unidentifiable. One explanation for this is that academics and memoirists will research such texts before writing about them, ensuring that their childhood paracanons can be named and identified; for general readers reporting to a research project, it is uncomfortable and unwieldy to discuss books without the tangible hook of a title or author.

Eventually, we discover Dorothy Clewes's little-known novel *Guide Dog* (1956) and, although the edition is not the same one Jillie borrowed from her friend as a girl, so that after reading the first page she worries that is going to be 'another dead end', she agrees on rereading the full text that 'it must be the same book'. If I were concentrating on Jillie's rereading attitude here, I would note that she displays characteristics of a renovationist stance, highlighting the differences between her remembered and very engaged childhood responses and her adult assessment of Clewes's novel. She reports disappointment because *Guide Dog* feels 'one-dimensional' in comparison with the children's literature she currently loves reading and because it does not have the same 'impact' upon her as it did when she was younger; but she also recognizes that her skills in understanding plot development have improved in ways that have rendered the narrative less confusing – and, ironically, less emotionally involving. I shall look more closely now at the moments of uncertainty, misremembering, and errors in memory surrounding her account, to push beyond her own appraisal that as a child she had not read *Guide Dog* 'properly' and had feasibly got it 'totally wrong'.

There are a number of key aspects of Clewes's novel that Jillie brings up in her remembering account that can be evaluated against her account of rereading. She recalls the main protagonist being the 'same sort of age as me', living near the moors, and suddenly going blind. She recalls 'his resentment at everything, how he hit out, and he was angry' and focuses on his frustrating relationship with a guide dog he resents, which she thinks is a female golden retriever. Most vivid is her memory of one or possibly two specific scenes of high drama in which the bond between boy and animal is tested, one of which she thinks was also represented on the front cover of her original edition:

> He was horrible to this guide dog, he really resented it, he used to kick it and [. . .] then one day the guide dog saved his life. He was at the top of a cliff and he was kicking the dog, and someone came along and said, that dog stopped you falling off the cliff [. . .]
>
> I have a vision of a blond boy standing at the top of a cliff or tor with a pair of glasses on, to indicate he's blind I suppose [. . .] but with a golden retriever by him [. . .]
>
> I have another image of him walking along the road and falling. And that's when he lashed out at the dog because the dog hadn't warned him that something [. . .] or he hadn't listened.

While Jillie's image of the dog is proven to be fairly accurate – she is actually a female golden Labrador called 'Mick' – other aspects of this scene have been misremembered and have to be reconfigured as she rereads and reflects on the experience. Several details appear as familiar in the rereading, although they were not part of her active recollection: for instance, she recognizes the moment in which the protagonist, Roley Rolandson, is blinded by a parcel bomb, and also a subsequent episode when he is depicted in hospital talking about training to be a doctor; however, she is surprised to realize that Roley is nineteen years old, since 'in my mind he was no more than fourteen'. This kind of 'error' might be explained, not as a deficit of memory, but as remembrance of early reading encounters in which the reader fits the text more directly to their own situation. It is quite likely that eleven-year-old Jillie sought to make the text more relevant to her life and experience by aligning the main character's age more closely to her own, for instance.

Such processes of alignment are more significant when plot or character is played out in an imaginative projection onto the reader's life. As with the representational space I described in Chapter 2, this projection overlays textual events onto real-life contexts. According to Jillie's account of remembering, the suddenness of Roley's blindness in the novel provoked a good deal of reflexive thinking in her younger self, causing her to imagine that the same fate might befall her and encouraging her to play-act being blind by 'walking around with my eyes shut'. Her anxiety that, like Roley, she could wake up not being able to see is the major affective thread connecting her to the text, and being so intimately woven into fantasies about her own life and body it saturates other aspects of the accounts of remembering and rereading, even though Jillie claims that she did not 'get the same emotions at all from it really'. The falling incident represents a good example of the way in which this kind of implicated reading can work towards shaping textual memories and reforming the reading scene. Jillie comes back to the scene of falling several times: it is either on a cliff top or on a road, and in her remembering account it is a climactic moment of high drama and risk. On rereading, however, she finds that the episode involves an altogether less dangerous incident. At the residential centre where he being trained to work with his guide dog, Roley has decided to take his first independent walk and during this outing he ignores Mick's canine guidance, walking into an off-bound area where drainage pipes are being laid, 'suddenly the lane was giving way underneath him. He flung his arms wide, clutching nothing as the ground came up at him with a slap of water' (Clewes, 1956/1964, p. 129). The scene is mildly dramatic and results in a change of heart from Roley, who begins to accept Mick's assistance and move towards positive growth in his new situation, but it hardly represents a life-threatening incident, nor does it feature any kind of cliff.

Jillie's minor memory error of the scene in *Guide Dog* could have been influenced by other, more dramatic literary or filmic moments where a hero is imperilled at the edge of a cliff or on a narrow ledge. Such merging of textual and extratextual content often occurs in the process of remembering childhood fiction, as I noted earlier. In some cases, the act of remembering conflates presentification of two or more textual episodes from the same book or merges episodes from different books or other forms of transmediated texts. This phenomenon is often evident in memories of series books, which can function in retrospect in some ways like a single narrative, but which also often include rich content of generic patterns and incidents that can easily be transposed across single titles. For example, Tom, remembering Arthur Ransome's *Swallows and Amazons* (1930), recalls a specific section of the story where the young protagonists 'cut something and exchange blood'. Although this event does not occur in the fairly gentle adventures of the Walker children in this first novel in the sequence, there is an instance of blood mixing in Ransome's later *Secret Water* (1939). Tom may have read the whole series and merged mental images in his account of remembering, or he may simply have been adding detail from his own set or schema of generic expectations. Jillie insists that she cannot think of any other fictional instance of danger on a cliff top that might have resulted in her having 'merged the two stories together', although broader, generic images might have been in play.

Misremembering in this form can also be a result of merging memory images of early life events with the remembered book. An uncannily similar sequence of remembering and rereading is reported by Crago as part of his rereading experiment. In attempting an accurate reconstruction of the plot of one of his significant childhood texts, W. H. G. Kingston's *Old Jack* (1861), Crago misremembers one scene about a dead man set on a cliff-top, merging it with an earlier, much more powerful one, in which the hero's father dies. The subsequent, reconstructed scene is one filled with horror in Crago's memory. On rereading the novel in adulthood, he reports that the actual textual version now reminds him of his own grandfather's death, which his parents had avoided talking about when he was a child. Crago argues that his misremembering is a form of unconscious suppression of the painful autobiographical memory, and for Jillie too, the heightened emotion and anxiety she recalls feeling about the novel as a child and her practice of imagining the events of the narrative into the reality of her own existence, increases the likelihood that this moment of the protagonist slipping into a drainage ditch has been merged with existing fantasies of being blind and subsequently exaggerated in the reading scene.

The process can be likened to 'imagination inflation', a phenomenon in which richly made fantasies or imaginings become so vivid that they are recalled as autobiographical memories of personal experiences (Fernyhough, 2012, pp. 157–8). In remembering childhood books the process works slightly differently, since fictional content is already imagined rather than remembered autobiographically, but the same principle of memory reconstructed from imagination applies. Textual evidence from Clewes's narrative also invites speculation that a reader might be tempted to enhance the key moment of peril later in the lifelong reading act, since he or she has already been encouraged to link Roley's dealings with dogs with the trauma of his blindness. In the first chapter, at the moment when Roley tries to deliver the package that explodes in his eyes, a dog runs up to the door and starts barking. He later transfers his anxiety from this single incident onto any encounters with dogs in general, so that when the idea of a guide dog is suggested he responds with terror: 'as clearly as if it were happening all over again he could feel the sudden impact of the heavy body, hear again the explosion ringing in his ears, see in his mind's eye the blinding flash. "A dog. I couldn't", he gasped' (Clewes, 1956/1965, p. 54). Remembering the dramatic impulses of this description and overlaying them onto what should be an exciting point of peril later in the story is certainly a plausible explanation for inflating the setting of a ditch to a thrilling cliff-top environment.

The spatial context for this reconstructed event – the remembered cliff – also works to situate this textual episode against a more general backdrop of high peril and epic drama, which in turn has to be reimagined in more down-to-earth terms when the scene is reread as occurring in rather mundane surroundings. Jillie recalls the cliff textually and also as part of the visuals of the front cover art. The 1964 US hardback edition published by Coward-McCann does feature quite an atmospheric cover, illustrated with a boy and dog walking through a dangerous-looking forest path. The British Hamish Hamilton edition of 1965 (which Jillie is perhaps more likely to have encountered) depicts no rural location, simply featuring a rather creepy close-up illustration of a dog. One of Peter Burchard's illustrations shows a boy walking with his dog across moors with hills in the background (Clewes, 1956/1964, p. 117). None of these images represents a cliff-top scene. As with scene construction theory, discussed in Chapter 1, this relocation of events to the 'top of a cliff' acts as a trope that allows Jillie to marshal actual details of the novel against scenery meaningful to her, and is no doubt one of the reasons that this otherwise unremarkable literary work has entered into her paracanon.

Those affective traces binding text to reading scene throughout the lifelong reading act are not always easy to identify or understand. There are not always good psychical explanations for why certain affective packages – of love, fear, or more ambivalent feelings – allow a childhood book to resonate over time and become paracanonical. Even more uncertain is why some books seem to be scratched away from the reading scene, either disintegrating in memory or disappearing altogether. In the last part of this chapter, I turn to precisely those forgotten objects and explore what it might mean to think about a lost paracanon.

Forgetting and *anamnesis*

Wendy Lesser rereads Stendhal's *The Charterhouse of Parma* (1839) in anticipation of gathering material for her autobibliography, but in the process discovers she 'couldn't recall the slightest thing about the book itself' (2002, p. 5). She finds the experience curious yet not intellectually interesting enough for her study, and it leads her to suggest that successful rereading only takes place if a book can actually be remembered 'well enough to get something new out of the rereading' (p. 5). Forgotten books are, therefore, not included in her project. Clearly, there is some logic to this position since any comparison between *now* and *then* requires at least some point of connection otherwise it becomes meaningless. While a 'null result', such as Lesser's response to Stendhal's work, technically adds to findings from any rereading experiment, most rereaders (and researchers) are looking for more detailed insights into earlier encounters with books. Some elements of forgetting are still useful for any rereading endeavour, however. Victoria is 'quite pleased' about how much she had actually remembered about *Heidi* from her childhood encounter, at the same time pointing out that 'there was enough forgotten that made my rereading very pleasurable and rather a roller-coaster for me'. As William Brewer argues, a great deal of the satisfaction of reading fiction comes from moments of suspense and not-knowing and, while rereading can pose a threat to this aspect of the experience, processes of forgetting and limited remembering ensure that readers may still be able to enjoy a book throughout their life course, especially when there is a long period between encounters (1996, p. 122). Remembering a childhood book in total fullness runs the risk of boring a rereader. There is delight in surprise as well as in familiarity and recognition.

Conversely, there can be vexation in the realization that matter has been forgotten. During our discussion about her memories of *Little Women*, Sue declares, 'I just wish I could remember more, it's rather upsetting', and although we subsequently discover that there is very good reason she cannot remember much substance, since she never read the novel in the first place, her distress at the apparent loss is not uncommon. Georgina makes a telling comment when she says that she had been 'feeling bad' for not remembering more about

Falkner's *Moonfleet* (1898), a book she claims she read in the early 1970s around the age of eleven and loved as a child. Her reading history provides some clues as to why forgetting so much of *Moonfleet* feels painful. She was an enthusiastic reader as a girl, relating to me her remembered childly identity as 'the nutcase who read books', who considered books her friends and the small bookcase she owned her 'pride and joy'. Her paracanon is rich and diverse, ranging from illustrated classics such as Kenneth Grahame's *The Wind in the Willows* (1908) to Blyton's popular *Malory Towers* series (1946–51), and including adult texts such as *Jane Eyre*, which she read in her teens. She also has fairly rich textual and contextual memories of other childhood books, including *Heidi* (she recalls descriptions of 'wonderful fresh milk and cream' and the character of the 'lovely, big, bear-like grandfather'[5]) and *The Swiss Family Robinson* (she distinctly remembers making lists of unusual and archaic words that featured in the text). In contrast, she complains that although she can remember that she read *Moonfleet*, that there were descriptions of smuggling, good and bad men, and that it made her feel 'frightened and exhilarated', she 'cannot remember anything else about it'.

Georgina's forgetfulness is, in fact, neither unusual nor particularly severe: as Bayard has noted, the process of forgetting begins as soon as one starts rereading and is 'unavoidable' (2008, p. 47) and so it would be strange if some content had *not* been lost over time. She is also aware of some of the functionality of memory that might have inflected her own recollection of *Moonfleet*, especially the potential for merging and reconstruction, and she worries in our interview that she might be confusing Falkner's novel with Robert Louis Stevenson's *Treasure Island*. It is therefore the affective interpretative scheme that she brings to her accounts that reveals the extent of her forgetting and how the loss of memories of this paracanonical book sits within her sense of her lifelong reading act. In concluding her rereading account, Georgina writes, 'I had forgotten almost every incident in the book and given the awfulness of John's fate I am surprised and a bit shocked that I didn't recall more'; this shock of betrayal infuses her reading scene.

In this expression the idea of betrayal, a responsibility towards a loved object emerges, and the ethics of remembering are brought into play. Although the book she struggles to recall is at no risk itself from Georgina's failure to re-energize it in her reading scene, the idea that a beloved book that once provoked strong emotions has left almost nothing of its substance in reach feels like a form of treachery. This is a different form of betrayal to that proposed by Lynne Pearce, in which it is part of the 'sequel' of the reading romance, encompassing disappointment and disenchantment with a previously beloved text (1997, pp. 169–80; see Chapter 4); although for Pearce too, the reader is implicated in any failure of a textual relationship and has to 'face up' to her responsibilities through 'painful acknowledgement' (p. 171). Georgina's bad feeling can also be interpreted as a result of failing me as researcher, and not having enough material to present in her remembering account (she describes herself as 'hopeless', an assessment I am quick to refute).

I am making the case in this book for the importance of paracanonical texts in all their variety of effects on the reader: these are the books that recur in the reading scene across the life space, rather than those books that touch an individual only once and then are lost. It is also part of my argument that the influence of childhood books across the lifespan can be proposed and supported by their continued existence in the reading scene through rememberings and re-encounters. Why, then, attempt to interpret any kind of forgetting as part of the lifelong reading act? One reason is that forgetting can be understood as merely a hidden corner in the terrain of autotopography. There is always the possibility of emerging from this spot through remembrance at some later stage. This potential is acknowledged in wider thinking on memory: although Daniel Schacter subscribes to biological research suggesting that memory engrams 'fade away over time', he also admits that 'the idea that all experiences are recorded forever, requiring only a Proustian taste, sight, or smell to come dancing into consciousness, can never be disproved on purely psychological grounds' (1996, p. 78). Rosemary Sutcliff's memories of L. M. Montgomery's *Emily of New Moon* and Marcel Proust's fictional account of his hero rediscovering *François le Champi*, discussed in the Chapters 3 and 4, are founded on half-forgotten childhood books, properly recalled in the context of a younger reading self only through the process of triggering. Proust's hero stumbles across Sands's novel by chance on a library shelf (1927/2002, p. 191), and Montgomery's novel can only be set down in Sutcliff's autobiography in adulthood because one of her Canadian friends reminded her who wrote the work and sent her a copy in the post (Sutcliff, 1983, p. 97). Until that moment, *Emily* was practically a lost childhood book, and signified erased affective traces. Even more obscured in what she calls the 'murk' of memory, is Mackey's 'keystone book', *The Children's Wonder Book* (1933), which she only half-recalled in its material reality before she began her project, knowing, however, that she had encountered many of the classic stories, folk tales, fairy stories, legends and myths that are anthologized within it (2016, p. 209). She is subsequently reacquainted with it when she gathers up her mother's collection of children's books, although has to employ the services of an astute librarian to identify the title and publisher, since its cover and front matter are missing. She describes it as the 'most forgotten book' (p. 213) of all those she has been able to retrieve throughout her rereading odyssey, acknowledging that there may be others that have completely faded away in the 'murk' of her past. As with Lesser, she recognizes that rereading is constrained by having to remember earlier reading encounters in the first place, and notes 'it is inevitable that I have no idea what is missing' (p. 47).

What is not immediately apparent in accounts, either produced by my participants or published in autobibliographies and bibliomemoirs, is the body of work once read by children in the twentieth century but not remembered even in passing in their adult lives. Remembering that some childhood books are forgotten can be, in its paradoxical way, an opening for further research and memory work. Mark Currie explains the 'paradox of remembered forgetting' (2013, p. 155), noting how elusive forgetting really is since to remember an instance of forgetting is 'to fail to remember it as it was' (2006, p. 64). To remember even the title or front cover image of a childhood book is to fail to forget it completely. As well as acknowledging the provisional nature of forgetting, then, I also want to foreground the fact that it is a source of affective anxiety as well as a potential spur to action. Once more, I have focused primarily on the phenomenological practices of individuals, and the effect of remembering and forgetting on their personal reading scene across the life course. There is, however, a wider cultural question to be asked: are those forgotten texts worth remembering? Recent and contemporary literary scholarship works hard to reclaim and recover authors and texts that have fallen out of fashion or for reasons of ideology, production, or reception, have been left without strong traces in the public consciousness. Is it necessary to try to do the same for forgotten childhood books on the level of individual reading histories, or is it enough to get mere glimpses of the gaps and fragments reported by ordinary readers, themselves for so long a hidden set of voices? I would not want to make claims that my project achieves the impossible and revives faded engrams. Nevertheless, if a childhood book can be thought of as a relic worth excavating, then not even recognizing that it is there, deeply buried, risks keeping the practice of early reading, and the former child him- or herself, hidden in oblivion (to turn Proust's formulation – discussed in the last chapter – on its head).

If only to salve the fear that something important is forgotten and missing, it is worth exploring methods for accessing lost books in the interests of experimental phenomenological rereading research. As I have explained elsewhere, 'remembering, misremembering or forgetting can all be ways of noticing and acknowledging meaningful details about a book, a reading stance, or an affective response in childhood and beyond' (Waller, 2017b, p. 144). The method might be called *anamnesis*: that is, the conscious recalling of forgotten knowledge from a previous life. Drawn from Socrates's theory, recorded by Plato, that learning is simply a form of remembering information already gained in an earlier incarnation of the self, anamnesis can be applied in some parts to the process of remembering lost paracanons, the texts of which were part of the knowledge base and identity of younger selves. Some of my rereaders offer up strategies for proactive recovery of the past. Written records are suggested as useful tools: for example, Sue recognizes her tendency to forget quickly and easily and explains that she has 'got into the habit of keeping a note' about current books she encountered to avoid any further decay in knowledge of her reading history. Other written records – such as Joanna's diary of the series books she collected and read throughout childhood (see Chapter 1) – are invaluable sources for autobibliographers was well as for other researchers, and offer up new approaches to book history.[6]

Plato's method involves dialogue, so that the youthful student is helped to retrieve previous knowledge through careful and generous questioning by his tutor. For adults remembering childhood books, family members and peers or friends may offer the same service. Some defer to others to help them triangulate memories and excavate missing or forgotten texts from their childhood reading histories. Philippa confers with her daughter and negotiates a shared remembering account of *The Wind on the Moon* (see Chapter 4), while, on being asked what books he was reading alongside *Swallows and Amazons* as a boy, Tom says 'I shall have to ask my parents actually'. These tactics do not always work. Jillie's attempt to conjure her past reading through discussion with her mother simply reveals further gaps and silences. When she asks what books her mother used to read aloud to her, her mother apparently responds 'well I can't remember' and on further prompting, she reiterates 'well we didn't really have books and we didn't go to the library. So I don't remember'. The triple loss of tangible evidence here – the absence of physical books in the home, the impossibility of public records through library usage, and the fading of a communal memory shared with a parent – leaves Jillie in a potentially destabilizing situation and adds a further layer of meaning to the crucial position the books she *does* remember have established in her new reading history. My own practice as researcher aims to fill some of the gaps, probing memories of childhood reading through loosely structured workshops and open interview techniques,[7] and explicitly allowing for material in 'the murk', as Mackey would say, to rise to the surface when it can.

Conclusion

Not everything has to be remembered, or remembered in full, of course. Jorge Luis Borges's short story 'Funes, the Memorious' (1942) recounts the experiences of a man who has a complete and precise memory of everything he has ever experienced and encountered. The scenario in this story results in a chaotic and dysfunctional life for Funes because 'to think is to forget differences, generalize, make abstractions' (1942/1970, p. 94). Since modern theories of remembering are founded on the premise that past experience and knowledge must be reconstructed, the notion of absolute memory disrupts ideas of a logical and reasoned understanding of the world. Remembering every single detail from the full life course would prevent any possibility of sense-making. Friedrich Nietzsche goes further with his philosophy, arguing that 'he who cannot sink down on the threshold of the moment and forget all the past [. . .] will never know what happiness is' (1874/1997, p. 62). Not only is forgetting important for humans to fully function in the diurnal world, it is also a prerequisite for contentment. Where avid readers cannot retrieve books from their past, a certain amount of therapeutic 'letting go' might be encouraged. Kevin Crossley-Holland provides an anecdote that goes some way to demonstrating the drama that might entail from such release. In his memoir, he relates the guilty secret that he has held on to a childhood book borrowed from his local library for over forty years. As part of his repentance for this terrible sin, he takes a pilgrimage to his old village, not to return the book, which is itself lost and tragically forgotten ('I could see exactly how it looked [. . .] but I could no longer even remember what it was about or its name'; Crossley-Holland, 2009, p. 67), but to make penance by offering a full set of his own writings to be placed on the shelves in its stead. However, when he returns, hoping to avoid a gigantic fine from the librarian, Miss Hill, the library 'had simply vanished. The books all the books, the wooden barn that housed them, Miss Hill: they had all disappeared. There was just a gap – a hole in my heart – where they had been' (p. 67).

Seeking the shadows and probing instances of transformation and mutation offers up a different kind of analytical work to other chapters in this book by recognizing that lifelong reading is not constituted by processes of remembrance across the life course, but is complex, often messy and disputed, or even hidden from view. The model I carefully built in the first part of my study provides robust potential for childhood books to inhabit the reading scene in partial or deformed ways, or to draft outside its boundaries, promising to break through and surface into consciousness when the faculties of memory shift in some acute manner. What I hope this chapter has shown is that narratives of transformation, misremembering, and forgetting have as central part to play in a history of reading as those well-nurtured and well-rehearsed accounts of vividly remembered paracanonical childhood books. The space around the reading scene will always be bigger than the space within, and any shadows cast by the half-remembered, half-forgotten texts of the past that drift there add texture to our understanding of the lifelong reading act.

Conclusion: The lifelong reading act

> *For a week you were wholly given up to the soft drift of the text, which surrounded you as secretly, densely, and unceasingly as snow. You entered it with limitless trust. The peacefulness of the book that enticed you further and further! [. . .] The child seeks his way along the half-hidden paths [. . .] To him the hero's adventures can still be read in the swirling letters like figures and messages in drifting snowflakes. His breath is part of the air of the events narrated, and all the participants breathe it. He mingles with the characters far more closely than grown-ups do. He is unspeakably touched by the deeds, the words that are exchanged; and, when he gets up, he is covered over and over by the snow of his reading.*
>
> (Benjamin, 1996/1928, p. 463)

Remembering and rereading are complex practices linking adults to their past reading selves. Walter Benjamin's major insight into childhood reading was that it is a serious business, one that is integrated into a child's very being as he or she grows, and one that has an effect on emotions as much as cognitive development. Although lifelong reading can originate at any point in the life course, childhood books have a special place in reading histories, providing touchstones for future reading and giving shape to a sense of self over time. The 'soft drift' of books embraces each reading child, and not only in moments of textual absorption. The 'snow of [. . .] reading' (p. 463) continues to swirl and settle as children become adults, and adults age. This beautiful image contrasts dramatically with the hard labour of digging Benjamin uses to explore memory as a form of excavation, and these metaphors offer complementary ways of thinking about the influence of early reading and the manner in which adults continue to engage with paracanonical texts over time.

Rereading Childhood Books has placed readers at the centre of an investigation of these practices and, in doing so, has argued for recognition of a lifelong reading act within the field of children's literature studies. Throughout, I have given priority to paracanons, rather than canons, discussing childhood books that have been deemed significant by individuals remembering their early reading. This focus on personal memory and the affective traces linking readers to texts has allowed me to put canonical, popular and ephemeral texts on an equal footing, and to nod to a new kind of accounting of children's literature in Britain during a long twentieth century.

The kernel of the lifelong reading act is a first encounter with a book, but this act spreads beyond the initial moment of reading (or being read to) into other points of engagement in the following hours, days, months, years, and decades. Sparks of involuntary memory, conscious attempts at recollection, and instances of textual recognition; imaginative re-enactments and the incorporation of books into real or virtual environments; feelings reignited through glimpses of character or atmosphere; rereading projects and autotopographical reminiscence: all these activities play a part. The lifelong reading act can also contract, as books are lost, misremembered, or forgotten. In the first three chapters of this book, I outlined a model of lifelong reading: a working tool meant to help me – and hopefully others – to understand the workings of this phenomenon. My starting point was temporal, as I wanted to consider the way that childhood books and early reading experiences continue to play a part in adult life, and are remembered, re-enacted, and reread at different moments in time throughout the life course. However, I also embraced the premise that 'journeying into memory is actually more about travelling through an imaginative space than about zooming back and forwards along a personal timeline' (Fernyhough, 2012, p. 152), and as I probed this concept further, increasingly a model emerged that dealt more meaningfully in spatial dimensions. In order to understand an individual's relationship with childhood books over time, I needed to identify sites of readerly interaction, both internal and external, and show how these interrelate as a reader moves through the life course. My model thus describes the reading scene, the life space, and the affective traces that reveal connections between them.

The reading scene is the conceptual space in which all the cognitive activities of lifelong reading take place, from initial decoding and interpreting (including presentification, concretization and concretion), to responses related to memory and rereading, such as recollection and recognition. While nostalgia in the form that Sylveta Boym describes as 'a yearning for a different time' (2001, p. xv) is at the heart of many autobibliographic endeavours and often shapes the reading scene, alternative forms of remembrance can be accessed or foregrounded through phenomenological research, using methods of re-memorying. The reading scene can also be a conceptual backdrop and a descriptive account of those activities as it appears in literary memoir or interview transcript. In this way, my model maintains a natural tension between specific memory functions pertaining to remembered childhood reading and the autobiographical urge to organize these into narrative forms.

The reading scene is surrounded by the life space. This element of the model refers to the 'time-space relational networks' that encompass each individual person and his or her psychological events (Reavey, 2017, p. 109; see also Lewin, 1936). As a concept it allows us to locate a single reading act within a matrix of linked experiences, places, objects, and other actors, rather than as an event on a timeline. It therefore addresses sociocultural aspects of reading throughout a lifetime, and also works to relate phenomenological acts of reading, remembering reading, and rereading to material objects (books and related artefacts), places (textual, imaginative, and real), and people (co-readers, for example). Through the process of autotopography – linking reading self to the life space – it is possible to disrupt the dominant notion of reading histories as linear journeys from youth to adulthood and show instead how remembering adults traverse a more complex terrain relating to childhood books.

Affective traces cause textual encounters to resonate across the life space, connecting individuals and their reading scenes. Bundles of emotional response work according to the theory of mood-congruent recall, allowing specific moments from the past to chime with the remembering present through affective vibrations. Since paracanons are by definition made up of texts that are emotionally significant in some way, remembering and rereading accounts are often saturated with affect. Passionate responses can be found most often when readers recall experiencing 'make-believe' attitudes that mimic the emotions felt by characters within a childhood book. More pervasive than these are moods and ambivalent feelings, such as anxiety, desire, and boredom, that emerge in childhood and in digging down the reading memories in adulthood.

In building this model and exploring its different components, I have paid close attention to academic and literary voices who have reflected on their childhood reading in published criticism, autobibliography, and memoir. I have also heeded the voices of everyday readers who have told me how they remember paracanonical texts and what has happened when they have returned to reread them. Such data have allowed me to make some cautious generalizations about how adults interact with childhood books throughout the life course and to draw out specific insights about the relationship between child readers and children's literature in the late nineteenth and into the twentieth centuries.

This approach has also aided me in moving beyond a binary conception of adult reading practices. The distinction between 'book people' and 'child people', or literary and educational concerns, famously identified by John Rowe Townsend in 1968 (and subsequently problematized by him in 1971)[1] has shaped much subsequent debate around the relationship between adults and children in the sphere of their books and reading, remaining 'a standard categorisation in children's literature studies', according to David Rudd (2012, p. 249).[2] While most recent criticism seeks to reformulate the dichotomy by renaming Townsend's terms, showing the overlaps, or demonstrating the way these types of approach co-exist within the work of individual scholars, I have developed instead a tripartite categorization of autotopographical attitudes to help describe the way that adults respond to childhood books when these are re-encountered later in life. The restorationist, preservationist, and renovationist stances introduced in Chapter 4 offer a more nuanced way of parsing the complex reactions adults reveal when they remember or return to familiar books from youthful reading days. These attitudes help us cast remembered reading and rereading as processes of excavation, illuminating the strata of texts and self that may be uncovered. They describe the way that different rereading acts will privilege different types of unearthing, by celebrating layers of response, by attempting to keep childhood books and reading buried and intact, or by reworking response to fit with current beliefs or abilities. These attitudes may also help to complicate ideas about the adult–child relationship in the context of reading and books more generally, as they open up a wider spectrum of possible responses and speak to the growing sense within children's literature criticism that 'our younger and older selves are multiple and interlinked, akin to one another rather than wholly distinct' (Gubar, 2013, p. 454).

A major purpose of this book has thus been to add re-memorying, and its companion method of anamnesis, as a fifth strategy to supplement Peter Hunt's list of adult 'ways of reading children's literature' (1991, p. 45), demonstrating how adults can approach certain childhood books with pseudo-archaeological intentions and dig up shards of cognitive, emotional, and autotopographical connection to those texts. Re-memorying is a methodological approach that invests meaning in the process of revisiting through memory work and attentive rereading, while anamnesis represents the conscious recalling of forgotten knowledge about childhood reading. *Rereading Childhood Books* straddles reading studies and children's literature studies in this way, contributing new insights to both.

Hunt himself, in a personal correspondence with me on this topic, offered up a metaphor of excavation to explain his own experience of returning to old favourites from his youth: '[books] are time-capsules of who and what you are when you read them, and the experience of the book and the experience of you reading the book are locked together'. This metaphor points to the complex and entangled relationships that exist between young readers and texts and indicates that on returning to a childhood book in adulthood one might unearth fragments about both a remembered narrative and remembered self that necessitate puzzling over and interpreting. The time-capsule hints at a potentially moribund, museumized, or preservationist version of the past that risks dealing solely in nostalgic desires, as I discussed in Chapter 4; but, it is also a charmingly intimate and amateur intervention into archaeological practice (Brian Durrans goes so far as to state it is a primarily 'embarrassing' phenomenon; 2014, p. 183), mirroring something of the central role of readers and their personal paracanons I have attempted to foreground in this book. In addition, throughout the twentieth century, time-capsules have been increasingly linked to childhood, with schoolchildren often actively involved in the selection of memorable objects for inclusion and children's TV shows such as the BBC's *Blue Peter* hosting high-profile burials.[3] As children are given agency in a hands-on form of memorializing the past, so, too, do childhood books provide new ways for a culture to look back on itself through a mixture of the private and the public.

Time-capsules do not necessarily follow the clear chronology of ancient to modern we might expect from more obvious relics. Memories of childhood books are also unstable and non-linear, erupting involuntarily or proving frustratingly elusive, shattering into meaningless fragments when touched or emerging from the ground quite unlike the reality of the reread and revisited text. In Chapter 5, I explored the peculiar effects of transformed texts on the lifelong reading act, noting that misremembering and forgetting must be incorporated into the model for it to be complete. Shadows and black holes in the reading scene can represent rich sites for excavation of hidden meanings, as well as a chance to interrogate re-memory methods. The imperative to dig up the past is by no means the only ethical choice for adult readers and researchers, however, and, for some, paracanons are necessarily shaped by childhood books that remain hidden from view because they throw up troubling material.

In February 2017, the 1998 *Blue Peter* time-capsule buried under London's Millennium Dome was excavated by mistake by builders preparing a new housing development (Siddique, 2017). As well as entertaining a nation divided in its attitudes towards icons of British nostalgia and future thinking (such as the BBC and The Millennium Dome), this embarrassing cultural faux pas highlighted something of what Durrans calls the 'ontologically ambiguous' nature of time-capsules (2014, p.183). These objects exist just under the surface and reveal past identities that are neither whole nor always wholly desirable. Childhood books too can unearth uncomfortable or unappealing aspects of readerly identity. If, as Boym argues, 'nostalgic love can only survive in a long-distance relationship' (p. xiii), then paracanonical books that come along with us as we age often transcend nostalgia and move into other spheres of influence on the self. Excavation of artefacts so closely bound to the near past is also as likely to tell us about our own memories as it is to reveal truths about the historical period from which these objects originate. Nevertheless, the theoretical findings presented in this monograph provide the foundations for further research that engages more directly with history and other areas of investigation.

Future directions

The focus of this study has been British readers who were children in the long twentieth century – from around 1860 to 2000 – although I have consulted material that falls outside of these perimeters where necessary (in analysing

Marcel Proust's account of childhood reading in France, for instance, and dipping back in time to Charles Dickens's reading experiences). Future researchers will be able to begin with the model proposed in *Rereading Childhood Books* and look further afield. Using archives and online resources such as the Reading Experience Database to gather adult accounts of remembering and rereading from earlier periods, investigators are already offering alternative reading histories (see in particular, Matthew Grenby's *The Child Reader, 1700–1840* [2011]), and these can be enriched by an understanding of the lifelong reading act. Comparative work about the memories and rereading experiences of adults from different parts of the world is also an important part of this developing picture (see Parameswaran, 2003, for an Indian case study on memories of the *Nancy Drew* books, and Jensen, 2018, for memory work from a Danish context, for instance). Although I took into account the effects of translations and adaptations in Chapter 5, the fluidity of children's literature content in the context of publishing transformations is an area I have not been able to focus on as much as I would have liked. Subsequent enquiry should certainly tackle the issues of response to source and target texts as they have been encountered in various sequences by lifelong readers (Sanjay Sircar's account of his relationship with Helen Bannerman's 1899 picture book *The Story of Little Black Sambo* (2004) is an excellent example of the nuanced readings of reading against a changing cultural backdrop that might provide a model for such work).

I considered some elements of the social contexts for childhood reading: within the family and among interpretative communities of children's literature scholars. Since reading childhood books for pleasure, rather than for education or academic study, has often had an overtly social drive, there are many other aspects of shared, civic, and communal reading that might be explored, including rereading in local reading groups, mass reading events focused on children's literature, and media tie-ins with an element of social improvement at their heart (the University of Roehampton's AHRC 'Memories of Fiction' project undertakes some of this work, as does do Danielle Fuller and DeNel Rehberg Sedo in *Reading Beyond the Book: The Social Practices of Contemporary Literary Culture* [2013]). Common reading experiences of generations growing up in specific locales and historical moments might be considered along the lines of work already done by regional projects, such as

Australian Readers Remember 1890–1930 (Lyons and Taksa, 1992), *Scottish Readers Remember, Rereading Sheffield*, the University of the Third Age's 'You Must Remember This' survey (de Bóo, 2008), or Mel Gibson's recent study of comic book readers (2014). Other areas worthy of study include implicit communities of co-readers who have shared an ongoing bond with a particular classic novel or popular series but have no actual meeting point (work I have begun in exploring the memories of men who read Frances Hodgson Burnett's *The Secret Garden* as boys [Waller 2017a]), or communities of online fan forums or author societies (research I am currently undertaking with the Enid Blyton Society). All provide rich starting points for research drawing on the model of the lifelong reading act and incorporating methodologies of re-memorying, anamnesis or autotopography.

It is evident that as child readers of the twenty-first century mature and become participants in the lifelong reading act, different types of engagement with paracanonical books will emerge as significant and memorable. In her introduction to *Reinventing Childhood Nostalgia: Books, Toys, and Contemporary Media Culture* (2017), Elizabeth Wesseling points out that in an era of electronic and digital mass media, the remediation of children's cultural artefacts, including children's literature, is 'quite unprecedented' (2018, location 43), and quotes Linda Hutcheon's observation from 1998 that 'nostalgia no longer has to rely on individual memory or desire: it can be fed forever by quick access to an infinitely recyclable past' (Hutcheon, 2000, p. 196). Future research will need to take into consideration the greater availability of childhood books in multiple formats in a digital world and their increasingly fragmented and plural forms of consumption. Vladimir Nabokov's famous formulation that 'one cannot *read* a book; one can only reread it' (1966/1969, p. 3)[4] may take on new meanings for future adults who are likely to encounter their childhood paracanons in endlessly mediated ways. Whether memory itself is affected by shifts from material to digital is a larger question that I suspect will require sustained interdisciplinary collaboration between scholars of reading and researchers working in psychology, neuroscience, and philosophy.

A final area that I could not address in *Rereading Childhood Books* but is burgeoning elsewhere is the intersection between reading and ageing. Many of my participants fall into the category of the 'third age' (Laslett, 1989) and were often keen to spend time reflecting on their youthful pasts as part of a broader personal reminiscence project. A number commented on the way their memories of childhood reading differed from other parts of their life experience, and these reflections chime with Ballard's observation: 'As I grow older – I'm now in my early sixties – the books of my childhood seem more and more vivid, while most of those that I read ten or even five years ago are completely forgotten' (1992/2015, p. 88). Less easily accessible, but perhaps more pressing, is the ongoing relationship with paracanonical childhood books that individuals might hold on to in their 'fourth age' (Higgs and Gilleard, 2015), when declining powers of memory (including the possibility of disease and memory loss) are more prevalent. I hope that my poetics of remembering and rereading will provide a platform for future interdisciplinary research into this topic, as well as offering a starting point for promoting the therapeutic potential of memories of childhood books. As such, *Rereading Childhood Books* contributes to – and draws from – memory studies more broadly. This lively and diverse field includes empirical and theoretical disciplines of psychology, biomedicine, and neuroscience, and also intersects with philosophical, ethical, and psychoanalytical discourses as well as cultural or sociological debates that consider shared memories, traumatic memory, and the role of history and memorialization. Literary critics have long been drawn to memory as a crucial theme in narrative fictions and a dynamic structure for writing; increasingly, we can extend our discussions into reading as both a cultural form of remembering and a phenomenological act inflected by remembrance. Benjamin's understanding that memory work itself is a form of excavation, both systematic and thrillingly exploratory, indicates the need for a plan for future investigation as well as initial 'cautious probing'.

Final words

My own lifelong reading act is as winding and textured as anyone's. Like other academics with an interest in revisiting books from their own childhood with an eye to the reading process rather than interpretation of texts – such as Hugh Crago, Margaret Mackey, Rachel Falconer – I have performed re-memory experiments on myself, sometimes in public.[5] Yet I am reluctant to focus in on my own narrow reading history alone and have preferred to survey other accounts in order to develop an understanding of process. I recognize the limitations of this approach, agreeing in part with Mackey when she notes that 'retrospective, edited, and reduced accounts of other readers describing what happens inside their own minds as they construe the material before them' (2016, p. 9) only offers part of the picture, but have considered the breadth and objective distance gained sufficient benefit to press ahead. I should come clean and admit that my own paracanon has pursued me throughout this book. At each turn, I have privately checked my findings against the memories of my own significant childhood books. When possible, I have looked up at the shelf to get a familiar glimpse of those I still own: Blyton's *The Mystery of the Pantomime Cat*, Robert Cormier's *Fade*, and Dianna Wynne Jones's *Fire and Hemlock*. When I think of this latter volume, I identify with Polly's attempts to reaccess the secrets of her own forgotten past. I remember her encountering her own paracanonical childhood book and rereading it in a manner that suggest the effort of digging. She runs through her memories time and time again, 'across the jolt where she had done God alone knew what, and on into the plain, single four years back beyond. Back and forth' (Jones, 1985, p. 318), in the manner of the repetitive turning over of matter that Benjamin sees as key to productive memory work. Benjamin calls for remembering to be 'epic and rhapsodic' as well as systematic in order to reach new places and 'delve to ever deeper layers' (1939/1999, p. 611), and in this way Polly manages to access knowledge of her childhood self and the fictional worlds she has been immersed in through her own 'heroic act of honest recollection', as Charles Butler puts it (2006, p. 267). Many of the adults I have encountered in the course of writing this book – either in their published works or in interview and discussion – have managed the same feat of excavation through the acts of remembering and rereading. Their reading histories are testament to the lifelong reading act.

Appendix: Participants

This study draws on reading accounts produced during a broad research project I called 'Rereading Childhood Books', carried out in the UK between 2009 and 2014. Approximately 120 adults between the ages of eighteen and eighty took part in this project, which was constructed in two phases. All participants completed an initial questionnaire about their childhood reading habits and histories, detailing specific books they read as children as well as those they had returned to as adults. They were then invited to identify one significant text they had not read since childhood. Forty-five individuals agreed to continue with this second phase, which involved using re-memorying methodology to create an 'account of remembering' and an 'account of rereading', either in interview with me or in written notes. More details of this methodology, which is based in the tenets of interpretative phenomenology, are provided in my chapter 'Re-Memorying: A New Phenomenological Methodology in Children's Literature Studies' (2017).

I found participants through a range of approaches, from direct contact with groups I considered to be committed to childhood reading or interested in memory work (including librarians, schoolteachers and University of the Third Age groups), to general advertising in bookshops and libraries in my local environment (mostly London and Bath). Personal contacts and 'snowballing' – the process in which existing participants suggest friends or colleagues as potential future participants – also played a part, and further cohorts of rereaders were marshalled as part of smaller sub-projects (one on rereading *Swallows and Amazons*, and one focused on male memories of *The Secret Garden*: see separate studies of these projects in Maine and Waller, 2011 and Waller, 2017a). A representative set was not the purpose of my research design, since my main aim was to work with participants who were invested in the idea of remembering childhood books. Nevertheless, age, gender and occupation were identifiers of interest to me in this study, and I provide data related to these in the table below. I did not explicitly gather other data such as details of race, sexuality, socioeconomic status or region. I also did not request information about nationality, but most individuals were British. Participants offered their own terms for occupation, although I have standardized these for clarity.

Age	Decade of birth	Gender	Occupation
80+	1920s	Female	Retired teacher
80+	1930s	Female	Retired physiotherapist
70+	1930s	Female	Housewife
70+	1930s	Male	Retired chartered accountant
70+	1930s	Female	Retired
80+	1930s	Female	Retired head of children's and schools library service
70+	1930s	Female	Retired teacher
70+	1930s	Female	Retired
70+	1930s	Female	Retired teacher
70+	1930s	Female	Retired nurse
70+	1930s	Female	Retired speech therapist
70+	1930s	Male	Retired
70+	1930s	Male	Retired senior lecturer
70+	1930s	Female	Retired teacher
70+	1930s	Male	Retired technical insurance manager
70+	1930s	Male	Retired teacher
60+	1930s	Male	Not given
70+	1930s	Female	Retired
70+	1940s	Male	Retired clergyman
70+	1940s	Female	Retired secretary
70+	1940s	Female	Retired bank manager
70+	1940s	Female	Retired teacher
60+	1940s	Female	Retired
60+	1940s	Male	Retired
60+	1940s	Female	Retired
60+	1940s	Female	Retired nurse
70+	1940s	Female	Retired
60+	1940s	Male	Not given
60+	1940s	Female	Retired higher education equality and diversity officer
60+	1940s	Male	Retired NHS director
60+	1940s	Male	Retired BBC producer
60+	1940s	Female	Learning support assistant
60+	1940s	Female	Retired probation officer
60+	1940s	Male	Retired
60+	1940s	Male	Retired
60+	1940s	Female	Retired teacher

Age	Decade of birth	Gender	Occupation
60+	1940s	Female	Retired
60+	1940s	Female	Retired teacher
60+	1940s	Female	Retired
60+	1940s	Female	Editor
60+	1940s	Female	Retired library assistant
60+	1940s	Female	Not given
60+	1940s	Male	Not given
60+	1940s	Female	Retired teacher
60+	1940s	Female	Retired
60+	1940s	Male	Retired chartered engineer
60+	1940s	Male	Educational consultant
60+	1940s	Male	Not given
60+	1940s	Female	Grandmother
60+	1940s	Male	Computer consultant
60+	1940s	Male	Retired civil servant
60+	1940s	Female	Retired
60+	1940s	Female	Educational consultant
60+	1940s	Female	Retired
60+	1940s	Female	Retired
60+	1940s	Female	Retired teacher
60+	1940s	Male	Retired
60+	1940s	Female	Retired headteacher
60+	1940s	Female	Retired teacher
60+	1940s	Female	Retired headteacher
60+	1940s	Female	Retired
60+	1950s	Female	Retired entepreneur
60+	1950s	Female	Clinical psychologist
60+	1950s	Female	Not given
60+	1950s	Female	Retired teacher
50+	1950s	Female	Chemist
50+	1950s	Male	Not given
50+	1950s	Female	Librarian
50+	1950s	Female	Teacher
50+	1950s	Female	Librarian
50+	1950s	Female	Behaviour support assistant
50+	1950s	Female	Primary deputy headteacher
50+	1950s	Female	Retired senior lecturer
50+	1950s	Female	Housewife
40+	1950s	Female	Not given
50+	1960s	Female	Social worker
50+	1960s	Female	Freelance translater
40+	1960s	Female	Senior children's library assistant

Age	Decade of birth	Gender	Occupation
40+	1960s	Male	Not given
40+	1960s	Female	Teacher
40+	1960s	Male	Not given
40+	1960s	Male	Not given
40+	1960s	Female	Teacher
40+	1960s	Female	Teaching assistant
40+	1960s	Female	Nurse
50+	1960s	Female	Not given
40+	1960s	Female	Hospital pharmacist
40+	1960s	Female	Teacher
40+	1960s	Female	Children's book publisher
40+	1960s	Female	Not given
40+	1960s	Female	Housewife
30+	1960s	Female	Not given
30+	1970s	Female	Educational consultant
30+	1970s	Female	Teacher
30+	1970s	Female	Not given
30+	1970s	Male	Teacher
30+	1970s	Female	Director
30+	1970s	Male	Not given
30+	1970s	Female	Civil servant
30+	1970s	Female	Recruitment consultant
30+	1970s	Female	Illustrator
30+	1970s	Female	Commercial manager
30+	1970s	Female	Teacher
30+	1970s	Female	Not given
30+	1970s	Male	Not given
20+	1970s	Female	Not given
30+	1970s	Female	Not given
30+	1980s	Female	Teacher
30+	1980s	Female	Teacher
20+	1980s	Female	Not given
20+	1980s	Female	Assistant head teacher
20+	1980s	Female	Recruitment consultant
20+	1980s	Male	Not given
20+	1980s	Female	Not given
20+	1980s	Female	Teacher
18+	1990s	Female	Student
18+	1990s	Male	Not given
18+	1990s	Male	Not given
18+	1990s	Male	Not given

Notes

Introduction: Excavating

1 Academics have considered the autobiographical, psychological and cultural implications of looking back on early experiences in terms of later responses to literary artefacts, however. See, for instance, Elizabeth Wesseling's recent edited collection, *Reinventing Childhood Nostalgia: Books, Toys, and Contemporary Media Culture* (2018), as well as Jacqueline Rose's *The Case of Peter Pan: Or the Impossibility of Children's Literature* (1984), Betty Greenway's *Twice-Told Children's Tales: The Influence of Childhood Reading on Writers for Adults* (1995), and Valerie Krips's *The Presence of the Past: Memory, Heritage, and Childhood in Postwar Britain* (2000).

2 Călinescu admits his lack of expertise in children's literature, noting that in discussing children's reading he has had to, for the most part, 'improvise, to make guesses and hypotheses which [he] cannot scientifically verify' (1993, p. 93).

3 Useful reflections on children's rereading practices include Donald Fry's *Children Talk about Books: Seeing Themselves as Readers* (1985), Jan Susina's 'Children's Reading, Repetition, and Rereading: Gertrude Stein, Margaret Wise Brown, and *Goodnight Moon*' (1998) and Mavis Reimer et al.'s *Seriality and Texts for Young People: The Compulsion to Repeat* (2014).

4 Unless they requested that their real names be used, all participants are referred to by pseudonyms throughout.

5 Pearce in turn finds the term in Toni Morrison's *Beloved* (1988), where it is deployed to explain the tangible reconstruction of the past through a conscious return to a conceptual space or place.

6 See Kuhn (1995/2000); Haug (2000); and Onyx and Small (2001). Re-memorying has also provided groundwork for those examining traumatic experience, such as Felman and Laub, 1992.

7 See also Crago's practical application of personal reader response in a reading of Jill Patton Walsh's *The Chance Child*, in which he methodically analyses his own moment-by-moment reactions to the novel ('The Readers in the Reader', 1982).

8 Crago does mention Jared Curtis's 1984 article 'On Re-Reading *The Hobbit*, Fifteen Years Later' in *Children's Literature in Education*, which looks like a similar personal project but is actually an exploration of his changing sense of identification with Tolkien's work across two *adult* encounters with the text.

9 Gekoski also deploys this trope. However he works with it in relation to his lifelong library rather than a specifically youthful one. With a perceptibly ironic tone, he explains his reaction when his ex-wife retains custody of his book collection: 'I cursed Barbara and I cursed God. These weren't books, things of paste and ink and paper. They were as close as I came to a *soul*, they contained my history, my inner voices and connections to the transcendent, and she had excised it' (2009, p. 5). Gekoski compares the process to that of intercision in Philip Pullman's *Northern Lights* (1995), and in the association with demons who change shape throughout youth, a neat point might be made about the transmutability of texts into imagination (although Gekoski does not make it).

10 American essayist Sven Birkerts uses a similar metaphor when he claims that rereading a novel 'it's always a different river and always a different I stepping into it' (1998, p. 340).

11 Benjamin's ambivalence over the reporting of a simple 'inventory of discoveries' and his promotion of 'fruitless searching' as having intrinsic value set his insights apart from Sigmund Freud's use of excavation as a metaphor for memory and the practice of psychoanalysis. In *Studies on Hysteria* 1895), for instance, Freud wrote of clearing away psychical material as one might excavate 'a buried city' (p. 139), an approach that, as Steen Larsen (1987) has argued, oversimplifies the underpinning assumptions of both memory studies and archeological practice. For this reason, Freud's ideas about memory play a much lesser role in this book.

12 Alongside a story about King Arthur, a book of fairy stories, *The Oxford Book of Ballads* and *The Golden Bough*, the full list of children's novels Polly reads is: *The Wizard of Oz*; *Five Children and It*; *The Treasure Seekers*; *The Wolves of Willoughby Chase*; *The Box of Delights*; *The Lion, the Witch, and the Wardrobe*; *The Sword in the Stone*; *The Hundred and One Dalmations*; *Black Beauty*; *Tom's Midnight Garden*. Although not strictly written with a child audience in mind, *Uncle Tom's Cabin*, *The Three Musketeers* and *The Lord of the Rings* might also be included in Polly's reading history.

13 Fans of Jones's novel will know that the narrative is somewhat complicated by the fact that Polly's remembered childhood book – *Fire and Hemlock* – has *actually* become a different text to the one she read in childhood, as it has been rewritten by Tom's colleagues to help attract Polly's attention; however, I do not think this detail detracts from the main points I draw out from the textual example.

1 The reading scene

1 Some critics have suggested that new forms of understanding of this most intricate aspect of human consciousness have been reached by testing literary representations against neurological methods. For instance, psychologist Charles Fernyhough turns to the insights of literary authors, who have 'much to tell us about memory', but also looks to scientists 'to set them straight' when they do not conform to current theories (2012, p. 7).
2 See also Hassabis and Maguire (2007).
3 See, for example, Jonah Lehrer's *Proust Was a Neuroscientist* (2007) and Suzanne Nalbantian's *Memory in Literature: From Rousseau to Neuroscience* (2003).
4 The essay appeared first as 'Sur la lecture' in an edition of *La Renaissance Latine* in 1905, then as 'Journées de lecture' in Proust's unpublished collection of essays *Contre Sainte-Beuve*, which formed the basis of his *À la Recherche du Temps Perdu*. The description is adapted and included rather more famously in the first volume of *À la Recherche du Temps Perdu*. See Proust (1913/2002, pp. 85–90).
5 In another translation it is 'days that have vanished' (Proust, *On Reading Ruskin*, 1906/1987, p. 100).
6 Amy Holdsworth offers a parallel insight in her study of remembered TV viewing. She notes that it is the world of television and its associated activities that adults most often recall, rather than the programmes themselves, astutely stating that '"remembering television" is by no means synonymous with "remembering television viewing"' (2011, p. 12).
7 The Collect for the last Sunday before Advent includes the lines from the *Book of Common Prayer*, 'Stir up, we beseech thee, O Lord, the wills of thy faithful people', and is traditionally a reminder for the congregation to prepare their Christmas pudding (1852, p. 76).
8 Norton's novel is also published as *Daybreak*.
9 Damion Searl argues that footnotes are not in the slightest irrelevant in Proust's work, but act as his method of 'establishing relationships and plumbing depths' (2011, p. xv), and are therefore certainly worth examining.
10 See Yow (2015, pp. 162–4).

2 The life space

1 There are other sources, such as surveys and interviews with child readers, library and bookselling statistics, ethnographic observation of classroom reading.

2 Jacalyn Eddy identifies the journey as a common metaphor for reading among her 'bookwomen' (2006, p. 89).

3 Kate, in Sarah Pyke's doctoral project 'Textual Preferences: The Queer Afterlives of Childhood Reading' (2018, unpublished thesis, University of Roehampton), explains that as a young person, reading often presented her with material that did not equate with her own sense of herself as a gendered, and that books presented a challenge to her desire to orient herself.

4 'I am almost inclined to set it up as a canon that a children's story which is enjoyed only by children is a bad children's story' (Lewis, 1966/1982, p. 24). Other children's authors have made similar assertions: P. L. Travers argues that children's literature should not be siphoned off as a separate entity and offers a rather wonderful image to support her idea: 'if it is literature indeed, it can't help being all one river and you put into it, according to age, a small foot or a large one' (1975, p. 22).

5 Ransome does not specify the edition of *Robinson Crusoe* he was given and, of course, it is possible that he was handed one of the many abridged versions for children that would have been more accessible to a young boy in the late nineteenth century. See Chapter 5 for more discussion of children's editions of classic literature.

6 See Jackie Horne's 'Epilogue' to *History and the Construction of the Child in Early British Children's Literature* (2011) for a detailed account of Salmon's report.

7 Calls to examine and encourage reading for pleasure are common in both children's literature and educational scholarship. See, for example, Meek (1988), Chambers (1991) and Cremin (2007).

8 An early indication of the mismatch between set texts at school and pleasurable memories of early reading can be found in Anne Mozely's 1870 article 'Fiction as Educator', featured in *Blackwoods*, in which she writes that adults remembering influential books from childhood must realize that they came to them through chance and not through the 'authority' of a teacher (cited in Price, 2012, p. 88).

9 It is worth noting that many autobiographical accounts conversely mention the sick bed in passing as unexceptional: Adams remembers reading a book of songs with his mother 'once, being convalescent in bed' (1990, p. 21), for instance.

10 See www.secondlife.com. The platform has been in existence since 2003.

11 Rumer Godden, author of *The Doll's House* (1947), also relates in her co-written childhood memoir, *Two Under the Indian Sun* (1966), how she and her sisters role-played *Robinson Crusoe* in the garden of their home in Bengal, giving the role of goat and parrot to Nancy and Rose because 'there wasn't anybody on the island except Crusoe and Man Friday' (1966, p. 51).

12 See Maine and Waller (2011).

3 Affective traces

1 Michael Ward makes the point that atmosphere is 'a somewhat inadequate word' in the context of this essay (2012, p. 13).
2 Rachel apparently read an edition – possibly an American copy – that combined Alcott's first two volumes, *Little Women* (1868) and *Good Wives* (1869) in one text, since Beth does not die until towards the end of the latter.
3 See Waller (2016).
4 See Kimberley Reynolds's 'Introduction' to Reynolds, Brennan and McCarron's *Frightening Fiction* (2001) for a discussion of such concerns in the 1990s (pp. 1–5).
5 Blyton's assumption would probably be roundly rejected by Judith Kerr, who found the Grimms's stories 'totally unfrightening' (Kerr, 1992/2015, p. 52).
6 Probably either *Fairy Tales from Hans Christian Andersen*, published by Dent in 1899 and illustrated by Thomas, Charles and William Heath Robinson, or *Hans Andersen Fairy Tales*, published by Constable in 1913 and illustrated by William Heath solely.
7 Mel Gibson touches upon the potential for sexual gratification very briefly in her study of remembered reading of post-war comics, noting the assumption reported by her participants that parents considered romance comics 'common and vulgar' because they encouraged 'an interest in sexual relationships' (2015, p. 120).
8 Lewis's discussion of joy and desire broadens out to lead towards his Christian apologetics in this and other works, but it maintains relevance for his poetics of reading and it is this element I have focused upon in this chapter.
9 It also does not take into account the fact that the 'Just William' stories were originally published in a magazine for adults.

4 Rereading attitudes

1 The same adults might also be taken aback by Diana Wynne Jones's account of her encounter with the real Potter on a childhood holiday, in which she describes the author simply as 'an old woman with a sack over her shoulders' who stormed out of her house to hit Jones's sisters 'for swinging on her gate' (1988/2012, p. 217).
2 See Chapters 2 and 5 for more discussion of Miller's accounts. Curiously, in an earlier version of this account included in his book, *On Literature* (2002), Miller celebrates rather than mourns the loss of first-time reading, since the loss primes the reader for later acts of critical deconstruction, which would not otherwise be possible. The later, preservationist, essay appears in a collection of children's

literature scholarship and this context may perhaps have persuaded the critic to be more accepting of a child's eye view (although it is worth noting that this particular collection of essays claims it is an attempt to get away from perceived conventions of children's literature scholarship and its reliance on 'the real child' [Lesnik-Oberstein, 2004, p. 20]).

3 A cursory search for 'rereadings' of children's fiction mostly turns up articles and book chapters presenting not memories of childhood reading, but fresh critical analyses of classic and canonical texts: two such items are John Clement Ball's article 'Max's Colonial Fantasy: Rereading Sendak's *Where the Wild Things Are*' (1997) and Suma Gupta's book-length study, *Re-Reading Harry Potter* (2003).

4 See Clémentine Beauvais's *The Mighty Child* (2015) for a comprehensive working through of these debates.

5 Peter Hollindale describes her attack as 'crusty impatience' (1997, p. 33).

6 In my study, half of my participants were born in or before 1950 and around 60 per cent of the total had had children.

7 George Sands's novel has, however, been published in children's editions, for instance, in the Bibliothèque Verte imprint (1951).

8 Since Philip Pullman's infamous attack on Lewis's 'impertinen[t]' deployment of the Passion to garner sympathy for Aslan, and the series's 'misogyny . . . racism [. . .] sado-masochistic relish for violence' (1991), current young readers of Narnia might be more alert to underlying Christian narratives in the series as well as potentially suspect ideologies and, therefore, may not experience the same feelings of having been 'duped' as children if they return to it in adulthood.

9 See Waller (2017a).

10 Aiken's translation is *The Angel Inn* (1976).

11 Dusinberre argues that Woolf's imagination is 'peopled with Carrollean figures', but she also quotes Woolf's statement in an essay on Carroll that 'the two Alices are not books for children' (p. 2) ('Lewis Carroll' in Woolf, 1947, pp. 70–1).

5 Transforming, misremembering, forgetting

1 The literal translation is 'Push-Me, Pull-You'.

2 Victoria's youthful naivety in all things international can be compared with Philip Pullman's account of reading translated books in childhood, in which he claims that he 'felt at home' in 'the valleys and forests and coastlines' known to fictional characters from the Moomin books and *Emil and the Detectives*, and that he was 'European before I'd discovered whether I was English or British' (Pullman, 2001, p. 6).

3 My searches of abridged and adapted versions of *Heidi* have not yet revealed an edition that uses the word 'dirndl'.
4 I have avoided the term 'false memory' because of its association with false memory syndrome, which is primarily based in research about child abuse cases and is not appropriate for my study (see Loftus, 1993).
5 Georgina might also be half-remembering the name of the brown goat, which features in the text: Little Bear.
6 The Reading Experience Database includes a range of diary entries as part of its evidence base for forms of reading. The diary of Hilary Spalding, daughter of a clergyman, writing in 1943 is a good example.
7 See Waller (2017b) for detailed information about this methodology.

Conclusion: The lifelong reading act

1 Townsend's original statement about 'book people' and 'child people' was included in an article in the *Wilson Library Bulletin* in October 1968 and then discussed and nuanced in the article 'Standards of Criticism for Children's Literature' in *Top of the News* in June 1971 (later reprinted in *Signal* in 1974 and Aidan Chambers's collection of *Signal* articles, *The Signal Approach to Children's Literature* in 1980).
2 See Hollindale (1988); Lesnik-Oberstein (1994); Meek (1995); Lyon (2003); and Nodelman (2008).
3 The first *Blue Peter* time-capsule was buried in 1971, followed by further capsules in 1984, 1998 and 2000. The 1998 capsule includes a novel by Roald Dahl.
4 Nabokov's phrase is taken from an unpublished lecture given at Wellesley College in the late 1940s.
5 See Waller (2005).

Bibliography

Memoirs/autobiographies by children's writers

Adams, R. (1990), *The Day Gone By: An Autobiography*. London: Hutchinson.

Aiken, J. (1974), 'Joan Aiken', in *Pied Pipers: Interviews with the Influential Creators of Children's Literature*, ed. J. Wintle and E. Fisher. London: Paddington Press, pp. 161–8.

B. B. (1978), *A Child Alone: The Memoirs of 'BB'*, illus. D. J. Watkins-Pitchford. London: Michael Joseph.

Bawden, N. (1994), *In My Own Time: Almost an Autobiography*. London: Virago.

Blyton, Enid ([1952] 1986), *The Story of My Life*. London: Grafton Books.

Boston, L. (1979), *Perverse and Foolish*. London: Bodley Head.

Buchan, J. ([1940] 1984), *Memory Hold-the-Door*. London: Dent.

Crossley-Holland, K. (2009), *The Hidden Roads: A Memoir of Childhood*. London: Quercus.

Farjeon, E. ([1935] 1960), *A Nursery in the Nineties*. London: Oxford University Press.

Garner, A. (1974), 'Alan Garner', in *Pied Pipers: Interviews with the Influential Creators of Children's Literature*, ed. J. Wintle and E. Fisher. London: Paddington Press, pp. 223–9.

Garnett, E. ([1982] 1985), *First Affections: Some Autobiographical Chapters on Early Childhood*. Oxford: Isis.

Gavin, J. (2007), *Walking on My Hands: Out of India – The Teenage Years*. London: Hodder Children's Books.

Godden, J. and Godden, R. (1966), *Two Under the Indian Sun*. London: Macmillan.

Goudge, E. (1974), *The Joy of the Snow: An Autobiography*. London: Hodder and Stoughton.

Grahame, K. ([1898] 1929), *Dream Days*. London: Thomas Nelson.

Hughes, S. (2002), *A Life Drawing: Recollections of an Illustrator*. London: Random House.

Kerr, J. ([1992] 2015), 'Judith Kerr', in *The Pleasure of Reading: 43 Writers on the Discovery of Reading and the Books That Inspired Them* (2nd edn), ed. A. Fraser. London: Bloomsbury, pp. 51–8.

Kipling, R. ([1937] 1991), *Something of Myself and Other Autobiographical Writings*, ed. T. Pinney. Cambridge: Cambridge University Press.

Lewis, C. S. ([1955] 2012), *Surprised by Joy: The Shape of My Early Life*. London: HarperCollins.

Lively, P. ([1994] 1995), *Oleander, Jacaranda: A Childhood Perceived*. London: Penguin.

McGough, R. ([1992] 2015), 'Roger McGough', in *The Pleasure of Reading: 43 Writers on the Discovery of Reading and the Books That Inspired Them* (2nd edn), ed. A. Fraser. London: Bloomsbury, pp. 150–5.

Mitchison, N. (1973), *Small Talk: Memories of an Edwardian Childhood*. London: Bodley Head.

Potter, B. ([1929] 1977), '"*Roots*" of the Peter Rabbit Tales', in *The Cool Web: The Pattern of Children's Reading*, ed. M. Meek, A. Warlow and G. Barton. London: Bodley Head, pp. 188–91.

Pullein-Thompson, J., Pullein-Thompson, C. and Pullein-Thompson, D. (1996), *Fair Girls and Grey Horses*. London: Allison and Busby.

Pullman, P. (2001), 'Shedding Light: The Marsh Award for Children's Literature in Translation 2001'. *School Librarian*, 49(1), 6–7.

Ransome, A. ([1976] 1985), *The Autobiography of Arthur Ransome*, ed. R. Hart-Davis. London: Century Publishing.

Sutcliff, R. (1983), *Blue Remembered Hills: A Recollection*. London: Bodley Head.

Townsend, S. ([1992] 2015), 'Sue Townsend', in *The Pleasure of Reading: 43 Writers on the Discovery of Reading and the Books That Inspired Them* (2nd edn), ed. A. Fraser. London: Bloomsbury, pp. 219–24.

Uttley, A. (1937), *Ambush of Young Days*. London: Faber and Faber.

Westall, R. (2006), *The Making of Me: A Writer's Childhood*. London: Catnip.

Wilson, J. ([2009] 2010), *My Secret Diary: Dating, Dancing, Dreams and Dilemmas*. London: Corgi.

Childhood books

Details of specific editions referred to in this book are included in the References.

Adams, R. (1972), *Watership Down*.

Alcott, L. M. (1869), *Little Women*.

Alcott, L. M. (1869), *Good Wives*.

Ally Sloper's Half Holiday comics (1884–1916).

Andersen, H. C. (1843), 'The Ugly Duckling'.

Andersen, H. C. (1845), 'The Little Match Girl'.

Andersen, H. C. (1858), *The Marsh King's Daughter.*

Ballantyne, R. M. (1858), *The Coral Island.*

Bates, L. (1975), *Little Rabbit's Loose Tooth*, illus. D. de Groat.

Beecher Stowe, H. (1852), *Uncle Tom's Cabin.*

Blackmore, R. D. (1869), *Lorna Doone.*

Blyton, E. (1943), *The Magic Faraway Tree.*

Blyton, E. (1946–51), *Mallory Towers* series.

Blyton, E. (1947), *Enid Blyton's Treasury.*

Blyton, E. (1949), *The Mystery of the Pantomime Cat.*

Bourne, L. R. (1927), *Coppernob Second Mate.*

Brontë, C. (1847), *Jane Eyre.*

Buckley, A. (1901), *Eyes and No Eyes.*

Bunyan, J. (1678), *The Pilgrim's Progress.*

Burnett, F. H. (1911), *The Secret Garden.*

Carroll, L. (1865), *Alice's Adventures in Wonderland.*

Carroll, L. (1871), *Through the Looking Glass, and What Alice Found There.*

Carry, C. E. (1885), *Davy and the Goblin: Or What Followed Reading 'Alice's Adventures in Wonderland'.*

The Children's Wonder Book (1933).

Christopher, J. (1970), *The Guardians.*

Clewes, D. (1956), *Guide Dog.*

Cormier, R. (1988), *Fade.*

Crompton, R. (1921–70), *Just William* series.

Davison, F. D. (1936), *Children of the Dark People.*

Dearmer, M. (1914), *The Cockyolly Bird.*

Defoe, D. (1719), *Robinson Crusoe.*

De la Mare, W. (1924), *Three Royal Monkeys.*

De Segur, Mme (1858), *Les Malheurs de Sophie.*

Dickens, C. (1839), *Nicholas Nickleby.*

Dumas, A. (1845), *The Count of Monte Cristo.*

Falkner, J. M. (1898), *Moonfleet.*

Fisk, N. (1973), *Grinny.*

Gallico, P. (1950), *Jennie.*

Garfield, J. B. (1957), *Follow My Leader.*

Gautier, T. (1863), *Captain Fracasse.*

Golding, W. (1954), *The Lord of the Flies.*

Goudge, E. (1946), *The Little White Horse.*
Grahame, E. (1938), *The Children Who Lived in a Barn.*
Grahame, K. (1908), *The Wind in the Willows.*
Haggard, H. R. (1885), *King Solomon's Mines.*
Hardy, T. (1872), *Under the Greenwood Tree.*
Harnett, C. (1949), *The Great House.*
Hay, I. (1907), *Pip: A Romance of Youth.*
Haywood, C. (1939), *'B' Is for Betsy.*
Heidi, Girl of the Alps anime series (1974).
Henry, M. (1949), *King of the Wind.*
Hill, L. (1950–63), *Sadler's Wells* series.
Jacobs, J. (1890), 'Jack and the Beanstalk'.
James, M. R. (1904), 'Lost Hearts'.
Jefferies, R. (1879), *Wild Life in a Southern Country.*
Jefferies, R. (1879), *The Amateur Poacher.*
Jefferies, R. (1882), *Bevis.*
Jefferies, R. (1884), *Life of the Fields.*
Jones, D. W. (1985), *Fire and Hemlock.*
Kingsley, C. (1863), *The Water Babies.*
Kingston, W. H. G. (1901), *Old Jack.*
Ladybird. (1964–) *Key Words* reading scheme.
Ladybird. (1946), *Downy Duckling.*
Lang, A. (1889–1930), *Fairy Books.*
Lee, H. (1960), *To Kill a Mockingbird.*
Lewis, C. S. (1950–56), *The Chronicles of Narnia* series.
Lewis, C. S. (1953), *The Silver Chair.*
Lewis, C. S. (1954), *The Horse and His Boy.*
Letts, W. M. (1907), *The Story Spinner.*
Linklater, E. (1944), *The Wind on the Moon.*
Linklater, E. (1949), *Pirates of the Deep Green Sea.*
Linnet, B. (1906), *Why-Why and Tom-Cat*, illus. G. Brown.
Lofting, H. (1920–52), *Dr Doolittle* series.
London, J. (1903), *Call of the Wild.*
Lubbock, J. (1882), *Ants, Bees and Wasps.*
Meade, L. T. (1892), *Four on an Island: A Story of Adventure.*
Mee, A. (1910–64), *The Book of Knowledge: The Children's Encyclopedia.*
Milne, A. A. (1924), 'At Home'.

Milne, A. A. (1924), *When We Were Very Young.*

Milne, A. A. (1926), *Winnie-the-Pooh.*

Milne, A. A. (1927), *Now We Are Six.*

Milne, A. A. (1928), *The House at Pooh Corner.*

Montgomery, L. M. (1908), *Anne of Green Gables.*

Montgomery, L. M. (1923), *Emily of New Moon.*

Muir, F. (1981), *What-a-Mess and the Cat Next Door*, illus. J. Wright.

Nabokov, V. (1950), *Lolita.*

Norton, A. (1952), *Star Man's Son: 2250 AD.*

Potter, B. (1903), *The Tale of Squirrel Nutkin.*

Puck comics (1904–40).Pullman, P. (1995), *Northern Lights.*

Ransome, A. (1930), *Swallows and Amazons.*

Ransome, A. (1939), *Secret Water.*

Rogerson, J. (1980), *Crown* readers.

Salinger, J. D. (1951), *The Catcher in the Rye.*

Schonell, F. (1939), *Happy Ventures* readers.

School Friend comics (1919–29).

Scott, W. (1817), *Rob Roy.*

Segur, Comptess de (1863), *L'Auberge d l'Ange-Gardien.*

Sewell, A. (1877), *Black Beauty.*

Sherwood, M. (1818), *The Little Woodman and His Dog Caesar.*

Smith, D. (1948), *I Capture the Castle.*

Spyri, J. (1880–81), *Heidi.*

St. John, P. M. (1950), *Treasures of the Snow.*

Stevenson, R. L. (1883), *Treasure Island.*

Stevenson, R. L. (1885), *A Child's Garden of Verses.*

Streatfeild, N. (1936), *Ballet Shoes.*

Streatfeild, N. (1962), *Apple Bough.*

Streatfeild, N. (1968–9), *Gemma* series.

Swift, J. (1726), *Gulliver's Travels.*

Thompson Seton, E. (1898), *Wild Animals I Have Known.*

Trimmer, S. (1786), *Fabulous Histories.*

Turner, E. (1894), *Seven Little Australians.*

Wetherell, E. (1850), *The Wide Wide World.*

Wilder, L. I. (1932–43), *Little House* series.

Wyss, J. D. (1812), *The Swiss Family Robinson.*

References

Abrams, L. (2014), 'Liberating the Female Self: Epiphanies, Conflict and Coherence in the Life Stories of Post-War British Women'. *Social History*, 39(1), 14–35.

Adams, R. (1972), *Watership Down*. London: Rex Collings.

Adams, R. (1977), *The Plague Dogs*. London: Allan Lane.

Ahmed, S. (2004), *The Cultural Politics of Emotion*. Edinburgh: Edinburgh University Press.

Aiken, J. (1975), *The Angel Inn*. London: Cape.

Alcott, L. M. ([1868] 1957), *Little Women*. London: Dean and Son.

Alcott, L. M. and Farrer, M. (1947), *Little Women by Louisa M. Alcott; Retold by Marjorie Rowe*, illus. G. King. Maidenhead: Purnell.

Alcott, L. M. and Page, J. (1950), *Little Women: Retold by Josephine Page*. London: Oxford University Press.

Andersen, H. C. (1899), *Fairy Tales from Hans Christian Andersen*, trans. E. Lucas, illus. T. Robinson, C. Robinson and W. H. Robinson. London: Dent.

Andersen, H. C. (1913), *Hans Andersen Fairy Tales*, trans. unknown, illus. W. H. Robinson. London: Constable.

Anon. ([1744] 1760), *A Little Pretty Pocket-Book, Intended for the Instruction and Amusement of Little Master Tommy and Pretty Miss Polly*. London: Newbery.

Appleyard, J. A. (1991), *Becoming a Reader: The Experience of Fiction from Childhood to Adulthood*. Cambridge: Cambridge University Press.

Armstrong, J. (2003), 'New Anticipations of the Past'. *Children's Literature in Education*, 34(3), 249–55.

Attebery, B. (2014), *Stories about Stories: Fantasy and the Remaking of Myth*. Oxford: Oxford University Press.

Attenborough, D. (1993), *Shadowlands*. Paramount Pictures.

B. B. (1942), *The Little Grey Men*. London: Eyre & Spottiswoode.

B. B. (1944), *Brendon Chase*. London: Hollis & Carter

Ball, J. C. (1997), 'Max's Colonial Fantasy: Rereading Sendak's *Where the Wild Things Are*'. *Ariel*, 28(1), 167–79.

Ballard, J. G. ([1992] 2015), 'J. G. Ballard', in *The Pleasure of Reading: 43 Writers on the Discovery of Reading and the Books that Inspired Them* (2nd edn), ed. A. Fraser. London: Bloomsbury, pp. 88–95.

Barnett, T. (2013), '"Reading Saved Me": Writing Autobiographically about Transformative Reading Experiences in Childhood'. *Prose Studies*, 35(1), 84–96.

Barthes, R. (1975a), *The Pleasure of the Text*, trans. R. Miller, with a note on the text by R. Howard. New York: Hill and Wang. First published in French 1973.

Barthes, R. (1975b), *S/Z*, trans. R. Miller. London: Jonathan Cape. First published in French 1970.

Barthes, R. (1977), 'The Death of the Author', in *Image Music Text*, trans. S. Heath. London: Fontana Press, pp. 142–8. First published in French 1968.

Barthes, R. (1979), *A Lover's Discourse*, trans. R. Howard. London: Cape. First published in French 1977.

Bauer P. ([2007] 2014), *Remembering the Times of Our Lives: Memory in Infancy and Beyond*. New York: Psychology Press.

Bayard, P. (2008), *How to Talk about Books You Haven't Read*, trans. J. Mehlman. London: Granta Books.

Beauvais, C. (2015), *The Mighty Child: Time and Power in Children's Literature*. Amsterdam: John Benjamin.

Benjamin, W. ([1926] 1996), 'A Glimpse into the World of Children's Books', in *Selected Writings: Volume 1, 1913–1926*, ed. M. Bullock and M. W. Jennings. Cambridge, MA: Harvard University Press, pp. 435–43.

Benjamin, W. ([1928] 1996), 'One Way Street', in *Selected Writings: Volume 1, 1913–1926*, ed. M. Bullock and M. W. Jennings. Cambridge, MA: The Belknap Press of Harvard University Press, pp. 444–88.

Benjamin, W. ([1939] 1999), 'Berlin Chronicle', in *Selected Writings: Volume 2, 1927–1934*, ed. M. W. Jennings, H. Eiland and G. Smith, trans. R. Livingstone et al. Cambridge, MA: The Belknap Press of Harvard University Press, pp. 595–637.

Benjamin, W. (2014), 'Children's Literature', in *Radio Benjamin*, ed. L. Rosenthal, trans J. Lutes, L. Harries and D. K. Reese. London: Verso. First broadcast in 1929.

Bernstein, R. (2011), 'Children's Books, Dolls, and the Performance of Race; Or the Possibility of Children's Literature'. *PMLA*, 126(1), 160–9.

Blue Peter (1958–). British Broadcasting Corporation.

Blyton, E. ([1943] 2007), *The Magic Faraway Tree*, illus. P. Hess. London: Egmont.

Book of Common Prayer of the Church of England: Adopted for General Use in Other Protestant Churches, The (1852) (2nd edn). London: E. T. Whitfield.

Borges, J. L. ([1942] 1970), 'Funes the Memorious', in *Labyrinths: Selected Stories and Other Writings*, ed. D. A. Yates, trans. J. E. Irby. Harmondsworth: Penguin, pp. 87–95.

Bornat, J. (1989), 'Oral History as a Social Movement: Reminiscence and Older People'. *Oral History*, 17(2), 16–24.

Boruah, B. H. (1988), *Fiction and Emotion: A Study in Aesthetics and the Philosophy of Mind*. Oxford: Clarendon Press.

Boscagli, M. (2014), *Stuff Theory: Everyday Objects, Radical Materialism*. London: Bloomsbury.

Boym, S. (2001), *The Future of Nostalgia*. New York: Basic Books.

Brannen, J. and Nilsen, A. (2002), 'Young People's Time Perspectives: From Youth to Adulthood'. *Sociology*, 36(3), 513–38.

Brewer, W. F. (1986), 'What Is Autobiographical Memory?', in *Autobiographical Memory*, ed. D. C. Rubin. Cambridge: Cambridge University Press, pp. 25–49.

Brewer, W. F. (1996), 'The Nature of Narrative Suspense and the Problem of Rereading', in *Suspense: Conceptualizations, Theoretical Analyses, and Empirical Explorations*, ed. P. Voderer et al. London: Routledge, pp. 107–27.

Brown, S. and Reavey, P. (2015), *Vital Memory and Affect: Living with a Difficult Past*. London: Routledge.

Bruner, J. (1986), *Actual Minds, Possible Worlds*. Cambridge, MA: Harvard University Press.

Butler, C. (2006), *Four British Fantasists: Place and Culture in the Children's Fantasies of Penelope Lively, Alan Garner, Diana Wynne Jones, and Susan Cooper*. Lanham, MD: Scarecrow Press.

Călinescu, M. (1993), *Rereading*. New Haven: Yale University Press.

Calvino, I. ([1991] 1999), *Why Read the Classics?*, trans. M. McLaughlin. London: Jonathan Cape.

Campbell, N. (2017), *Children's Neo-Romanticism: The Archaeological Imagination in Post-War Children's Fantasy*. PhD thesis, University of Roehampton.

Carroll, J. S. (2012), *Landscape in Children's Literature*. London: Routledge.

Carroll, N. (1990), *The Philosophy of Horror; Or Paradoxes of the Heart*. London: Routledge.

Carruthers, M. (2008), *The Book of Memory: A Study of Memory in Medieval Culture*. Cambridge: Cambridge University Press.

Chambers, A. (ed.) (1980), *The Signal Approach to Children's Literature*. London: Kestrel Books.

Chambers, A. (1991), *The Reading Environment: How Adults Help Children Enjoy Books*. Stroud: Thimble Press.

Cheatley, F. (1994), 'Revisiting Some Icons of the Golden Age'. *Papers*, 5(2), 104–8.

Clark, C. and Teravainen, A. (2017), *Celebrating Reading for Enjoyment: Findings from Our Annual Literacy Survey 2016*. London: National Literacy Trust.

Clewes, D. ([1956] 1964), *Guide Dog*, illus. P. Burchard. New York: Coward-McCann.

Clewes, D. ([1956] 1965), *Guide Dog*. London: Hamish Hamilton.

Cliff-Hodges, G., Nikolajeva, M. and Taylor, L. (2010), 'Three Walks Through Fictional Fens: Multidisciplinary Perspectives on *Gaffer Samson's Luck*'. *Children's Literature in Education*, 41(3), 189–206.

Coats, K. (2009), 'Wet Work and Dry Work: Notes from a Lacanian Mother', in *A Narrative Compass: Stories That Guide Women's Lives*, ed. B. Hearne and R. Seelinger Trites. Urbana: University of Illinois Press, pp. 68–79.

Coats, K. (2017), 'Empathy and the Early Reader', in *The Bloomsbury Introduction to Children's and Young Adult Literature*, ed. K. Coats. London: Bloomsbury, pp. 391–9.

Corcoran, B. and Evans, E. (eds) (1987), *Readers, Texts, Teachers*. Milton Keynes: Open University Press.

Crago, H. (1979), 'Cultural Categories and the Criticism of Children's Literature'. *Signal*, 30, 40–50.

Crago, H. (1982), 'The Readers in the Reader: An Experiment in Personal Response and Literary Criticism'. *Signal*, 39, 172–82.

Crago, H. (1986), 'A Signal Conversation'. *Signal*, 50, 122–40.

Crago, H. (1990), 'Childhood Reading Revisited'. *Papers*, 1(3), 99–115.

Crago, H. (2014), *Entranced by Story: Brain, Tale and Teller, from Infancy to Old Age*. New York: Routledge.

Crago, M. and Crago, H. (1983), *Prelude to Literacy: A Preschool Child's Encounter with Picture and Story*. Carbondale: Southern Illinois University Press.

Cremin, T. (2007), 'Revisiting Reading for Pleasure; Diversity, Delight and Desire', in *Understanding Phonics and the Teaching of Reading*, ed. K. Goouch and A. Lambirth. Berkshire: McGraw Hill, pp. 166–90.

Cremin, T., Bearne, E., Mottram, M. and Goodwin, P. (2008), 'Primary Teachers as Readers'. *English in Education*, 42, 8–23.

Culler, J. ([1975] 2002), *Structuralist Poetics*. London: Routledge.

Currie, M. (2006), *About Time: Narrative, Fiction and the Philosophy of Time*. Edinburgh: Edinburgh University Press.

Currie, M. (2013), *The Unexpected: Narrative, Temporality and the Philosophy of Surprise*. Edinburgh: Edinburgh University Press.

Curtis, J. (1984), 'On Re-Reading *The Hobbit*, Fifteen Years Later'. *Children's Literature in Education*, 15(2), 113–20.

Darnton, R. (1990), 'First Steps Toward a History of Reading', in *The Kiss of Lamourette: Reflections in Cultural History*. London: Faber and Faber, pp. 154–88.

de Bóo, M. (ed.) (2008), *You Must Remember This*. London: Third Age Trust.

Dennett, D. (1991), *Consciousness Explained*. Boston: Little, Brown.

Denzin, N. K. (2013), *Interpretative Autoethnicity*. London: Sage.

Dickens, C. ([1843] 2006), 'A Christmas Carol', in *A Christmas Carol and Other Christmas Books*, ed. R. Douglas-Fairhurst. Oxford: Oxford University Press, pp. 9–83.

Dickens, C. ([1860] 1958), 'Nurse's Stories', in *The Uncommercial Traveller*. Oxford: Oxford University Press.

Dickinson, P. (1970), 'A Defence of Rubbish'. *Children's Literature in Education*, 1(3), 7–10.

Dolan, F. E. (2013), 'Mastery at Misselthwaite Manor: Taming the Shrews in *The Secret Garden*'. *Children's Literature*, 41, 204–24.

Durrans, B. (2014), 'Time Capsules as Extreme Collecting', in *Extreme Collecting: Challenging Practices for 21st Century Museums*, ed. G. Were and J. C. H. King. Oxford: Berghahn Books, pp. 181–202.

Dusinberre, J. (1987), *Alice to the Lighthouse*. Basingstoke: Macmillan.

Eddy, J. (2006), *Bookwomen: Creating an Empire in Children's Book Publishing 1919–1939*. Madison: University of Wisconsin Press.

Edgeworth, M. ([1796] 1854), *The Parent's Assistant*. New York: C. S. Francis & Co.

Eich, E., Macaulay, D. and Ryan, L. (1994), 'Mood Dependent Memory for Events of the Personal Past'. *Journal of Experimental Psychology*, 123, 201–15.

Ellis, S. (2014), *How To Be a Heroine: Or What I've Learned from Reading Too Much*. London: Vintage Books.

Emrys, E. (1987), 'Readers Recreating Texts', in *Readers, Texts, Teachers*, ed. B. Corcoran and E. Emrys. Milton Keynes: Open University Press, pp. 22–40.

Ender, E. (2005), *Architexts of Memory: Literature, Science, and Autobiography*. Ann Arbor: University of Michigan Press.

Esrock, E. J. (1998), 'Taking a Second Look: The Reader's Visual Image', in *Second Thoughts: A Focus on Rereading*, ed. D. Galef. Detroit, MI: Wayne State University Press, pp. 152–66.

Even-Zohar, I. (1979), 'Polysystem Theory'. *Poetics Today*, 1(1–2), 287–310.

Fadiman, A. (2005), *Rereadings: Seventeen Writers Revisit Books They Love*. New York: Farrar, Straus and Giroux.

Fair, T. (2014), '19th-Century English Girls' Adventure Stories: Domestic Imperialism, Agency, and the Female Robinsonades'. *Rocky Mountain Review of Language and Literature*, 68(2), 142–58.

Falconer, R. (2008), *The Crossover Novel*. London: Routledge.

Feagin, S. L. (1996), *Reading with Feeling: The Aesthetics of Appreciation*. Ithaca, NY: Cornell University Press.

Felman, S. and Laub, D. (1992), *Testimony: Crises of Witnessing in Literature, Psychoanalysis, and History*. London: Taylor & Francis.

Fernyhough, C. (2012), *Pieces of Light: The New Science of Memory*. London: Profile Books.

Fish, S. (1999), 'Just Published: Minutiae without Meaning', *New York Times*, 7 September. http://www.writing.upenn.edu/~afilreis/88v/fish-biography.html (accessed 3 February 2016).

Fisher, P. (2002), *The Vehement Passions*. Princeton: Princeton University Press.

Flint, K. (2012), 'What Can Reading Do?' *Novel*, 45(1), 19–22.

Foster, S. and Simons, J. (1995), *What Katy Read: Feminist Re-readings of 'Classic' Stories for Girls*. Basingstoke: Macmillan.

Fraser, A. (ed.) ([1992] 2015), *The Pleasure of Reading: 43 Writers on the Discovery of Reading and the Books That Inspired Them* (2nd edn). London: Bloomsbury.

Freud, S. ([1899] 1959), 'Screen Memories', in *The Standard Edition of the Complete Psychological Works of Sigmund Freud: Early Psychoanalytic Publications* (vol. 3), trans. and ed. J. Strachey, ed. A. Freud. London: Hogarth Press, pp. 303–22.

Freud, S. and Breuer, J. ([1895] 2004), *Studies on Hysteria*, trans. N. Luckhurst. London: Penguin.

Fry, D. (1985), *Children Talk about Books: Seeing Themselves as Readers*. Milton Keynes: Open University Press.

Fuller, D. and Rehberg Sedo, D. (2013), *Reading Beyond the Book: The Social Practices of Contemporary Literary Culture*. London: Routledge.

Gaiman, N. (2002), *Coraline*. London: Bloomsbury.

Gallico, P. ([1950] 1973), *Jennie*. London: Michael Joseph.

Geertz, C. (1973), 'Thick Description: Toward an Interpretative Theory of Culture', in *The Interpretation of Cultures: Selected Essays*. New York: Basic Books, pp. 3–30.

Gekoski, R. (2009), *Outside of a Dog: A Bibliomemoir*. London: Constable.

Gibson, M. (2015), *Remembered Reading: Memory, Comics and Post-War Constructions of British Girlhood*. Leuven: Leuven University Press.

González, J. A. (1995), 'Autotopographies', in *Prosthetic Territories: Politics and Hypertechnologies*, ed. G. Brahm, Jr and M. Driscoll. San Francisco: Westview Press, pp. 133–50.

González-Ruibal, A. (2013), *Reclaiming Archaeology: Beyond the Tropes of Modernity*. Abingdon: Routledge.

Greenway, B. (ed.) (1995), *Twice-Told Children's Tales: The Influence of Childhood Reading on Writers for Adults*. London: Routledge.

Grenby, M. O. (2009), 'The Origins of Children's Literature', in *The Cambridge Companion to Children's Literature*, ed. M. Grenby and A. Immel. Cambridge: Cambridge University Press, pp. 3–18.

Grenby, M. O. (2011), *The Child Reader, 1700–1840*. Cambridge: Cambridge University Press.

Groube, L. (1981), 'Black Holes in British Prehistory: The Analysis of Settlement Distribution', in *Patterns of the Past: Studies in the Honour of David Clarke*, ed. I. Hodder, G. Isaac and N. Hammond. Cambridge: Cambridge University Press, pp. 185–210.

Gubar, M. (2013), 'Risky Business: Talking about Children in Children's Literature Criticism'. *Children's Literature Association Quarterly*, 38(4), 450–57.

Gupta, S. (2003), *Re-Reading Harry Potter*. London: Palgrave.

Guthrie, J. T. and Wigfield, A. (2000), 'Engagement and Motivation in Reading', in *Handbook of Reading Research* (3rd edn), ed. M. L. Kamil, K. B. Mosenthal, P. D. Pearson and R. Barr. Longman: New York.

Hacking, I. (1995), *Rewriting the Soul: Multiple Personality and the Sciences of Memory*. Princeton: Princeton University Press.

Haigh, J. D. (1991), 'C. S. Lewis and the Tradition of Visionary Romance', in *Word and Story in C. S. Lewis*, ed. P. J. Schakel and C. A. Huttar. Columbia: University of Missouri Press, pp. 182–98.

Halbwachs, M. ([1952] 1992), *On Collective Memory*, ed. and trans. Lewis Coser. Chicago: University of Chicago Press. First published in German 1941.

Handy, B. (2017), *Wild Things: The Joy of Reading Children's Literature as an Adult*. New York: Simon and Schuster.

Harde, R. and Kokkola, L. (2017), *The Embodied Child: Readings in Children's Literature and Culture*. London: Routledge.

Hassabis, D. and Maguire, A. E. (2007), 'Deconstructing Episodic Memory with Construction'. *Trends in Cognitive Sciences*, 11, 299–306.

Haug, F. (2000), 'Memory-Work as a Method of Social Science Research: A Detailed Rendering of Memory Work Method', in *Dissecting the Mundane: International Perspectives on Memory-Work*, ed. A. E. Hale et al. Lanham, MD: University Press of America, pp. 21–41.

Heddon, D. (2002), 'Autotopography: Graffiti, Landscapes and Selves'. *Reconstruction: Studies in Contemporary Culture*, 2(3), n.p.

Hennegan, A. (1998), 'On Becoming a Lesbian Reader', in *Sweet Dreams: Sexuality, Gender and Popular Fiction*, ed. S. Radstone. London: Lawrence and Wishart, pp. 165–90.

Higgs, P. and Gilleard, C. (2015), *Rethinking Old Age: Theorising the Fourth Age*. Basingstoke: Palgrave Macmillan.

Hill, S. (2009), *Howards End Is on the Landing: A Year of Reading from Home*. London: Profile.

Hodder, I. (2014), *Archaeological Theory Today*. Oxford: Wiley/Blackwell.

Holdsworth, A. (2011), *Television, Memory and Nostalgia*. Basingstoke: Palgrave Macmillan.

Hollindale, P. (1988), *Ideology and the Children's Book*. Stroud: Thimble Press.

Hollindale, P. (1997), *Signs of Childness*. Stroud: Thimble Press.

Horne, J. (2011), *History and the Construction of the Child in Early British Children's Literature*. Farnham: Ashgate, pp. 239–46.

Hunt, P. (1991), *Criticism, Theory, & Children's Literature*. Oxford: Blackwell.

Hunt, P. (2001), *Children's Literature*. Oxford: Blackwell.

Hunt, P. (2009), Personal correspondence. 7 May.

Hutcheon, L. (2000), 'Irony, Nostalgia and the Postmodern', in *Methods for the Study of Literature as Cultural Memory*, ed. R. Vervliet and A. Estor. Amsterdam: Rodopi, pp. 189–207.

Immel, A. (2013), 'Children's Books', in *The Book: A Global History*, ed. M. F. Suarez and H. R. Woudhuysen. Oxford: Oxford University Press, pp. 220–30.

Ingarden, R. (1973), *TheCognition of the Literary Work of Art*, trans. R. A. Crowly and K. R. Olsen. Evanston, IL: Northwestern University Press. First published in Polish 1937.

Inglis, F. (1981), *The Promise of Happiness: Value and Meaning in Children's Fiction*. Cambridge: Cambridge University Press.

Iser, W. (1974), *The Implied Reader*. Baltimore: Johns Hopkins University Press.

Jansson, T. ([1945–70] 1950–78), *The Moomin* series. London: Ernest Benn.

Jensen, H. S. (2018), 'Making Children's "Classics", Making Past Childhoods: Children's "Classics" as Sites for Memory Politics and Nostalgia', in *Reinventing Childhood Nostalgia*, ed. E. Wesseling. London: Routledge, British Library digital collection (accessed 24 March 2018), location 323–77.

Jones, D. W. ([1985] 2000), *Fire and Hemlock*. London: HarperCollins.

Jones, D. W. ([1988] 2012), 'Something about the Author', in *Reflections on the Magic of Writing*. Oxford: David Fickling Books, pp. 210–41.

Jones, K. (2006), 'Getting Rid of Children's Literature'. *The Lion and the Unicorn*, 30(3), 287–315.

Kästner, E. (2015), *Emil and the Detectives*. London: Penguin. First published in German 1929.

Kidd, K. (2011), 'The Child, the Scholar, and the Children's Literature Archive'. *The Lion and the Unicorn*, 35(1), 1–23.

Klinkenborg, V. (2009), 'Some Thoughts on the Pleasures of Being a Re-Reader', *New York Times*, 29 May.

Knoepflmacher, U. C. (1983), 'Little Girls without Their Curls: Female Aggression in Victorian Children's Literature'. *Children's Literature*, 11, 14–31.

Knoepflmacher, U. C. (2002), 'The Critic as Former Child: A Personal Narrative'. *Papers*, 12(1), 5–9.

Krips, V. (2000), *The Presence of the Past: Memory, Heritage, and Childhood in Postwar Britain*. New York: Garland.

Kuhn, A. ([1995] 2000), *Family Secrets: Acts of Memory and Imagination* (2nd edn). London: Verso.

Lamarque, P. (1981), 'How Can We Fear and Pity Fictions?' *British Journal of Aesthetics*, 21(4), 291–304.

LaMotta, V. M. (2012), 'Behavioral Archaeology', in Archaeological Theory Today, ed. I. Hodder. Oxford: Polity Press, pp. 62–92.

Larsen, S. (1987), 'Remembering and the Archaeology Metaphor'. *Metaphor and Symbolic Activity*, 2(3), 187–99.

Laslett, P. (1989), *A Fresh Map of Life: The Emergence of the Third Age*. London: Weidenfeld and Nicolson.

Lathey, G. (2010), *The Role of Translators in Children's Literature: Invisible Storytellers*. London: Routledge.

Lathey, G. (2015), *Translating Children's Literature*. London: Routledge.

Le Guin, U. (2006), 'Imaginary Friends', *New Statesman*, 18 December. www.newstatesman.com/node/166019 (accessed 3 April 2018).

Leavis, Q. D. (1932), *Fiction and the Reading Public*. London: Chatto & Windus.

Lehrer, J. (2007), *Proust Was a Neuroscientist*. New York: Houghton Miffin.

Lesnik-Oberstein, K. (1994), *Children's Literature: Criticism and the Fictional Child*. Oxford: Clarendon Press.

Lesnik-Oberstein, K. (ed.) (2004), *Children's Literature: New Approaches*. Basingstoke: Palgrave Macmillan.

Lesser, W. (2002), *Nothing Remains the Same:Rereading and Remembering*. Boston: Houghton Mifflin.

Lessing, D. (1999), 'Doris Lessing', in *For the Love of Books: 15 Celebrated Writers on the Books They Love Most*, ed. R. B. Shwartz. New York: Berkely Books, pp. 149–53.

Lewin, K. (1936), *Principles of Topological Psychology*. New York: McGraw Hill.

Lewis, C. S. ([1945] 1970), 'Meditation in a Toolshed', in *God in the Dock: Essays on Theology and Ethics*, ed. W. Hooper. Cambridge: Eerdmans, pp. 212–15.

Lewis, C. S. (1950), *The Lion, the Witch, and the Wardrobe*. London: Geoffrey Bles.

Lewis, C. S. ([1954] 1980), *The Horse and His Boy*. London: Armada Lions.

Lewis, C. S. ([1961] 1969), *An Experiment in Criticism*. Cambridge: Cambridge University Press.

Lewis, C. S. ([1966] 1982), *Of Other Worlds: Essays and Stories*. London: Bles.

Littau, K. (2006), *Theories of Reading: Books, Bodies, and Bibliomania*. Oxford: Polity Press.

Loftus, E. (1993), 'The Reality of Repressed Memories'. *American Psychologist*, 48, 518–37.

Longfellow, H. W. (1850), 'Tegnér's Death', in *The Seaside and the Fireside*. London: Ticknor, Reed and Fields, pp. 77–81.

Lyon, B. (2003), *Kiddie Lit: The Cultural Construction of Children's Literature in America*. Baltimore: Johns Hopkins University Press.

Lyons, M. and Taksa, L. (eds) (1992), *Australian Readers Remember: An Oral History of Reading, 1890–1930*. Oxford: Oxford University Press.

Mackey, M. (2013), 'The Emergent Reader's Working Kit of Stereotypes'. *Children's Literature in Education*, 44(2), 87–103.

Mackey, M. (2016), *One Child Reading: My Auto-Bibliography*. Edmonton: University of Alberta Press.

Maguire, E. A., Intraub, H. and Mullally, S. L. (2016), 'Scenes, Spaces, and Memory Traces: What Does the Hippocampus Do?' *Neuroscientist*, 22(5), 432–9.

Mahy, M. (1987), 'Joining the Network'. *Signal*, 54, 151–60.

Mahy, M. (2000), 'Touchstones: The Interpretation of Adult Experience by the Images of Childhood Reading', in *A Dissolving Ghost: Essays and More*. Wellington: Victoria University Press, pp. 81–91.

Maine, F. and Waller, A. (2011), '*Swallows and Amazons Forever*! How Adults and Children Engage in Reading a Classic Text'. *Children's Literature in Education*, 42(4), 354–71.

Mangan, L. (2018), *Bookworm: A Memoir of Childhood Reading*. London: Square Peg.

Manguel, A. (2010), *A Reader on Reading*. New York: Yale.

Manlove, C. N. (2003), *From Alice to Harry Potter: Children's Fantasy in England*. Christchurch: Cybereditions.

Martens, L. (2011), *The Promise of Memory: Childhood Recollection and Its Objects in Literary Modernism*. Yale: Harvard University Press.

Maynard, S., MacKay, S., Smyth, F. and Reynolds, K. (2007), *Young People's Reading in 2005: The Second Study of Young People's Reading Habits*. London: Roehampton University and Loughborough University.

Meade, L. T. ([1892] n.d.), *Four on an Island: A Story of Adventure*, illus. W. Rainey. London: W&R Chambers.

Meek, M. (1988), *How Texts Teach What Readers Learn*. Stroud: Thimble Press.

Meek, M. (1995), 'The Constructedness of Children'. *Signal*, 76, 5–19.

Miall, D. S. and Kuiken, D. (2002), 'A Feeling for Fiction: Becoming What We Behold'. *Poetics*, 30, 221–41.

Miller, J. H. (2002), *On Literature*. London: Routledge.

Miller, J. H. (2004), 'Reading *The Swiss Family Robinson* as Virtual Reality', in *Children's Literature: New Approaches*, ed. Karin Lesnik-Oberstein. Basingstoke: Palgrave Macmillan, pp. 78–92.

Miller, L. (2008), *The Magician's Book: A Skeptic's Adventure in Narnia*. New York: Little, Brown.

Milne, A. A. ([1926] 2000), *Winnie-the-Pooh*, illus. E. H. Shephard. London: Egmont.

Montgomery, L. M. ([1908] 1964), *Anne of Green Gables*. London: Penguin.

Moore, A. C. (1920), *Roads to Childhood: Views and Reviews of Children's Books*. New York: George H. Doran.

Morrison, T. (1987), *Beloved*. New York: Knopf.

Moss, E. ([1974] 1977), 'The Adult-eration of Children's Books', in *The Cool Web: The Pattern of Children's Reading*, ed. M. Meek, A. Warlow and G. Barton. London: Bodley Head, pp. 333–7.

Nabokov, V. ([1966] 1969), *Speak, Memory: An Autobiography Revisited*. Harmondsworth: Penguin.

Nabokov, V. (1980), Lectures on Literature, ed. F. Bowers. New York: Harcourt.

Nalbantian, S. (2003), *Memory in Literature: From Rousseau to Neuroscience*. Basingstoke: Palgrave Macmillan.

Nell, V. (1988), *Lost in a Book: The Psychology of Reading for Pleasure*. New Haven: Yale University Press.

Ngai, S. (2005), *Ugly Feelings*. Cambridge, MA: Harvard University Press.

Nietzsche, F. ([1874] 1997), 'On the Uses and Disadvantages of History for Life', in *Untimely Mediations*, ed. D. Breazale, trans. R. J. Hollingdale. Cambridge: Cambridge University Press.

Nikolajeva, M. (2009), 'Theory, Post-Theory, and Aetonormative Theory'. *Neohelicon*, 36(1), 13–24.

Nikolajeva, M. (2013), '"Did You Feel as if You Hated People?": Emotional Literacy Through Fiction'. *New Review of Children's Literature and Librarianship*, 19(2), 95–107.

Nodelman, P. (2008), *The Hidden Adult: Defining Children's Literature*. Baltimore: Johns Hopkins University Press.

Norcia, M. (2004), 'Angel of the Island: L. T. Meade's New Girl as the Heir of a Nation-Making Robinson Crusoe'. *The Lion and the Unicorn*, 28(3), 345–62.

Norton, A. ([1952] 1968), *Star Man's Son: 2250 AD*, illus. V. Mordvinoff. London: Victor Gollancz.

Oatley, K. (1994), 'A Taxonomy of the Emotions of Literary Response and a Theory of Identification in Fictional Narrative'. *Poetics*, 23, 53–74.

Oatley, K. (2010), 'Re-reading Swallows and Amazons', *OnFiction*, 8 July. www.onfiction.ca/2010/07/re-reading-swallows-and-amazons.html (accessed 3 April 2018).

Odden, K. (1998), 'Retrieving Childhood Fantasies: A Psychoanalytic Look at Why We (Re)Read Popular Literature', in *Second Thoughts: A Focus on Rereading*, ed. D. Galef. Detroit, MI: Wayne State University Press, pp. 126–51.

Oittinen, R. (1989), 'On Translating for Children: A Finnish Point of View'. *Early Child Development and Care*, 48(1), 29–37.

Oittinen, R. (2014), 'No Innocent Act: On the Ethics of Translating for Children', in *Children's Literature in Translation: Challenges and Strategies*, ed. V. Coillie and W. P. Verschueuren. London: Routledge, pp. 35–45.

Onyx, J. and Small, J. (2001), 'Memory-Work: The Method'. *Qualitative Inquiry*, 7, 773–86.

Panksepp, J. (1998), *Affective Neuroscience: The Foundations of Human and Animal Emotions*. New York: Oxford University Press.

Parameswaran, R. (2003), 'Reading Nancy Drew Books in Urban India: Gender, Postcolonialism, and Memories of Home', in *Defining Print Culture for Youth: The Cultural Work of Children's Literature*, ed. A. H. London and W. Weignd. Westport, CT: Libraries Unlimited, pp. 169–95.

Paul, L. (2009), 'Learning To Be Literate', in *The Cambridge Companion to Children's Literature*, ed. M. Grenby and A. Immel. Cambridge: Cambridge University Press, pp. 127–42.

Pearce, L. (1997), *Feminism and the Politics of Reading*. London: Arnold.

Pearce, L. (2017), *Devolving Identities: Feminist Readings in Home and Belonging*. London: Routledge.

Potter, B. (1902), *The Tale of Peter Rabbit*. London: Frederick Warne.

Presner, T., Shepard, D. and Kawano, Y. (eds) (2014), *HyperCities: Thick Mapping in the Digital Humanities*. Cambridge, MA: Harvard University Press.

Preston M. J. (1995), 'Rethinking Folklore, Rethinking Literature: Looking at *Robinson Crusoe* and *Gulliver's Travels* as Folktales: A Chapbook-Inspired Inquiry', in *The Other Print Tradition: Essays on Chapbooks, Broadsides, and Related Ephemera*, ed. C. L. Preston and M. J. Preston. New York: Garland, pp. 19–73.

Price, L. (2012), *How To Do Things with Books in Victorian Britain*. Princeton: Princeton University Press.

Prior, K. S. (2012), *Booked: Literature in the Soul of Me*. New York: T. S. Poetry Press.

Proust, M. ([1906] 1987), *On Reading Ruskin: Prefaces to* La Bible d'Amiens *and* Sésame et le Lys *with Selections from the Notes to the Translated Texts*, ed. and trans. J. Autret, W. Burford and P. J. Wolfe. New Have: Yale University Press.

Proust, M. ([1913] 2002), *The Way by Swann's*, trans. L. Davis. London: Penguin.

Proust, M. ([1927] 2002), *Finding Time Again*, trans. I. Patterson. London: Penguin.

Proust, M. (2011), 'On Reading: Translator's Preface to *Sesame and Lilies*', in *Marcel Proust and John Ruskin: On Reading*, ed. and trans. D. Searls. London: Hesperus, pp. 3–44.

Pullinger, K., Joseph, C. and Campbell, A. (2005–2018), *Inanimate Alice*. Bradfield Company. https://inanimatealice.com (accessed 3 April 2018).

Pullman, P. (1991), 'The Dark Side of Narnia', *The Guardian*, 1 October, n.p.

Pullman, P. (1995), *Northern Lights*. London: Scholastic.

Pullman, P. (2001), 'Shedding Light: The Marsh Award for for Children's Literature in Translation 2001'. School Librarian, 49(1), 6–7.

Pyke, S. (2018), 'Textual Preferences: The Queer Afterlives of Childhood Reading'. PhD thesis, University of Roehampton.

Rathbone, C. J., Conway, M. A. and Moulin, C. J. A. (2011), 'Remembering and Imagining: The Role of the Self'. *Consciousness and Cognition*, 20(4), 1175–82.

Reading Experience Database, The (1995–). The Open University. http://www.open.ac.uk/Arts/reading/UK (accessed 3 April 2018).

Reavey, P. (2017), 'Scenic Memory: Experience Through Time-Space'. *Memory Studies*, 10(2), 107–111.

Reimer, M. et al. (2014), *Seriality and Texts for Young People: The Compusion to Repeat*. Basingstoke: Palgrave Macmillan.

Reynolds, K. (2011) 'Child-Oriented Criticism', in *Children's Literature Studies: A Research Handbook*, ed. M. O. Grenby and K. Reynolds. Basingstoke: Palgrave MacMillan, pp. 128–32.

Reynolds, K., Brennan, G. and McCarron, K. (2001), *Frightening Fiction*. London: Continuum.

Richmond, A. and Bracker, A. (2010), *Conservation: Principles, Dilemmas, and Uncomfortable Truths*. London: Routledge.

Ricoeur, P. (1988), *Time and Narrative*, trans. K. Blarney and D. Pellauer. Chicago: University of Chicago Press.

Rizvi, U. Z. (2015), 'Crafting Resonance: Empathy and Belonging in Ancient Rajasthan'. *Journal of Social Archaeology*, 15(2), 254–73.

Rodgers, B. (2016), *Adolescent Girlhood and Literary Culture at the Fin de Siecle: Daughters of Today*. Basingstoke: Palgrave MacMillan.

Rose, J. (1984), *The Case of Peter Pan, Or the Impossibility of Children's Fiction*. Basingstoke: Macmillan.

Rose, J. (2001), *The Intellectual Life of the British Working Classes*. New Haven: Yale University Press.

Rosen, H. (1998), *Speaking from Memory: The Study of Autobiographical Discourse*. Stoke on Trent: Trentham Books.

Rosenblatt, L. (1938), *Literature as Exploration*. New York: Appleton-Century.

Rosenblatt, L. ([1978] 1994), *The Reader, the Text, the Poem: The Transactional Theory of the Literary Work*. Carbondale: Southern Illinois University Press.

Rosenblatt, L. (1985), 'The Transactional Theory of the Literary Work: Implications for Research', in *Researching Response to Literature and the Teaching of Literature: Points of Departure*, ed. C. Cooper. Norwood, NJ: Ablex Publishing, pp. 33–53.

Rousseau, J.-J. (1907), *Émile: Or, Treatise on Education*, trans. W. Wayne. New York: D. Appleton. First published in French 1762.

Rudd, D. (ed.) (2012), *The Routledge Companion to Children's Literature*. London: Routledge.

Rudd, D. (2013), *Reading the Child in Children's Literature: An Heretical Approach*. Basingstoke: Palgrave Macmillan.

Ruskin, J. ([1849] 1903), 'The Lamp of Memory', in *The Seven Lamps of Architecture: The Works of John Ruskin* (vol. 8), ed. E. T Cook and A. Wedderburn. London: George Allen, pp. 221–47.

Ruskin, J. ([1865] 2002), *Sesame and Lilies*, ed. D. E. Nord. New York: Yale University Press.

Said, E. (1999), *Out of Place: A Memoir*. London: Granta.

Sale, R. (1978), *Fairy Tales and After: From Snow White to E. B. White*. Cambridge, MA: Harvard University Press.

Salmon, E. (1888), *Juvenile Literature as It Is*. London: Drane.

Sánchez-Eppler, K. (2011), 'Castaways: *The Swiss Family Robinson*, Child Bookmakers, and the Possibility of Literary Flotsam', in *The Oxford Handbook of Children's Literature*, ed. J. Mickenberg and L. Vallone. Oxford: Oxford University Press, pp. 433–54.

Sartre, J. P. (1967), *Words*, trans. I. Clephane. London: Hamish Hamilton. First published in French 1964.

Schacter, D. (1996), *Searching for Memory: The Brain, the Mind, and the Past*. New York: Basic Books.

Schacter, D. ([2001] 2002), *The Seven Sins of Memory*. New York: Houghton Mifflin.

Schakel, P. J. (2002), *Imagination and the Arts in C. S. Lewis: Journeying to Narnia and Other Worlds*. Columbia: University of Missouri Press.

Scottish Readers Remember: Project Overview. http://sapphire.ac.uk/scottish-readers-remember--(ahrc-funded)/ (accessed 3 April 2018).

Searle, D. (2011), 'Introduction' to *Marcel Proust and John Ruskin: On Reading*. London: Hesperus, pp. xi–xxii.

Seelinger Trites, R. S. (2009), 'Academic Grief: Journeys with *Little Women*', in *A Narrative Compass: Stories That Guide Women's Lives*, ed. B. Hearne and R. Seelinger Trites. Urbana: University of Illinois Press, pp. 8–18.

Seelye, J. (1990), 'Introduction: *The Swiss Family Robinson*'. Children's Literature Association Quarterly, 4–12.

Dr. Seuss (1986), *You're Only Old Once: A Book for Obsolete Children*. Toronto: Random House.

Shannon, G. (1986), 'All Times in One'. *Children's Literature Association Quarterly*, 10(4), 178–81.

Shavit, Z. ([1978] 1981), 'Translation of Children's Literature as a Function of Its Position in the Literary Polysystem'. *Poetics Today*, 2(4), 171–9.

Sherwood, M. ([1818] 1827), *The Little Woodman and His Dog Caesar*. Philadelphia: American Sunday School Union.

Shweder, R. A. (1990), 'Cultural Psychology – What Is It?', in *Cultural Psychology: Essays of Comparative Human Development*, ed. J. We. Stigler, R. A. Shweder and G. Herdt. Cambridge: Cambridge University Press, pp. 1–43.

Shweder, R. A. (1994), '"You're Not Sick, You're Just in Love": Emotion as an Interpretative System', in *The Nature of Emotion: Fundamental Questions*, ed. P. Ekman and R. J. Davidson. New York: Oxford University Press, pp. 32–44.

Shweder, R. A. (2004), 'Deconstructing the Emotions for the Sake of Comparative Research', in *Feelings and Emotions: The Amsterdam Symposium*, ed. A. S. R. Manstead, N. Frijda and A. Fischer. Cambridge: Cambridge University Press, pp. 81–97.

Siddique, H. (2017), 'Blue Peter Time Capsule Dug Up by Builders 33 Years Early', *The Guardian*, 2 July. www.theguardian.com/tv-and-radio/2017/feb/02/blue-peter-time-capsule-dug-up-by-builders-33-years-early (accessed 3 April 2018).

Sircar, S. (2004) 'Little Brown Sanjay and *Little Black Sambo*: Childhood Reading, Adult Rereading; Colonial Text and Postcolonial Reception'. *The Lion and the Unicorn*, 28, 131–56.

Smith, S. and Watson, J. (2010), *Reading Autobiography: A Guide for Interpreting Life Narratives*. Minneapolis, MN: University of Minnesota Press.

Solnit, R. (2013), *The Faraway Nearby*. London: Granta.

Spacks, P. M. (1996), *Boredom: The Literary History of a State of Mind*. Chicago: University of Chicago Press.

Spacks, P. M. (2011), *On Rereading*. Cambridge, MA: The Belknap Press of Harvard University Press.

Spalding, H. (1943), 'Private Collection of Mrs Hilary Adams. www.open.ac.uk/Arts/reading/UK/record_details.php?id=6625 (accessed 3 April 2018).

Spufford, F. (2002), *The Child That Books Built*. London: Faber and Faber.

Spyri, J. (1884), *Heidi's Early Experiences* and *Heidi's Further Experiences*. London: W. Swan Sonnenschein.

Spyri, J. ([1956] 2002), *Heidi*, trans. E. Hall, illus. A. Rinaldi. London: Kingfisher Classics. First published in German 1884.

St. John, P. M. (1950), *Treasures of the Snow: A Story of Switzerland for Children*, illus. unknown. London: C.S.S.M.

Steig, M. (1981), 'At the Back of *The Wind in the Willows*: An Experiment in Biographical and Autobiographical Interpretation'. *Victorian Studies*, 24(3), 303–23.

Stendhal ([1839] 1997), The Charterhouse of Parma, trans. M. Mauldon. Oxford: Oxford University Press.

Stevenson, R. L. (1883), *Treasure Island*. London: Cassell.

Stimpson, C. (1990), 'Reading for Love: Canons, Paracanons, and Whistling Jo March'. *New Literary History*, 21(4), 957–76.

Stockwell, P. (2009), *Texture: A Cognitive Aesthetics of Reading*. Edinburgh: Edinburgh University Press.

Streatfeild, N. ([1962] 1986), *Apple Bough*. London: Puffin.

Susina, J. (1998), 'Children's Reading, Repetition, and Rereading: Gertrude Stein, Margaret Wise Brown, and *Goodnight Moon*', in *Second Thoughts: A Focus on Rereading*, ed. D. Galef. Detroit, MI: Wayne State University Press, pp. 115–25.

Tally, R. (2013), *Spatiality*. London: Routledge.

Tarlow, S. (2000), 'Emotion in Archeology'. *Current Anthropology*, 41(5), 713–46.

Tatar, M. (2009), *Enchanted Hunters: The Power of Stories in Childhood*. New York: W. W. Norton.

Todorov, T. (1981), *Introduction to Poetics*, trans. R. Howard. Minneapolis: University of Minnesota Press. First published in French 1968.

Tolkien, J. R. R. ([1947]1964), 'On Fairy Stories', in *Tree and Leaf*. New York: HarperCollins.

Townsend, J. R. (1968), 'Present State of English Children's Literature'. *Wilson Library Bulletin*, 43, 126–33.

Townsend, J. R. (1971), 'Standards of Criticism for Children's Literature'. *Top of the News*, 27(4), 373–87.

Travers, P. L. (1975), 'On Not Writing for Children'. *Children's Literature*, 4(1), 15–22.

Tulving, E. (1985), 'Memory and Consciousness'. *Canadian Psychology*, 26, 1–12.

Tulving, E. (2000), 'Concepts of Memory', in *The Oxford Handbook of Memory*, ed. E. Tulving and F. I. M. Craik. New York: Oxford University Press, pp. 33–43.

Wall, B. (1991), *The Narrator's Voice: The Dilemma of Children's Literature*. Basingstoke: Macmillan.

Waller, A. (2005), '*Fade* and the Lone Teenager: Young Adult Fantastic Realism Shaping Modern Individualism', in *Children's Fantasy Fiction: Debates for the 21st Century*, ed. N. Moody and C. Horrocks. Liverpool: Association for Research in Popular Fictions, pp. 127–44.

Waller, A. (2016), 'Rereading the Self', in *Memory in the Twenty-First Century: New Critical Perspectives from the Sciences and Arts and Humanities*, ed. S. Groes. Basingstoke: Palgrave Macmillan, pp. 325–9.

Waller, A. (2017a), '"Girls Like It Most": Challenging Gendered Canons and Paracanons in the Case of *The Secret Garden*', in *Canon Constitution and Canon Change in Children's Literature*, ed. A. Müller and B. Küemmerling-Meibauer. London: Routledge, pp. 155–72.

Waller, A. (2017b), 'Re-Memorying: A New Phenomenological Methodology in Children's Literature Research', in *Companion to Children's Literature*, ed. C. Beauvais and M. Nikolajeva. Edinburgh: Edinburgh University Press, pp. 136–49.

Walton, K. L. (1978), 'Fearing Fictions'. *Journal of Philosophy*, 75(1), 5–22.

Ward, M. (2012), '"Looking Along the Beam": Divine and Literary Hiddenness in C. S. Lewis's *The Voyage of the "Dawn Treader"*', in *C. S. Lewis and the Inklings: Discovering Hidden Truth*, ed. S. Khoddam, M. R. Hall and J. Fisher. Cambridge: Cambridge Scholars, pp. 10–32.

Warner, M. (1998), *No Go the Bogeyman: Scaring, Lulling and Making Mock*. London: Vintage.

Warnock, M. (1971), 'Escape into Childhood'. *New Society*, 17, 823.

Watt, A. (2009), *Reading in Proust's À la Recherche: 'le Délire de la Lecture'*. Oxford: Oxford University Press.

Webster, J. D. and Haight, B. K. (eds) (2002), *Critical Advances in Reminiscence Work: From Theory to Application*. New York: Springer.

Wesseling, E. (ed.) (2018), 'Introduction', in *Reinventing Childhood Nostalgia: Books, Toys, and Contemporary Media Culture*. London: Routledge. British Library digital collection (accessed 23 March 2018), location 33–79.

Wintle, J. and Fisher, E. (eds) (1974), *Pied Pipers: Interviews with the Influential Creators of Children's Literature*. London: Paddington Press.

Wood, N. (2005), 'God in the Details: Narrative Voice and Belief in *The Chronicles of Narnia*', in *Revisiting Narnia: Fantasy, Myth, and Religion in C.S. Lewis' Chronicles*, ed. S. Caughey. Dallas: BenBella Books, pp. 45–58.

Woodward, K. (1997), 'Telling Stories, Aging, Reminiscence and the Life Review', in *Dorren B. Townsend Centre Occasional Papers*. Berkeley: University of California, pp. 1–17.

Woolf, V. ([1925] 1984), *The Common Reader: First Series*, ed. A. McNeille. London: Hogarth Press.

Woolf, V. (1947), *The Moment and Other Essays*, ed. L. Woolf. London: Hogarth Press.

Wyss, J. D. (1814), *The Family Robinson Crusoe*, trans. M. Godwin. London: Baldwin and Craddock. First published in German 1812.

Wyss, J. D. (1879), *The Swiss Family Robinson*, trans. W. H. G. Kingston. First published in German 1812.

Wyss, J. D. (2010), *The Swiss Family Robinson*. London: Dent/readaclassic. First published in German 1812.

Young, D. (2016), *The Art of Reading*. Melbourne: Melbourne University Press.

Yow, V. (2015), 'Interviewing Techniques and Strategies', in *The Oral History Reader*, ed. R. Perks and A. Thomspon. London: Routledge, pp. 153–78.

Zipes, J. (2001), *Sticks and Stones: The Troublesome Success of Children's Literature from Slovenly Peter to Harry Potter*. London: Routledge.

Index

Lightning Source UK Ltd.
Milton Keynes UK
UKHW021808181019
351875UK00003B/180/P